Parents & Hypocrisy

IF TOY GUNS and the like are so healthy for boys and girls, then why are so many parents so adamantly opposed to them? Too often, parents prohibit toy guns not out of their conscious altruism but out of their unconscious neuroticism— an anxious intolerance for feelings of anger in their children and in themselves. As Bettelheim (a Holocaust survivor) writes, "Some parents, out of their abhorrence of war and violence, try to control and forbid altogether, any play with toy guns, soldiers, tanks, or other toys which copy and thus represent implements of war. While these feelings are most understandable, when a parent prohibits or severely criticizes his child's gun play, whatever his conscious reasons for doing so, he is not acting for his child's benefit, but solely out of adult concerns and anxieties."

An interesting irony is that the supposedly psychologically sophisticated generation of parents now in their thirties and forties, so prone to preach nonviolence, tolerates a great deal of it in their personal and professional lives, whether in the high national divorce rate or the "hostile takeover" trend. A parent will justify harsh arguments with a spouse in front of a 4-year-old because the child is "learning how to resolve conflict." A father may be seeing an analyst to deal with "unresolved anger," while a mother will think nothing of telling her therapist that "of course" she fantasizes about shooting her husband's head off.

One young, affluent woman recently told me that she would need a lot of convincing before she would "condone violence" in children. Ten minutes later, the conversation had wandered and she was recounting the final stages of a relationship in which she and her partner (a co-worker) had "nuked" one another by having affairs with others. Apparently she perceived children playing with toy guns as more "violent" than adults "nuking" each other in their personal and professional lives.

For some of today's parents who grew up with the Cold War, "duck-and-cover" drills, multiple assassinations and Vietnam, the "violent" play of children may touch deep-seated fears, giving rise to the conviction that the peace movement must live on in the playroom. But by prohibiting or becoming overly anxious at such play, parents simply pass on to their children the same irrational fear—that aggressive feelings can be overwhelming and uncontrollable.

—Glen David Skoler

side's demands. We have had 20 years of experience in demonstrating the reverse. It is true that a segment of West German political opinion favors the unilateral dismantling of the short-range missiles on German soil and will continue to do so even if we enter into negotiations with the Soviets on the subject. But it is also true that a majority of Germans favor maintaining the alliance and remaining useful partners with the rest of NATO including the United States. It should be the objective of U.S. policy to assist that majority, through our

somewhat reduce the e
it does not negate the
tiated equal solution to t
It is argued that a U.
exchange of nuclear w
itarily ineffective, will ac
the ladder of graduate
But is it not possible
weapons of any range d
quired is to be able to
change? We have an in
ons of every conceivable

'Go Home, Yank'

*The following editorial appeared with the above headline in the M
Spiegel, West Germany's most popular newsmagazine. It was written
editor-in-chief and translated for The Washington Post by John Glad.*

By Rudolf Augstein

AMERICAN TROOPS are not stationed on our territory by s
out of a desire to do the nice Germans a favor. They are here
are strictly their own. The French have their own motivatio
would be totally out of reach of the missiles she so heartily urges up

Actually, the West Germans are themselves to blame for having s
performance by sounding the alarm in 1977 over intermediate-rang
that we have negotiated them away, it is obvious that they were the
to let go . . . .

Up until now we have felt secure under the protection of the Ame
er, even though we had our doubts as to the doctrine of "flexible r
did its inventors. Even the doubts were not without value. The po
had to experience them in reverse fashion, so they were a plus for o

Now those doubts must be laid aside. Hard facts are being created
ing the door on this solidarity . . . .

It is true that the Russians have never attacked us, nor do we fee
ticularly threatened now. It is also true that we do not have the sli
turn our backs on NATO; how could we?

But it is also true that the insane thoughts of those who wish to
war. If the USA and the London Lady insist as a precondition fo
troops on German soil that the Germans shoulder a magnified risk
tually alone), then we must let our Anglo-Saxon allies take their
great our regret and inner resistance . . . .

WINNING WITH KIDS

WINNING

WITH

KIDS

TESSA ALBERT
WARSCHAW, PH.D., AND
VICTORIA SECUNDA

HOW TO
NEGOTIATE
WITH YOUR
BABY BULLY,
KID TYRANT,
LONER, SAINT,
UNDERDOG OR
WINNER SO
THEY LOVE
THEMSELVES
AND YOU, TOO

BANTAM BOOKS
TORONTO • NEW YORK • LONDON • SYDNEY • AUCKLAND

WINNING WITH KIDS

A Bantam Book / September 1988

Library of Congress Cataloging-in-Publication Data

Warschaw, Tessa Albert.
Winning with kids.

Includes index.
1. Child rearing. 2. Child psychology. 3. Parenting.
4. Negotiation. I. Secunda, Victoria. II. Title.
HQ772.W235 1988 649′.1 88-47515
ISBN 0-553-05282-9

Published simultaneously in the United States and Canada

PRINTED IN THE UNITED STATES OF AMERICA

WAK   0 9 8 7 6 5 4 3 2 1

To the winning kids in my life—Shelli and Tim, Mindy and Billy, Loren and Donna, and Jeff; to their winning kids—Adam, Jaclyn, and Travis; and to all other kids who pull red wagons.

—T.A.W.

To Judy Fox, who deepened my understanding of children, and of myself.

—V.S.

ACKNOWLEDGMENTS

This book would not have been possible without the help of the following people, whom we would like to thank:

Dr. Louise Bates Ames of the Gesell Institute of Human Development and Bill Honig, Superintendent of Schools for the State of California, for their extremely valuable interviews;

Carol Hyatt and Stephen L. Isaacs, director of the Development Law & Policy Program at the Center for Population and Family Health at Columbia University, for their editorial suggestions and generous research assistance;

Our agent, Elaine Markson and her colleague, Geri Thoma, for their unflagging enthusiasm and support;

Our editor, Toni Burbank, whose keen eye, insights, and friendly editorial persuasion contributed immeasurably to this project, and whose spirited belief in it made the book a reality;

Sonya Hamlin, who is always there with a steady hand;

Sandy Gabin, for her tireless and gracious help;

Jeri Rosenhaft and David Shane, for their cheerful computer expertise, admirable efficiency and problem-solving;

Ann Albert and Harriet Resnick, Tessa's mother and sister, for their lifelong love and encouragement;

Shel Secunda, Vicky's husband, who bailed us out editorially and logistically more times than we can count, and who gave unstintingly of his time and handholding;

Jennifer Heller, Vicky's daughter, who served as negotiating guinea pig and source of information and filial patience;

Jeanne Golly, Lynn Jacobson, Andrea Szmyt and Ernie Costaldo, who are cheerleaders all.

The greatest measure of our gratitude goes to those parents and children—whose real names we could not use—who were willing to fill out questionnaires and share with us, in lengthy interviews, intimate details of their family and personal lives. For their candor, courage and trust, we cannot thank them enough. Their interviews were alternately painful, hilarious, and joyous, and in all ways they enlarged our respect for the incalculable difficulties and rewards of being a parent, and of being a child.

Finally, we wish to thank the school administrators and faculty members who helped us conduct our study and find interview subjects. To further protect the identity of the students and their parents, we cannot name the school officials here, but we wish to express our admiration for their extraordinary work and faith in children.

—Tessa Albert Warschaw, Ph.D.
Victoria Secunda

CONTENTS

INTRODUCTION   1

PART I
PROLOGUE:
SETTING THE STAGE

1. NEGOTIATION: THE PARENTING TOOL FOR PREVENTING
    AND SOLVING PROBLEMS WITH YOUR CHILDREN   9

PART II
THE CAST OF CHARACTERS:
UNDERSTANDING PEOPLE'S STYLES

2. WHAT IS STYLE?   23

3. GETTING TO KNOW YOUR CHILD   32

4. CHILDREN'S STYLES   55

5. YOUR PARENTING STYLE   68

PART III
PREPARING THE NEGOTIATING SCRIPT

6. THE LANGUAGE OF NEGOTIATION   91

7. THE SKILLS OF NEGOTIATION   106

8. THE STRATEGIES OF NEGOTIATION   122

9.   STRATEGY WITH STYLE   133

10. WHEN PARENTING STYLES DIFFER   148

PART IV
SCENARIOS:
NEGOTIATING WITH YOUNGSTERS
(PRESCHOOL AND ELEMENTARY SCHOOL AGE)

11. NEGOTIATING WITH PRESCHOOLERS   171

12. NEGOTIATING WITH GRADE SCHOOLERS   200

PART V
NEGOTIATING WITH TEENAGERS
(JUNIOR AND SENIOR HIGH SCHOOL)

13. ADOLESCENCE: THE HOMESTRETCH   235

14. DEFIANCE (REBELLION)   247

15. GRADES
     (GEARING UP FOR COLLEGE OR FULL-TIME WORK)   267

16. PEER PRESSURE (DRUGS, ALCOHOL, SEX)   283

PART VI
EXPERIMENTAL THEATER:
SPECIAL NEGOTIATING SITUATIONS

17. DIVORCE   299

18. STEPPARENTING   327

     EPILOGUE   349
     INDEX   351

Allow children to be
happy in their own
way, for what better
way will they ever
find?
                —Dr. Johnson,
                   letter, 1780

INTRODUCTION

In conducting negotiating seminars and in my private counseling practice, my starting point often is this: How do you get what you want? Behind that question is the belief that in order to reach your goals, you have to help others to reach theirs as well—the definition of winning negotiation. When applied to the world of work, most people grasp the concept fairly easily.

But when that kind of question is applied to the family—that is, when I ask, "Are your hopes and dreams for your children coming true? Are your kids becoming the kinds of people you hoped they would? Are you as close as a family as you would like?" many people are stymied. Often the response is a reluctant, or even anguished, "No."

The reason is this: Many loving parents do not know how to negotiate with their kids.

The idea of applying negotiating skills to the parent–child relationship may seem, at first, to be crass and manipulative, because *negotiation* is a term often associated with management and labor, militants and dissidents. But *successful* negotiation is not simply a business or political concept—it is a human concept: you collaborate to reach a mutual goal—even with a child.

For example, I recall once talking with the CEO (chief executive officer) of a major corporation who said with obvious anger, "My daughter refuses to get going on her college applications. I keep reminding her that the deadline is coming up, and she keeps putting it off. I don't know what to do about it."

As we discussed his problem, I discovered that the man had not allowed his daughter the latitude of making her own decisions on the subject. So much was he pressuring her that the teenager's response—passivity—was the only way she had to exercise any control, to have a "say," however self-defeating.

I suggested that he tell her, "Here are some reference books on colleges. When you're ready to go visit them and to fill out applications, let me know." It took all his resolve to back off, but within a month, she said to him, "Okay, let's get started. Here's where I want to look. Will you help me set up the appointments?"

Only when he collaborated, rather than insisting that she do things solely his way, was he able to get the response he wanted. Only when he gave her some freedom of reasonable and acceptable choice could she begin to become more responsible.

Negotiating within the family, through collaboration, allows children to participate in their own destinies and to relate to their parents in a healthy, rather than destructive, way; control is *shared*.

Sharing control within the family, however, does not mean losing parental authority, and this brings up an important difference between negotiating in a business deal and negotiating with children. In the former case, there is the presumption of adult equality, if only chronologically; in the latter, children, because of their youth and inexperience, are not our equals and therefore need our direction and protection.

And so, while successful negotiation depends upon the ability to collaborate, within the family you as the parent *are in charge*. There are times when you negotiate with your child and times when you do not.

You cannot negotiate with someone—in this case, your child—unless you know him or her. Most negotiations fail because the two parties do not have a real understanding of one another. We discovered in our research that many parents do not know their children well enough to get beyond their disagreements with them in order to develop a closer relationship as a family, even when that is their deepest wish.

To determine how well American parents and children know one another, we conducted a survey to find out what parents and their children are thinking about—the gaps between what they want from their relationship and what they have and the ways in which they do, or do not, understand and collaborate with one another.

We developed two extensive questionnaires—one for parents and another for children age 10 through 18—in which we asked questions that would tell us the parent's and the child's typical ways of behaving and responding, as well as how they perceive themselves and each other.

These questionnaries were distributed in three suburban schools—elementary, middle, and high school, which, in the interest of the participants' privacy, we cannot name here—as well as to families in Arizona, California, Connecticut, Illinois, Michigan, New Jersey, New York, and Tennessee. We followed up by interviewing many of the parents and students who filled them out.

We also interviewed parents of children between the ages of 1 month and 9 years, because these children were too young to fill out the kids' questionnaire.

Our questionnaires and interviews illustrated two primary areas of unhappiness within the American family:

- The gap between parents' expectations for their children and the abilities of the children to meet those expectations
- The desire both of parents and of their children to reach one another, but the inability to do so

The reason for this unhappiness became apparent to us when we compared the questionnaires of children with those of their parents: we sometimes wondered whether or not we had made a clerical error, so little did they sometimes know about each other's hopes, dreams, fears, and longing for a loving relationship with one another. At times it was as if parent and child were total strangers.

Parents often do not know their children not because of neglect or indifference, but because they confuse a child's alternative way of thinking or doing things with contrariness, *rather than realize that the child may have a different way of perceiving himself, his parents, and the world—a different way of being.* This difference is what I call *style,* the key concept of my approach to negotiation.

The aim of this book is to close the gap between what parents and their children want from one another and what they have by giving them a method by which they can, in a new way, create a more rewarding and loving relationship. But it has an even larger purpose: to help parents develop their children into Win/Win negotiators, people who believe that winning, in love or in work, is meaningless unless others win as well. Children who are raised with this philosophy will, when they are grown, be able to impart to their colleagues, their relationships, and the world around them a spirit of collaboration and goodwill.

Winning with Kids will show you how to use negotiating skills to solve current differences and disputes, to prevent future ones, and to build stronger, more loving bridges to one another, whether the child is a toddler or a teenager. It will provide the tools, language, and strategies of successful negotiation within the family, defining:

- Who the family "players" are—the six styles each of parents and of children
- How to negotiate with children of each style from preschool through the high school years
- The developmental issues of each age group—from tantrums to dating—and how the strategies of negotiation can be tailored for them according to children's styles

My interest in negotiation began many years ago, when I was a teacher in California. I noticed that the children who learned best were those whose teachers engaged them in the learning process according to the students' abilities and interests—that is, when teacher and student collaborated through negotiation. When there was a stalemate in the classroom, often it was because teacher and student were temperamentally out of sync or the teacher was unable to alter his or her teaching skills to fit the child's style. It was as though they were speaking different languages.

My observations of and experience with negotiation evolved when I was appointed to the Curriculum Commission for the State of California. I left the teaching profession to pursue the negotiating process full-time, first in my practice, then in conducting seminars for corporations, professional associations, governmental agencies, and private groups, and I wrote about its benefits in my first book, *Winning by Negotiation.*

No amount of negotiating acumen works unless one's attitude is positive, embracing the belief that a fulfilled life is possible and is what each of us deserves. Without that optimism—which I described in *Rich Is Better*—people are unable to resolve their differences.

Although I am a psychotherapist and have been a stepparent, I am not a parent. For this project I needed the perspective of someone who has had experience raising children.

Victoria Secunda has looked at the parenting process from many angles—as a stepchild, as a stepparent, as a divorced and remarried mother. In addition, she has written extensively over the years, in magazine and newspaper articles and books, about parent–child relationships, specifically about readiness and change in child development.

In *By Youth Possessed: The Denial of Age in America,* she examined the pitfalls of age-related expectations in childhood—the disappointment of parents who feel their children should be behaving in a certain way by a certain age.

This combination of her parenting experience and her sensitivity toward what children are able to do, as opposed to what their parents think they *ought* to be doing, made her the perfect collaborator and coauthor for this book.

She and I are philosophically in tune, believing in the human capacity for change and in respect for individual differences in people, whatever their ages. She, as a mother and student of human behavior, and I, as a therapist, have seen firsthand the joy that results when parents can collaborate with their children to help them become the best that they can be.

This book is the result both of our separate experiences and of our conviction that negotiation according to style within the family profoundly improves, or creates, a sense of belonging and love and mutual regard.

Tessa Albert Warschaw, Ph.D.
New York

PART I

PROLOGUE:
SETTING
THE STAGE

CHAPTER 1

NEGOTIATION: THE PARENTING TOOL FOR PREVENTING AND SOLVING PROBLEMS WITH YOUR CHILDREN

Nancy and Greg Hanson* have three children: Cindy, an ebullient and active teenager; Karen, a sensitive and beguiling 11-year-old; and David, 9, who is studious and withdrawn.

The girls are, as the Hansons enthusiastically put it, "terrific kids," and seem custom-made for each parent: Karen is a miniature of her mother, and Cindy is her father's psychic twin.

When describing their son, however, Nancy and Greg grow grim: they are, they say, constantly at odds with him. Whenever they ask David to do something, he says "No," or "Not now," or seems not to have heard. He seldom wants to join the family on their outings. He has few friends. At the dinner table he gulps down his food, anxious to return to his room.

Not that his parents haven't tried to make it otherwise. They've read a variety of child-rearing books and used an assortment of parenting techniques—nothing worked. They've had him tested to find out whether or not his remoteness is the result of a learning disability or a deep-seated emotional conflict—he has neither.

The Hansons are stumped: "What," they ask, "are we doing wrong?"

It is a question that echoes in the kitchens and dens of countless families across the country. Parents of goodwill, eager to raise children

---

*The names and identifying characteristics of all parents and children interviewed for this book have been changed to protect their privacy.

who are loving, achieving, and confident, find that often they can't connect with one or more of their kids, and they don't know why. Unable to find solutions for parent–child discord, they feel confused, angry, and guilty.

Parenting is a risky business, particularly for mothers and fathers who care deeply about their children and what happens to them. Either they experience their children's pain as though it were their own, or they believe their kids are growing up nicely and are stunned to discover that they are having problems—as simple as needing a math tutor or as serious as an eating disorder. Whichever is the case, such parents think it's their fault.

But even when their children aren't in trouble, they worry. Acutely aware of the incidence among children of such stress-related illnesses as ulcers, of the continuing debate about whether or not kids are harmed when both parents work, and of the increase in substance abuse and suicide among teenagers, parents worry about what *might* happen to their kids, and are concerned about how to prevent it.

Whether the problem is major or minor, present or future, caring parents look for answers in parenting books and articles, talk to guidance counselors and child psychologists—and are often confounded by their efforts. To their consternation, they find that the child-rearing theory they choose, or advice they take, may work for someone else's kids, but frequently falls flat on its face with one or more of their own.

Part of the problem is that for decades much of that advice and many of those theories have been rooted in the idea that because children are so malleable, they can, if you begin early enough, be molded into ideal kids; if they don't turn out well, it follows, it's your fault. But the unqualified "nurture" approach leaves out almost entirely the reality of children's inborn traits, desires, talents, and other qualities—their "natures."

A good measure of your difficulties with your child, then, has to do with the mix of your styles. What amuses, or moves, or inspires, or annoys you may not be what produces the same responses in your child. Your youngster has his or her own ways of loving and learning and responding; if they are not like yours, you may think that there is something wrong with the youngster—or with you—when neither may be the case.

Rather, the two of you may not be a "fit." You may, in fact, be a "mis-fit," a no-fault dissonance that is bound to cause friction between you. It is the mis-fit—the mix of styles—that causes more problems in the family than almost anything else.

In friendship, people are drawn to one another because of their similarities, and where there is a mis-fit, intimacy rarely flourishes. Within the family, however, a mis-fit with your child is not something from which you can flee; but chances are you fight about it.

When you recognize that much of your exasperation and unhappiness is caused by your different rhythms and outlooks, and when you understand them, you can change your relationship. Instead of bringing out the beast in each other, you can bring out the best.

The vehicle for doing so is negotiation.

WHAT DO WE MEAN BY NEGOTIATION?

By *negotiation* we do not mean jockeying with your child for a strategic edge, as though you were both business tycoons hammering out a contract in a smoke-filled room.

Rather, we mean that you and your child both get what you want from each other—with respect for your differences and your rights as human beings—through joint problem solving.

When you negotiate, you reach for possibilities, instead of being mired in a fantasy of what you wish your child could be. Negotiation in the family eliminates unrealistic expectations and helps you set achievable goals. Rather than looking at your child and saying, "I wish this could happen," you say, "This is what *can* happen."

That middle ground—the goal of negotiation—is *collaboration*.

Collaboration within the family involves three parallel tracks. One is your short-term goals: working through day-to-day irritations with your child—his messy room, his talking back, his fights with his siblings, his sullenness, his not doing his share of chores—all the things that drive you crazy.

The second track is your long-range parental goals—molding your child's character, imparting to him your values, building his self-esteem, guiding him toward healthy independence.

Third, which is the most important goal, is your desire to get closer as a family and to be supportive of and loving toward one another.

Parents often lose sight of the second and third tracks because they get stuck on the first. Perhaps you find yourself repeating to your child the same requests over and over, like a tedious litany, with no change in his behavior. By the end of the day, you are exhausted from work and from heated exchanges—or strained silences—between you. You may feel, at such vulnerable moments, that your relationship has derailed, or that you have lost parental control.

The need for total control is as debilitating as having none. Negotiation makes it possible to eliminate your habitual silent suffering and/or arguments. Instead of abdicating or attempting to control—one-sided endeavors that do not produce change—you collaborate with your child so that you both get what you want.

How well parents are able to share control, without giving up authority, is what separates confident parents from unhappy and disappointed ones. Sharing control is equally important to children, because it gives them the self-esteem required to create positive change within themselves. Anorexia nervosa among adolescent girls is a tragic plea for control: children who are vulnerable to this illness are often those whose parents expect perfection at school and in their appearance, with little regard for the child's wishes, needs, and abilities. Not able to measure up, anorexics choose the one area that they *can* control: the food they eat.

But kids also beg for a sense of control over their lives in other destructive ways—biting you and/or the kids they play with, talking back, doing poorly in school, using drugs and alcohol.

When you can accept your children's styles—even and especially if they do not mirror your own—what seemed at first to be a battle for control becomes an awareness of differences, many of which are non-threatening. Put in the simplest terms, you generally wake up cheerful, your child generally wakes up grumpy. It's a difference that can be accommodated by both of you.

But you want more for your children than simply the ability to tolerate each other's differences. You also have a larger picture of the kind of persons they are and will be, and how you can help them develop into whole human beings, the second goal of negotiating with children. If you and your children are mis-fits, you may not know how that can be accomplished.

Let's say, for example, that your child is a jock, devoted to sports, and glued to the television set during the World Series and the Super Bowl. You, on the other hand, are happiest at the ballet. You'd like your athletic child to learn something about the cultural world to expand his experiences, and to spend time with him that is enriching to you both. But the gap between you may seem too great even to attempt such a goal.

Here's one way to negotiate these opposing preferences: you can discuss with your child the athleticism involved in becoming a dancer and invite him to go with you to a ballet whose program would appeal to his interests and demonstrate the physical training, power, and prowess of great dancers.

As for your child's interest—sports—you can take the collaborative initiative and say, "Let's watch a game on television together. Maybe there's something you can show me about sports that I'd like, that would help me see athletics in a different way."

He might point out the grace of Michael Jordan suspended in the air in a Baryshnikov-like leap as he slam-dunks a ball into the basket for the Chicago Bulls. Or he could cite the spinning and high-stepping choreography of running back Walter Payton as he artfully dodges tacklers on his way to a touchdown for the Chicago Bears.

In this scenario, neither parent nor child has relinquished his view of the world—rather, each has shared and enlarged it in his own way. They have used a powerful negotiating skill: finding commonalities, one of the ingredients in becoming closer as a family, the third parental negotiating goal.

Successful negotiation is the sensitive and intelligent use of certain specific skills, which we will outline in subsequent chapters, that are a means of coming together in a way that benefits you both. Once you learn these skills, you can apply them to nearly any scenario with your child; through interaction with you, he in turn will learn and apply them to his life apart from you—at school and with friends.

But negotiations depend upon more than skills: they require a thorough knowledge of your child, so that you will know which skills to use, and when.

STYLE: HOW WELL DO YOU KNOW YOUR CHILD?

The flaw in many child-rearing theories is that they employ a single, all-purpose, one-size-fits-all technique. Without attention to children's styles, these theories may succeed with some kids, but miss the mark with others. Strict discipline, for instance—about which we'll elaborate later in this chapter—motivates some children to work harder out of a kind of "I'll show you" attitude, but causes others to cave in out of fear.

If you and your child don't mesh, it may be because you don't understand his style—his typical way of behaving and responding—or recognize that his behavior patterns *form* a style. It is this gap between your perceptions and expectations of him, and who he really is, that creates both your disappointment in him and your inability to get what you want from him, and he from you.

The missing piece is this: you may simply not know him as well as you think. As we discovered in our survey and from our interviews with parents and children, parents often are unaware of, or fail to see, certain aspects of their children's interests, hopes, and fears.

To return to the Hanson family, Greg and Nancy need to get to know David better—to see him as he sees himself—in order to understand the heart of their troubles with him. They and their son have a clash of styles, a problem that does not occur with their daughters, with whom they are each a fit.

David's behavior is perceived by his parents as insubordination and disrespect, when often it is simply a different style from theirs and a different way of expressing himself. It is as though they have antennae that do not pick up his signals—he is sending them messages that they do not receive. In the same way, he is not receiving theirs.

And so, because they push David to do things their way, instead of communicating with him in a way that is geared to his style, they are constantly at loggerheads. By not recognizing or accepting his style—his view of himself, of them, and of the world, which is different from theirs—they are bringing out the worst in him: his liabilities.

David is not without virtues: he is an extraordinarily loyal friend, he keeps promises, he is self-motivated, he is tenacious and bright. His parents, however, see only his liabilities: he is insensitive, disinterested, rude, and uncommunicative.

When they are able to understand his style, they will be aware of and will draw on his virtues—his assets—in order to help him limit his liabilities. They can reach their goal, which is to have David become a participating, cooperative member of the family, by *negotiating with him according to his style*.

We believe that while style remains essentially the same throughout life, that does not mean that people cannot modify both the ways in which they behave and the attitudes that drive them. When people can accept their own styles and concentrate on their unique and individual assets, rather than their liabilities—and when they can find positive ways for making decisions—they can employ these skills in their relationships with others.

Negotiating by style within the family is a liberating enterprise. It replaces blame and guilt with a method for getting results without drawing psychic blood. It jettisons the "oughts" of parenting, of what you imagine your children (or you) should be feeling or doing, and concentrates instead on what is possible for them to do.

When you understand your children's styles, and when you know how to negotiate with them, you can intervene, and help your children bring out their best, instead of their—and your—worst.

WHAT DO WE MEAN BY INTERVENTION?

To intervene is to stop the thing that is damaging your child and/or your relationship to him or her in order to bring about change. Intervention through negotiation is showing kids how to get what they want in a healthy, positive way, rather than in ways that are destructive.

There may be times, however, when intervening through negotiation is inappropriate, and instead you may need to consult a psychotherapist. Professional help may be necessary in cases involving paralyzing and irrational fearfulness (e.g., the house will collapse), chronic isolation and remoteness, extremes in eating habits (constant gorging or starvation), self-infliction of bodily harm, constant fatigue, trauma (such as the death of a parent or child molestation), insomnia, persistent violence, and prolonged inconsolability.

These symptoms do not emerge full blown, except in response to trauma, and sometimes not even then; rather, they may appear in disparate pieces, or by increment. As a result, parents may overlook their importance and fail to pick up on a child's pathological behavior until it has reached crisis proportions; or, if they do recognize the mental disturbance, they may wait too long to act upon it.

The rule of thumb for psychological intervention is to pay attention to your child's atypical behavior in terms of the degree of its severity and duration. Sometimes the line between a child's problems and pathology is fine indeed; both possibilities cluster into four general areas of your concern about his or her behavior. These concerns go beyond individual style—that is, can apply to almost any style—and could be related to the way you interact with your child, which means that there may be something you can do about them:

LACK OF SELF-ESTEEM. Is your child unusually vulnerable to abuse by other children? Does he frequently make self-deprecatory remarks? Is he extremely needy? It could be that either you or your spouse are often unavailable to him and he is not being given sufficient psychic support to weather schoolyard and other storms.

FEAR OF FAILURE. Is your child an over- or an underachiever? The degree of either extreme depends on the amount of fear of failure he feels, and not just on his style. Perhaps he is unable to set realistic goals for himself because you or your spouse don't take the time to show him how to make decisions, or because he is given too much latitude in decision making and not enough guidance, or because each of you gives him a different set of expectations.

RISK TAKING. Is your child unable to take risks, afraid to do anything on his own? Or does he take inappropriate and perhaps dangerous risks? He may be trying to get your attention in a negative way, because that is the only way he can.

DISTRUST. Is your child unusually fearful of strangers, unable to form attachments with people, or is he lonely or uncharacteristically remote? Maybe you have failed to keep promises once too often, or he feels redundant in your life, and he doesn't feel he can rely on anyone.

It's possible that any of these areas of concern could be cleared up by a sympathetic discussion with you. On the other hand, it may be that *nothing* you do seems to help your child, and the troubles seem to be worsening in an alarming way. If that is the case, there is the possibility of pathology.

If any of the symptoms of mental illness we listed above persists and seems to be unrelieved by all your efforts, *it is imperative that you seek professional help.* When children require psychological intervention, often the entire family goes into therapy; sometimes a neutral professional is necessary to help reduce the emotionally charged climate at home.

Most problems within the family, however, *can* be solved through parental intervention in the form of negotiation. This works in almost any routine parent–child disagreement: the child won't take a bath; the child won't stop teasing his sister; the child won't take out the garbage; the child won't eat anything you fix.

And it works in serious situations: The child has temper tantrums; the child hangs out with an unsavory crowd; the child is flunking out of school.

Intervention, however, applies to more than just problem solving. You can also intervene to implement your values in the family partnership.

Many parents feel anguished because their children seem to lack altruism, or respect for others (including their parents), or respect for themselves, as in drug and alcohol abuse. Family members often seem to be spiraling into their own separate orbits—the gravitational pull is outward, rather than toward one another.

Intervention through negotiation helps you redirect that pull back into the home, and can give the family a sense of moral purpose. It is the method by which you can give your children the strength and optimism and value system with which to make decisions that reflect your values and their own.

No parenting technique, however, works without love, which can be expressed both by accepting your children as they are, rather than as you wish they could be, and by helping them to become their best selves.

In that spirit, love also means being able to "just say no" from time to time, and having the courage to set limits—to let your children know what is acceptable behavior and what is not, what is negotiable and what is not, so that they can *just say no* to choices that can hurt them.

"DISCIPLINE," REWARD, AND PUNISHMENT. Parents know in the abstract that they are the authorities within their families, but often they are unable to strike the delicate balance between authority and overkill or, alternatively, impotence. One of the questions we are often asked is, "What do you mean, 'negotiate'? What about discipline? If I don't lay down the law, how will my kids become responsible?"

In child rearing, there *are* some issues that are nonnegotiable. You don't use negotiation, for example, to intervene between your toddler and an oncoming car—you physically remove the child from danger. Safety is not a subject for negotiation.

Other nonnegotiable issues could include:

lying
stealing
rudeness
health
the law (drugs, alcohol, driving without a license)

What is and what isn't negotiable depends on certain variables; one of them is the age of your child. If lying heads your list of nonnegotiables, for example, you still need to consider the difference between a 2-year-old's fantasies, which the child often confuses with reality (and which could explain an "untruthful" explanation for a misdeed), and a 10-year-old's deliberate attempt, say, to transfer blame for an infraction onto a sibling. "The tooth fairy did it" means one thing to a toddler and another to an older child, with whom you would take a much harder line.

Age aside, the yardstick for nonnegotiability is your firmly held standards, which, at times, you believe must take precedence over your child's, without discussion. Let's say that your child likes to dress all in black; you might be able to tolerate this attire for school wear, but feel that it is entirely inappropriate for a family wedding, and so creativity in the clothing department is not open to debate in that situation.

Having said that, while some issues are not negotiable, they may be signs of a problem that *could* call for a negotiation. So you can begin to address, say, a child's use of an electric tool he's been told not to touch by saying, "You broke the rule, and you could have been hurt, and I'm very angry. We need to talk about why you seem to think you have to break every rule."

Negotiation with your child does not mean you do not exhibit displeasure, or withhold approval, when he or she does something that makes you angry or disappointed. But do you punish?

As psychologist Selma Fraiberg observed in *The Magic Years*, if "punishment" does not teach—that is, if it does not help children see for themselves the benefits of not misbehaving—then it is meaningless. Your children may not misbehave around you because they want to avoid punishment—instead, they'll do so at school, or with their friends.

Reward and punishment in the broadest sense do not teach; rather, they impose external, rather than internal, reasons for children to mend their ways. Punishment can, in fact, reinforce the children's misbehavior, because it is, after all, attention; it is not a learning experience.

Let's say your child always gives you an argument at bedtime—he wants to finish his TV program, or he wants a glass of water, or he has to go to the bathroom. You lose your temper, you get exasperated, you threaten, you take away TV privileges for a week—and still he won't go to bed when he should.

You now need to examine your behavior in order to find out why he doesn't take your request seriously. His wheedling has one of three causes:

1. It is possible that in other areas of his life, and at other times of the day, you are not giving him enough positive attention; this would surely be more pleasurable to him than getting your goat, and he would have less investment in provoking you.

2. He may be reacting to a new anxiety—say, a substitute teacher in school who has taken a real dislike to him and who criticizes him in front of his friends. If you have dismissed your child's anxiety by saying, "He's the boss, you'll have to learn to do what he asks," rather than supporting your child and either complaining to the school or showing him that you understand and are sympathetic, your child will need you more. And so he won't go to bed.

3. You threaten, or promise, but seldom follow through, and so your child knows that you do not mean what you say.

The ways to get your child to give up his need to run you ragged at bedtime is to give him sufficient positive attention at other times, to recognize the difference between anxiety and mere manipulation, and never to promise when you can't deliver. All three responses on your part are those of an authority—not an authoritarian or an abused parent.

Instead of reward and punishment, we believe in *logical consequences*, a child-rearing approach developed by psychiatrist Rudolf Dreikurs. By requiring that your child be responsible for his own actions and decisions (within limits), you inspire within him the desire to improve, and the need for punishment becomes moot.

For example, let's say that your 7-year-old never picks up his clothes but throws them on the floor or sleeps in them. If he complains that he has no clean clothes to wear, you point out that that is the result of his not putting his clothes away; wearing wrinkled or soiled clothes is the *logical consequence* of not taking care of them. If you follow up by having him do his own laundry—with your help, until he is old enough to run the washing machine alone—he will *learn* that the reason it is important to put his clothes away is so he won't have to devote so much time to doing laundry.

Parenting is not for the fainthearted and sometimes requires the resolve to be temporarily unpopular with your children for their greater good. When you can do that, they develop the courage to have the same resolve with their peers and others, in order to protect themselves and to mature.

Without loving limits, your children are set adrift. Negotiating by style helps you take the parenting helm and intervene, whether or not you work, whether or not you are married, whether or not you have ever negotiated before, and whatever your children's ages.

THE PREVENTIVE MEDICINE OF PARENTING

This three-tiered approach to parenting—negotiation, attention to style, and intervention—is *preventive medicine,* whereby you help your children set a steady course toward their futures.

When children are involved in the decision-making process and are allowed to make certain appropriate choices, they and their parents do not feel so estranged or redundant. Parents have only to release their tight grip on how they *think* they ought to behave, and instead rethink parenting in terms of collaboration.

Negotiation gives parents the skills required to achieve the best that family can provide: a sense of self-esteem and purpose, a celebration of each member's individuality, and a safe haven within which children can learn how to move into the world, in their own ways, with optimism and confidence.

PART II

THE CAST OF CHARACTERS: UNDER-STANDING PEOPLE'S STYLES

CHAPTER 2

WHAT IS STYLE?

$\mathbf{S}$arah and Rebecca share a room in their parents' home on a tree-lined street in Connecticut. Anyone who knows the girls could tell you which is Sarah's side of the room: the shoes in her closet are lined up in a precise row of matched pairs; her stuffed toys are placed just so on her neatly made bed; nothing clutters the top of her desk except a book, a lamp, and a Snoopy pencil holder. Sarah, her gleaming, shoulder-length hair brushed into a ponytail, sits studying at her desk, her white polo shirt tucked into her denim skirt.

Rebecca's side of the room looks like the wake of a storm. Clothes spill out of drawers and undulate in piles across the floor; her bed, the covers hastily thrown over it, is strewn with magazines. Rebecca has spiked hair and wears layered, wrinkled shirts, a dozen bracelets, and black high-top sneakers; she lolls on the floor applying blue polish to her fingernails.

Most parents will recognize this scenario and hazard a guess: Sarah's probably a couple of years older than Rebecca, hence her preppy, serious demeanor and resolute neatness. Rebecca? Classic, devil-may-care second born.

Most parents would be wrong.

Sarah and Rebecca are identical twins, right down to their tooth structure and the matched sequence of baby tooth loss. But the resemblance ends with their packaging, because the 12-year-old girls could not be more unalike in temperament, talent, tempo, and personality. In short, they are totally dissimilar in *style*, and have been ever since they were born. Says their mother with a wry smile, "The scientists who do research on twins have never talked to *us*."

THE COMPONENTS
OF STYLE

Style is your typical and characteristic way of behaving. And while it may fall into certain general categories, which will be outlined in this book, it is uniquely one's own.

Think of your own children: How do they compare to one another? That they are often vastly dissimilar is no surprise to most parents. As one woman put it, "My three girls couldn't be more different—you'd think they were all adopted. My oldest is no trouble—good grades, helpful around the house. The middle child is something out of the afternoon soaps—she's bouncing off walls or on the floor with the latest tragic event in her life, and she never stops talking. My little one is so quiet you forget she's around." But parents often don't know how to apply that awareness to family negotiations.

In the helping professions, however, such as teaching or psychotherapy, the most effective practitioners not only understand the concept of individuality, they are trained to apply it. The savvy teacher, for example, looks at her students and does not think of them simply as "kids," uniformly capable of mastering lessons; rather, she thinks of them as different kinds of learners. She knows that all kids are not alike, hence, one teaching *style* will not work for all of them.

It is one thing to recognize temperamental differences in our kids—it is quite another to act upon that knowledge. Just when you thought you had the parenting process and all its booby traps licked with your first kid, along comes another child who, because of his unpredictability, sends you limping back to square one; parenting is a humbling enterprise. But, by being aware of style, you can learn how to accommodate such surprises and to make sense of them.

Style comes from a variety of sources, which are discussed in the following sections.

TEMPERAMENT. Press your nose against the glass of a hospital nursery to gaze at the new arrivals, and you will see a variety of behavior in the bassinets; some infants slumber peacefully, not stirring; others fidget and grimace; still others, their faces crumpled in rage, cry and shudder at loud noises.

Each of us is born with a unique temperament determined by genes, physiology, physical health, and mental acuity. Temperament shows up almost immediately; studies show, for example, that infants are either thing- or people-oriented.

Sounds simple so far, right? But this component of style is the most complex of all. We can't change our temperaments, and we are baffled when people ask us to try. It follows, then, that when we ask our children to react, make decisions, or behave according to the dictates of our own temperaments, we *are also asking them to ignore their own*—rather like asking a research scientist to become an acrobat.

Psychiatrists Stella Chess and Alexander Thomas, who are researchers at the New York University Medical Center, have studied temperament for three decades and have found that it includes such facets as activity level, adaptability to new situations, distractibility, persistence, and intensity of mood. Some kids easily shift gears when their families move and they enter a new school; others seem to be undone by such changes. Some kids are fairly even-tempered; others seem one day to be jumping for joy and the next day cannot be jollied out of the dumps. Some kids can play happily for hours with a single toy; others have the attention span of a gnat.

Based on these temperamental differences, according to Chess and Thomas, most, but not all, children fall under three general headings, all of them normal: the "easy child," the "difficult child," and the "slow-to-warm-up child."

The easy child responds positively to new situations, adapts well to change, and is generally cheerful and even-tempered; he is not reluctant to go into the arms of someone he has just met. The difficult child, on the other hand, tends to recoil from new situations, does not adapt easily to change, and may have wide mood swings, and his outlook is usually negative; he may cry when a stranger tries to play with him. As for the slow-to-warm-up child, he is mildly averse to new situations and adapts slowly to them; he *might* sit on grandma's lap, or play with a child in the sandbox—but in his own sweet time.

You probably know about these differences in children from experience as a parent. As one woman put it, "My first kid was so *easy*, but the second one gets into everything—I can't leave him alone for a *second*." Problems start when we stereotype and make assumptions about kids—that an easy child is also lazy, or that a difficult child is also unmanageable, or that a slow-warmer-upper is also antisocial.

Differences in children are *normal*, and each kind of child has his own gifts. The easy child, for instance, may also be imaginative; the difficult child may also be inventive; the slow-to-warm-up child may also be brilliant (this kind of child is the most misunderstood—his slow reaction time is often construed as dim-wittedness, when in fact he may be extraordinarily intelligent).

All this means is that no one temperament is ideal: each has its assets and liabilities, positive and negative qualities that are unique to it. How you respond to a child's temperament, however, can encourage or discourage those qualities. You may have a difficult child, for instance, and only focus on his negative characteristics. Your child may be easy, and you may tend to ignore him, thinking he's always content. Or you may have a slow-to-warm-up child, and rivet only on how he compares to other children.

Put another way, one parent, who is affectionate, creative, and gentle, might say of a child who is aggressive, competitive, and self-critical, "This kid's different"; another parent, who is cautious, systematic, and dour, might say, "This kid's a problem." The disparity stems from how parents perceive the child's style.

It's important to look at your children as having a *range* of qualities, from annoying to endearing, some of which give you pleasure, others of which may give you grief, and consider the child as a *whole*.

Temperament is innate and is the template upon which everything else in one's character is built; awareness of it gives you the basis upon which to help your child, to understand the rhythms of his moods and help him achieve a balance in the extremes of his temperament.

EMOTIONAL NEEDS.   Observe a room full of toddlers and their mothers, and you will see some children wriggle off their parent's lap and eagerly crawl to the other side of the room, there to coo contentedly with other children for several minutes before crawling back to mom. Others will sally forth only for a minute or two before scurrying back to the parental embrace. Still others, wide-eyed and overwhelmed, won't leave their mothers' sides. Some of this behavior can be accounted for by inherent sociability; but much of it also depends on emotional well-being.

When children's emotional needs are met, they are able to voluntarily "leave" their parents for longer and longer periods of time—it is as though their emotional replenishment at home is stored up for journeys of varying duration. But children who are not given the psychic sustenance they need are often unable to "travel" very far; they keep returning for it (or are reluctant to leave because they are still waiting for it).

This inability to "leave home" can linger throughout childhood as, for example, the 6-year-old who is terrified of going to school, or the 10-year-old who can't make it through the weekend at grandpa's house without you, or the 12-year-old who never wants to spend the night at a friend's house.

This neediness can extend into adulthood. When less assertive children are denied the attention they need, they find it difficult as adults to achieve the independence that is part of maturity—they may, in fact, still be living at home, for other than economic reasons. As for aggressive children, withholding from them positive and firm attention when they're young could lead to run-ins with the law as adults, or abusiveness to their spouses.

That unsatisfied emotional neediness in childhood can have harmful results as the child grows up is fairly certain; how that neediness expresses itself depends on the child's style, as we will see in subsequent chapters.

PARENTAL INFLUENCE. Children are archivists of family dynamics, unless their memories are too painful to recall. They may sit quietly during a family gathering, but they are observing all the time: Mom may hold forth at the dinner table, spouting opinions and dominating the conversation, scowling at Dad's tentative attempts to participate, or talking over them. From this scenario girls may learn that they are privileged conversational characters and that boys are spineless (or at least Dad is). Boys might make a mental note that girls (and women) talk too much, and that they don't want to grow up to be like Dad.

Children learn at home what behavior is acceptable or preferred, based on their observations: Mom always hides the department store bills from Dad, ergo, I better not tell him what I spent my money on; Dad always makes sarcastic jokes about Aunt Harriet, the dotty artist, ergo, I better keep my sketchpad a secret. Kids carry these reactions with them into the classroom or playground, drawn to certain teachers and friends, repelled by others, depending on their styles—their needs to dominate, or to follow another's lead, or to have healthy, evenly balanced relationships.

Parents become mentors, the people we most want to imitate, or they become examples of the kind of person we don't ever want to become. "You're getting more like your mother every day" can be a compliment or an epithet. Children are seldom neutral about their mothers and fathers.

AGE. As numerous child psychologists, pediatricians, and social scientists have pointed out, people change through time according to their position in the life span, from infancy, through adolescence, to old age. But even with age, there are variables in development: *People grow and change at their own speed, and may not follow a predictable chronological route.*

Chronological age and behavior age are not always the same thing, and confusing the two can have lasting harmful consequences for children. Says Dr. Louise Bates Ames of the Gesell Institute of Human Development, "Up to half of all school failure could be prevented or cured if children were placed in the grades their behavior dictates, rather than the grade their age dictates."

Age is a part of style—*but so are its variables*. When parents understand that, and when they remove the yardstick of age from their expectations, their impatience with their children's differing timetables is vastly reduced. Two 10-year-olds or two 16-year-olds may be going through vastly different changes in their lives and cannot be lumped together in terms of our chronological predictions about them.

VALUES. One person, having cashed a check at a bank, counts the money while leaving, discovers an overage of $5, and goes back to the teller to return the redundant sum; another in the same situation pockets the windfall and leaves without comment. At home that night, each person regales his family with his experiences—the first with pride of honesty, the second with glee at having put something over on someone.

Honesty, courtesy, religious conviction, kindness, thoughtfulness, generosity, and a host of other values are first experienced, or not experienced, at home, and color how children make ethical choices, depending on their styles.

Values have an impact on style in these, among other, ways: if human dignity in others is not valued in the family, a competitive child will be encouraged to think that it's acceptable to try to win at any price. If cooperation is valued, a gregarious child will be encouraged to be a team player, and help other people achieve their goals. If kindness is valued, a generous child will be encouraged to offer to shovel the snow from an elderly neighbor's walk.

The impulse to do good, or to do ill, toward other people depends upon the amalgam of a child's style and the values he learns at home.

These five components—temperament, emotional needs, parental influence, age, and values—together generate style, and dictate how we deal with people. *But temperament is the bedrock of style.* The kid who was described as "sunny" at the age of 6 is, at 30, probably still a cheerful presence. The go-getter in third grade is, at 40, probably still charging after challenges.

What, then, is *personality*? Is it the same as temperament or style? No. Personality is the public expression of style. In school, kids have one-word nicknames for themselves and others that are monikers for personality—"grind," "wimp," "airhead," "nerd," "prince/princess," "jock," "screwball," and "greaser" among them—few of which are designed to flatter.

Still, the personality we project, through our speech mannerisms and body language, is like a red flag to other people and causes them to instantly categorize us. They may be wrong in their assessment, but at first that's all they have to go on. When we talk about "first impressions," we are really discussing personality.

Most of us when we were young realized that our personalities either resulted in popularity or banished us to social purgatory, and so, imitating the "in" crowd, we learned how to make our personalities more appealing (or wept in the attempt).

And we learned that the personality we exhibited to peers often did not wash with our parents. We could be hipper than thou at school, but dared not attempt it at home because the stakes were different; flippancy was cool with chums, but not with our mothers and fathers, who were not charmed by its implied disrespect.

Style is cultivated by our experiences and modifies or adapts, depending upon the circumstances in which we find ourselves and the people with whom we are involved; it has many faces. Think of the situations in which you find yourself during the week—with clients, your boss, in meetings or at business lunches, at family gatherings. Adults are one style while interviewing for a job, another style when in the company of relatives, a third with close friends, a fourth at parties, a fifth with a spouse and, often, a sixth with their kids.

For their parts, kids' styles also adapt to their surroundings—the classroom, the football field, at proms, with cliques, with trusted buddies, with siblings, and with their mothers and fathers. The slow-to-warm-up child, for instance, may be "slow" only in school, but not at home. Although one's basic style does not change, the *expression* of our style changes, depending on the setting, and even that expression has stylistic patterns.

Because of children's stylistic adaptability, many parents at parent–teacher conferences do not recognize their child in the teacher's comments—the kid, for instance, who breaks furniture or throws tantrums at home is described as angelic, fastidious, and cooperative in the classroom. More than one parent has reacted to such comments by saying, "Are you sure we're talking about the same kid?" This adaptability is one reason why parents may not know everything about their children.

While style may alter from situation to situation and also as we age, one's temperament—our general way of responding and behaving—does not. We learn to cope with our style; but while it may become refined or muted by experience over the life span, it does not undergo any major changes.

We spoke earlier of *fit*. People who are like us—with whom we have a fit—are generally easier to be with than people who are not. That's why, in human relationships, it takes more effort and understanding to create a friendship out of a mis-fit than a fit: rather than instantly connecting as though we've previously met, an intermediate step is required—we need to know more about the person, because his or her style is different from ours.

In families, however, being "different"—a mis-fit—is often misunderstood, treated as though it were disobedience or contrariness. For example, there always seems to be a dissenter in a family: everyone wants to go to a baseball game except for one child, who prefers to stay home to read. A dogmatic, single-minded parent might regard that child as a troublemaker who is deliberately trying to disrupt family plans, when, in fact, the child is simply expressing stylistic preferences. In another family, a child might be eager to go to a baseball game, but his unathletic, artistic parents would prefer anything but; the child, from his parents' verbal and nonverbal messages of reluctance or displeasure, might infer that he is "wrong" to have such interests.

The child's temperament does not change when there is a family mis-fit—only the positive or negative *expression* of that temperament does. And so where there is a mis-fit, the relationship between parent and child can be like the stripping of gears, because they don't mesh.

But "different" is not bad per se—it is only different. When parents are able to see their kids in this light, they can accept their children's unique views of the world, and be enriched by them—just as they, in turn, can enrich their children in the same way. Variety stimulates us; sameness does not.

When parents respect their children's different temperaments, emotional needs, mentors, age, and values, their children do not seem so alien to them. For instance, the theatrical, passionate kid, whose parents encourage and support his vigorously creative style, might grow up to become a fine actor, making the most of that style; a similarly sanctioned "bookworm" kid might grow up to become a professor who inspires his or her students; a shy, sensitive child whose parents value his empathy for others might grow up to become a psychotherapist, capitalizing on his sensitivity.

But in the family, style mixtures can seem confounding and irksome, because we cannot easily escape them. It is one thing to *know* what style is; it is quite another to know how to coexist and to negotiate with it.

When you recognize that your children's positive and negative behavior falls into certain constellations, you begin to see their particular styles, and from that awareness you are able to find the best way to understand and deal with them.

CHAPTER 3

GETTING TO
KNOW YOUR
CHILD

Natalie Carroll, 36, is the gregarious, charming, and vibrant mother of two children, Deborah, 10, and Robert, 7. Born in Europe, where she was raised with old school manners and discipline, her traditional approach to family matters mirrors her roots: the husband is the head of the household, girls should be virgins when they marry, and children should be obedient and show respect for their elders.

Natalie thrives on competition. In the sales department of the Chicago advertising agency where she works, she has for the last two years had top commissions; on the tennis court, she runs down every shot.

She could not be more unlike her daughter, Deborah, who is reserved, cautious, and excruciatingly sensitive to criticism. Says Natalie:

> We are basically two different characters. In the past, Deborah's shyness and hypersensitivity put me off, and when I saw her closing up, it irritated me.
>
> Whenever we had a conversation, I would insist that she agree with my point of view. But every time I did, she would be on the verge of tears. She was growing farther and farther away from me. She would never tell me what was going on in school, for instance—I'd have to hear it from the other mothers. It really hurt me.
>
> I was trying to get closer to her, but I was doing it the wrong way—I knew I had to stop pushing. So I changed. I may be traditional, but I'm very realistic.
>
> One day about six months ago, I said to her, "What is it that makes you not want to tell me what happens in school? Is it you're afraid that

I'll put pressure on you?'' She said, ''No. I just didn't think it interested you.'' I said, ''What interests you interests me.''

Now she tells me what goes on in her life, because I've learned to listen, without passing judgment on everything she says. We've come a long, long way.

Natalie recognized that temperamentally she and Deborah are opposites, and that to make their connection more loving, she had to get to know her better—to stop insisting that her daughter be her clone, and to start seeing Deborah through Deborah's eyes.

Parents generally want to know more about their children—indeed, they often consult their child's teacher, or the mother of their child's best friend, to try to get a better idea of how he or she is doing apart from them. Nevertheless, either they are still in the dark about certain details of their child's life, or they don't act upon the knowledge they have acquired.

Why? Some explanations:

First, it's hard to know how to draw the line between candor from children and full disclosure. When you ask for openness from your kids, what comes out may be more than you want to hear, and you may not be prepared for the information you get: finding out that your child has few or no friends, for example, can be anguishing, reminding you of little murders in your own childhood from which you thought you'd never recover, memories you'd prefer to leave behind. As one woman tearfully put it, in discussing her 9-year-old daughter's having been summarily dropped by a group of chums, ''You'd think it was happening to *me*, for God's sake.'' Some parents so identify with their children's problems that they are unable to gain perspective and distinguish the patterns in their children's behavior.

In addition, learning that your kids never share toys, or are flunking school, or that they have experimented with pot is news that you may not want to hear, because, having heard it, you have to address and act upon it.

Either way, it is easy to overreact, and to feel as though your children's difficulties are somehow your fault. Kids are aware of their parents' need *not* to know. Said a 15-year-old girl who has a sexual relationship with her boyfriend, ''My mom would go off the *wall* if she found out.'' A mother we interviewed has told her kids, ''Do not bring me any bad news.''

The second reason you may not know your children well is that you may not understand what their behavior means and are puzzled about what, if anything, to do about it, and so you file away the information without analyzing it. Let's say your child drops an after school activity, saying "I've taken on too much." You don't give it any more thought. Little by little, however, she rids herself of other activities, in which you know she has an interest. Because the shedding of enjoyable pastimes is so gradual, you may not understand its significance, so you don't think it requires action just yet—until one day you discover that she's become a recluse. Sometimes it's hard to determine when behavior should be considered "serious," and when it is relatively unimportant.

Third, you may have trouble recognizing that your child may have some flaws. According to Dr. Louise Bates Ames:

> If, for example, a child is always having trouble getting along with other kids, often parents think it's the other kids' fault. There are some kids the other kids pick on, and in general parents don't recognize that they may have a wimpy kid who antagonizes people; they think instead that the other kids are mean to their child. If you think your child hasn't got much going for him, it makes you anxious and nervous.

Fourth, the tugs and demands of work often distract parents from recognizing mood swings or changes in habits in their kids—you assume they'll be relatively the same from day to day or week to week. Exhaustion and stress sometimes make observation impossible. And so, there are days when you say to yourself, as did one parent we talked to, "I pray to God there's nothing amiss with my kids, because I don't think I could handle one more problem."

Fifth, parents sometimes ignore their own instincts because "facts" or "expert opinion" have persuaded them to do so. We know of one underweight adolescent whose parents were concerned about her becoming anorexic. Each week she was required to visit her doctor to weigh in; and each week she would stuff into her pockets small weights so that the scale would register the requisite amount. She continued to lose weight. Her parents, hearing that her weight was inching up, thought she looked robust and healthy.

Finally, most children have a secret self—as do adults—within which they retreat to think, fantasize, mull, or feel. It's hard to know the difference between an invasion of their privacy and the need to know what goes on in their lives in order to help them: whether or not to listen in on their conversations, read their mail or diaries, search their rooms—or simply wait until they volunteer information.

For these reasons, not knowing your child as thoroughly as you might is not at all uncommon, nor is it a reason for you to feel guilty. For the same reasons, you may need to gather more information, with this goal in mind: how that information can help you get closer to your child.

Not that the process is simple. As children mature, their styles evolve and undergo subtle changes. Just when you thought you had your child's number, he does something—say, standing up to a roughneck on the playground after months of being reduced to tears—that throws you off.

Kids take detours and go through variations all the time, in tandem with physical and emotional modifications of their development. One night your daughter needs a baby-sitter, the next night she's baby-sitting. One month your son is cuddly and playful, the next he ricochets from your touch.

Kids are testing and retreating, trying on an assortment of clothes and tastes and friendships and beliefs, hanging on to some and discarding others; and although they may be within the range of a style, they are also growing up within a range of time. You have to pay attention both to their temperament *and* their timetable. Mostly, you have to observe, and adjust as they hit each new developmental plateau.

Change—behavior that seems to be out of character for your child—can be either part of the normal growing up process and/or a giant leap forward for him, or a sign of trouble: a sudden loss of appetite, a drop in grades, the loss of friendships, or the acquisition of new friends may all be red flags.

Getting to know your children with all these things in mind is sometimes tricky, emotionally charged, or painful. Still, if you are to collaborate with your kids, you may need to get to know them in a new way and on a deeper level.

The purpose of learning more about your children is not simply so that you can know when and how to negotiate; it is so you and they can have a closer relationship. You can't establish that intimacy unless you know the trivial—say, your child's favorite album—as well as the profound—say, how he feels about losing a friend.

Negotiation is both a *way* of knowing someone and the *result* of knowing him or her. By negotiating, you become intimate because you are open about who you are, who your child is, and how you are together as a family. It was with this view of negotiating within the family in mind that we formulated the questionnaire we used in our survey.

HOW WELL DO YOU
KNOW YOUR CHILD?

As we have said, this questionnaire was constructed for children from seventh grade through high school. The questions were designed to elicit children's characteristic ways of responding and behaving from both the parents' and the children's points of view.

But even if your child is below the age of 11, as you read through the following questions you can still begin to get a sense of the patterns of his behavior. For example, if you have a toddler, you know how he typically behaves when he "is disappointed or fails at something": he may suck his thumb, or throw food, or bang his head against the wall, or whimper, or punch you. So while some of these questions may not apply to your child because he or she is too young, in time they will; others of them do apply right now.

To find out just how well they know their children, we asked the parents in our sample these questions:

1. **My child is known as ... (Check off *one* answer that best describes how your child is known at school and *one* answer that best describes how your child is known at home.)**

	AT SCHOOL	AT HOME
Miss/Mr. Popularity	_____	_____
a loner	_____	_____
a nonconformist	_____	_____
a wimp	_____	_____
a loser	_____	_____
a nerd/geek	_____	_____
a "winner"	_____	_____
a preppie	_____	_____
boring	_____	_____

	AT SCHOOL	AT HOME
a jock	————	————
a shadow (follows everyone around)	————	————
a big mouth	————	————
a show-off	————	————
a troublemaker	————	————
a leader	————	————
an airhead	————	————
a genius	————	————
a prince/princess	————	————

2. When my child is feeling blue, he/she ... (Check off how often your child does each of the items below.)

	OFTEN	SOMETIMES	RARELY	NEVER
eats too much	————	————	————	————
doesn't eat enough	————	————	————	————
talks to me	————	————	————	————
talks to other parent	————	————	————	————
drinks alcohol	————	————	————	————
uses drugs	————	————	————	————
cuts school	————	————	————	————
can't sleep	————	————	————	————
watches TV	————	————	————	————
talks to friend	————	————	————	————
talks to nonfamily adult	————	————	————	————

	OFTEN	SOMETIMES	RARELY	NEVER
talks to teacher or guidance counselor	_____	_____	_____	_____
goes for walk	_____	_____	_____	_____
writes (journal, a letter, poetry)	_____	_____	_____	_____

3. Check off which of the following is very important, somewhat important, and not important *to your child*.

	VERY IMPORTANT	SOMEWHAT IMPORTANT	NOT IMPORTANT
get good grades	_____	_____	_____
be attractive	_____	_____	_____
spend time with me	_____	_____	_____
be part of "in" group	_____	_____	_____
have girlfriend/ boyfriend	_____	_____	_____
make own decisions	_____	_____	_____
not be treated like a child	_____	_____	_____
be popular	_____	_____	_____
be a good person	_____	_____	_____
be respected as an individual	_____	_____	_____
that I trust him/her	_____	_____	_____
not be overprotected	_____	_____	_____

4. I suspect my child does the following: (Check off for each of the items listed below.)

	DAILY	WEEKLY	MONTHLY	NEVER
drinks alcohol	_____	_____	_____	_____
uses drugs	_____	_____	_____	_____
has sex	_____	_____	_____	_____

5. If my child were in serious trouble, the person he/she would run to *first* is . . . (Check off *one*.)

_____ mother or father (circle one)

_____ stepparent

_____ brother or sister

_____ teacher

_____ friend

_____ minister/rabbi

_____ coach

_____ therapist

_____ no one

6. When my child is disappointed or fails at something, he/she . . . (Check off *one*.)

_____ gives up

_____ tries harder

_____ takes it out on others

_____ analyzes it

_____ blames others

_____ talks about it

_____ cries

_____ doesn't tell me

_____ don't know

7. The first name of my child's best friend is . . . (Write in your answer.)_____

   I like the friend: Yes_____ No_____

   Don't know the friend_____

8. My child's favorite recording star is . . . (Write in your answer.)

   _____ Don't know_____

9. His/her favorite TV show is . . . (Write in your answer.)

   _____ Don't know_____

On the kids' questionnaire, we asked the same first five questions, but reworded them to find out how children feel about themselves. We wanted to know how the child believes he is best known at school and at home; what the child says he does when he is blue; what the child says is important to him; what the child says is the frequency with which he uses alcohol, takes drugs, or has sex; and whom the child says he would run to first if he were in serious trouble.

Questions 6 through 9 appeared on the parents' questionnaire only, and not on the kids'. We were more interested in whether or not parents would check off "don't know" than in the content of the information requested: when parents don't know that which consumes so much of their children's time (music and television), that's a symptom of poor communication, and a lost negotiating tool, as we will see later on.

RESULTS.   When kids and one or both of their parents filled out both questionnaires and we could compare their responses, the results were these:

Question 1: Over half the parents guessed incorrectly how their children perceive themselves at school and at home.

Question 2: Nearly half of parents and their children disagreed about what the child often does when he or she is feeling blue. According to the children surveyed, the top five activities, in order of importance, were:

talk to a friend
watch TV
talk to Mom
eat too much
go for a walk

Question 3: Parents underestimated or overestimated what was very important to children on half the items listed: they underestimated the importance children placed on getting good grades and overestimated the importance to children of being good looking, being part of the "in" group, and being popular.

The most surprising gap was this: while only 12 percent of parents thought that it was very important to their children that they spend time with them, *nearly 40 percent of the children said it was very important to them.*

Other items considered "very important" to the children in our sample were:

having their parents trust them
getting good grades
being respected as an individual
being a good person
not being treated like a child
making their own decisions

Question 4: Parents agreed with the frequency with which their children claimed to drink alcohol, use drugs, and be sexually active *only* when the children checked off "never," the response for the majority of the kids, and for all of the middle schoolers. But when there was any involvement in those activities—that is, among high schoolers—most parents of the teenagers were unaware of it, or if they were, it was nearly always to a lesser degree of frequency than the youngsters indicated.

Alcohol: While only 18 percent of high schoolers indicated that they never drink, 52 percent of their parents checked off "never" (44 percent of the teenagers drink weekly, 33 percent once a month; one student checked off "daily").

Drugs: While 77 percent of the high schoolers said that they never use drugs, 90 percent of their parents said "never" (14 percent of the teenagers claimed to use drugs weekly, 7 percent once a month; one student checked off "daily").

Sex: While 62 percent of the high schoolers claimed never to engage in sex, 76 percent of their parents said "never" (7 percent of the teenagers have sex weekly, 18 percent once per month; none checked off "daily").

(Note: National figures for teenage involvement with alcohol, drugs, and sex are higher than those in our study.)

Question 5: Slightly over half of the parents and their children disagreed on whom the child would run to first if he or she were in serious trouble. Of the kids, nearly half said they would go to a parent; approximately one third said they would go to a friend; and in third place, less than 1 percent said they would go to a brother or sister.

As for the questions put to parents only (6 through 9), a little more than half didn't know the name of their child's favorite rock star, and 27 percent didn't know which TV show their child watches most often. On the surface, these pieces of information seem trivial. But comes a negotiating crunch—when, for example, your child wants to watch a given program, and you know that it is his favorite, you have something to use as a trade-off, one of the negotiating tools we'll explore in Part III.

The parents in our sample *did* get high marks on the other two questions posed only to them: nearly all knew the name of their child's best friend and how their child responds to disappointment or failure.

In fairness to parents, these questions are not always easy to answer. Indeed, many of the parents we interviewed said either that filling out the questionnaire was difficult for them, that we had asked questions that they'd never thought about before, that they were embarrassed to admit there were some questions to which they simply did not know the answers, or that their intuition told them to check off one thing but, not trusting it, they checked off another instead.

Their reactions indicated not only the degree to which parents and children sometimes do not communicate well with one another, but also the difficulty of rectifying that situation. Communication can be a Pandora's box. When you're living with a child who is more than happy to tell you that you are too chunky to wear jeans, or that you're woefully uncool, or that you embarrass him in front of his friends simply by saying hello, it's hard to summon an eagerness to hear what he's *not* telling you. It's easy to become discouraged from continuing the communicating process when there is no hint of conciliation from the other person.

And so we also asked parents this on their questionnaire:

What stops me from negotiating with my child is . . . (Check off one.)

_____ his/her rudeness

_____ my anger

_____ our lack of communication

_____ lack of time

_____ his/her lack of responsiveness

_____ not knowing how

Of the parents who answered this question, the most frequent response was "my anger."

You may think you know your child well—what makes him cheerful or miserable, when he feels confident or shaky, whether he's having a spell of calm or has hit the rapids—but then you are surprised to hear from his teacher that he is doing well (when you thought he wasn't) or that he is a holy terror in the classroom (when you thought he would be a joy).

The point is this: do you know your child well enough to negotiate with him? Do you know, for example, that being sent to his room may be absolutely the worst way to set limits with him, because he loves to be alone, while it's the best for his more sociable brother? Do you know that he learns more from teachers who allow him to choose between projects than from those who allow him no options, because he recoils from strict structure? Do you know the best time to talk to him, and for how long?

In other words, *do you know his style?*

Even if you think you know him better than anyone else, it still may not be well enough to get him to want to meet you halfway, or to comprehend changes that might indicate that he is unhappy or troubled.

When you recognize what motivates or discourages him and how and why he responds the way he does—his style—you can use that knowledge to resolve current problems and prevent future ones, to accommodate a differing point of view, and to deepen your relationship to one another.

WHAT IS YOUR CHILD'S STYLE?

Spotting your child's style, as we have said, is like putting together the pieces of a puzzle: the data are all around you and need only to be culled and arranged into a certain order. No one is in a better position to gather that data than you are. Your own observations about your child's behavior over his lifetime so far will give you clues to his style.

The following exercise is designed to help you put those clues together to determine what your child's style is.

EXERCISE 1

Answer yes or no to the following questions:

Is your child able to disrupt the entire family?

Yes_____ No_____

Does your child frequently embarrass you in public by being bad-mannered?

Yes_____ No_____

Does your child clown around when it is not appropriate?

Yes_____ No_____

Does he/she become easily bored with one activity and jump to another?

Yes_____ No_____

Does he/she frequently disregard rules?

Yes_____ No_____

Is he/she volatile at the least provocation?

Yes_____ No_____

Does he/she want to win at everything—is he/she a poor loser?

Yes_____ No_____

Does your child intimidate his/her friends to get what he/she wants?

Yes_____ No_____

Does he/she suddenly—as though it were out of character—charm you to get what he/she wants?

Yes_____ No_____

Is your child emotional in the extreme—with great highs and lows?

Yes_____ No_____

If you answered yes to more than five of the above questions, your child may be a **Baby Bully**.

Answer yes or no to the following questions:

Does your child cooperate only when you agree with or promise him/her something?

Yes_____ No_____

Does your child try to make all the family decisions, such as who puts him/her to bed, who does which chores, who will drive him/her to baseball practice or on an errand?

Yes_____ No_____

Does your child become depressed if everything in his/her life is not running smoothly?

Yes_____ No_____

When you say no to your child, does he/she try to debate you into the ground?

Yes_____ No_____

Do you find that you almost never have to prod your child to complete a task he wants to perform?

Yes_____ No_____

Does your child always believe that his way of doing things is the right way?

Yes_____ No_____

Is your child extremely perfectionistic?

Yes_____ No_____

Does your child constantly grill you, particularly on issues that do not concern him/her, such as where you went and what you did?

Yes_____ No_____

Does your child think he or she has all the answers?

Yes_____ No_____

Is your child's room orderly, with everything in its place?

Yes_____ No_____

If you answered yes to more than five of the above questions, your child may be a **Kid Tyrant**.

Answer yes or no to the following questions:

Does your child have few, if any, friends?

Yes_____ No_____

Does your child rarely participate in group activities and, instead, select tasks to do alone or with only one other person?

Yes_____ No_____

Does your child rarely tell you what he/she likes or dislikes?

Yes_____ No_____

Does your child seldom express his/her emotions?

Yes_____ No_____

Does your child take a long time before responding to questions?

Yes_____ No_____

Does your child close up when asked questions about himself or herself?

Yes_____ No_____

Does your child find it hard to ask for help?

Yes_____ No_____

Does your child express stubbornness with silence?

Yes_____ No_____

Do day-care center staff or teachers comment on your child's quiet manner?

Yes_____ No_____

Is your child more interested in things than people?

Yes_____ No_____

If you answered yes to more than five of the above questions, your child may be a **Loner**.

Answer yes or no to the following questions:

Does your child frequently bring home stray animals and lonely kids?

Yes_____ No_____

Do teachers and other adults adore your child (describing the child as "sweet," "helpful," "considerate," etc.)?

Yes_____ No_____

Does your child often manipulate you with charm, kindness, or flattery?

Yes_____ No_____

Is your child involved in clubs or activities?

Yes_____ No_____

Is your child disinterested in his/her appearance or the orderliness of his/her room?

Yes_____ No_____

Is your child prone to giving you sympathetic advice about your health, your friends, your job?

Yes_____ No_____

Does your child avoid competition in order to have lots of best friends?

Yes_____ No_____

Does your child tend to be bossy?

Yes_____ No_____

Does your child frequently complain of being taken advantage of by friends?

Yes_____ No_____

Does your child tend to embellish the truth?

Yes_____ No_____

> If you answered yes to more than five of the above questions, your child may be a **Saint.**

Answer yes or no to the following questions:

Does your child constantly seek approval?

Yes_____ No_____

Is your child often used or taken advantage of by his/her friends?

Yes_____ No_____

Does your child frequently ask you to repeat directions?

Yes_____ No_____

Does your child often call himself or herself "stupid," "dumb," "ugly," "too fat," "too thin," and the like?

Yes_____ No_____

Is your child chronically unable to make decisions?

Yes_____ No_____

Does your child make promises and then not follow through?

Yes_____ No_____

Is your child extremely sensitive to criticism?

Yes_____ No_____

Will your child do almost anything to avoid conflict?

Yes_____ No_____

Does your child too often assume blame when things go wrong?

Yes_____ No_____

Is your child the peacemaker in the family?

Yes_____ No_____

> If you answered yes to more than five of the above questions, your child may be an **Underdog.**

Answer yes or no to the following questions:

Is your child as interested in the playing of a game as winning it?

Yes_____ No_____

Is your child more interested in people than things?

Yes_____ No_____

Is your child at ease with new situations, new tasks, new people?

Yes_____ No_____

Is your child able to see options?

Yes_____ No_____

In group endeavors, does your child seek the opinions of other people before making decisions?

Yes_____ No_____

Does your child know and accept his/her own limitations?

Yes_____ No_____

Is your child willing to participate in family discussions and problem solving?

Yes_____ No_____

Does your child easily accept and give love or affection?

Yes_____ No_____

Does your child make up his/her own mind about friends, rather than being swayed by what the "in" crowd thinks about people?

Yes_____ No_____

Is your child generally self-confident, even when he/she isn't able to handle something?

Yes_____ No_____

If you answered yes to more than five of the above questions, your child may be a **Winner**.

At first, it may seem as though your child fits into all six categories—kids are often a combination of styles—but one style predominates. Remember, when discussing any of the various nuances of style, we are always talking about *degree;* with children, we are also talking about growth and change. Nevertheless, you can observe patterns in their behavior that reveal their styles.

The following chart summarizes the assets and liabilities of each of the kids' styles. There may seem to be only slight differences between styles—the Baby Bully and Kid Tyrant appear to have a lot in common, as do the Saint and Underdog. You'll know the difference, however, when you discover that the negotiation that works for one style doesn't for another, as we will see in Chapter 8.

STYLE	ASSETS	LIABILITIES
Baby Bully	extrovert	gets into fights
	funny	brags
	creative	cheats and lies to win
	tireless	uncontrolled temper
	imaginative	extreme mood swings
	fearless	show-off
	gregarious	aggressive
	bright	cries "foul!"
	charismatic	bad loser, worse winner
	enthusiastic	daredevil
Kid Tyrant	resilient	smug
	leader	doesn't want help
	articulate	stubborn
	problem-solver	extreme fear of failure
	achiever	bad-tempered
	risk taker	unemotional
	decisive	martinet
	self-starter	impatient
	perseveres	oils you with charm
	responsible	gets others to do his/her work

Loner	keeps secrets	rarely talks
	trustworthy	ignores problems
	loyal	few friends
	superb student	immune to others
	independent	withholding
	neat	tactless
	polite	remote
	not underfoot	unfeeling
	hard worker	unresponsive
	rarely lies	secretive
Saint	cheerful	keeps score of favors
	helpful	often manic
	considerate	manipulative
	charitable	overextended
	observant	indiscriminate about
	available	pals
	popular	apple polisher
	generous	mini-social-worker
	open	throws tantrums
	loving	gossip
		busybody
Underdog	peacemaker	avoids problems
	devoted	eternal victim
	complimentary	bait for Bullies
	cooperative	slave for Tyrants
	grateful	caves in when criticized
	kind	doesn't commit
	solicitous	worrier
	tender	depressive
	compassionate	craves attention
	lovable	overwhelmed by own
		feelings

Winner	variety of friends	almost none
	great communicator	
	empathetic	
	can ask for help	
	optimistic	
	affectionate	
	leader by	
	consensus	
	dependable	
	can admit failure	
	honorable	

Having read each style's assets and liabilities, you may still need more information before you can decide the general category into which your child belongs. (Note: If you work full time, you can enlist the help of grandparents, baby-sitters, housekeepers, coaches, teachers, tutors—even your child's friends—to help you in your information gathering.)

As you know from the previous chapter, style reveals itself in a number of ways.

VERBAL LANGUAGE. Our children's speech patterns can be confounding: when they are infants, they *can't* talk; when they are toddlers, they are often unintelligible; when they are in elementary school, they often use slang that is either alien to you or makes you blanch; when they are teenagers, they try to maintain a low profile with their parents.

Still, there are styles of kidtalk. Here are some examples:

STYLE	VERBAL LANGUAGE
Baby Bully	"Me first!" (competitive)
Kid Tyrant	"I'll be captain, you play outfield." (controlling)
Loner	"What fire?" (caustic)
Saint	"I'm still your friend." (consoling)
Underdog	"I dunno, what do you want to do?" (compliant)
Winner	"Let's do it together." (collaborative)

LISTENING. Children hear what they want to hear, depending on their styles. You doubtless have felt like tearing out your hair because you've asked your kid to do something 85 times, and still he does not remember. But you may not have known what he was listening *for*. This chart illustrates how each style listens:

STYLE	LISTENS FOR
Baby Bully	other person giving in
Kid Tyrant	a chance to do it his way
Loner	a chance to terminate the conversation
Saint	signs of uncertainty (so he can advise you)
Underdog	direction and decisions
Winner	clarity and honesty

BODY LANGUAGE.   Children reveal themselves by the ways they move or gesture, because they have not yet learned how to conceal the physical reflection of their thoughts or feelings. This chart illustrates the typical body language of each style in childhood:

STYLE	BODY LANGUAGE
Baby Bully	restless runs, doesn't walk takes up excessive space (as on a couch) dramatic gestures
Kid Tyrant	deliberate movements frowns a lot unsmiling stiff
Loner	tense; clenches teeth standoffish flinches when touched unexpressive
Saint	smiles frequently nods in agreement loves touching and being touched sits close to you
Underdog	can't look you in the eye poor posture looks sad nervous mannerisms

Winner   alert
              relaxed
              poised
              maintains eye contact

You can probably find evidence of your child's body language in your family photo albums. Watch for patterns in what your child is doing when the shutter is snapped. Is he or she usually behind everyone else? Making faces? Standing in front of the group? Off to one side? Nearer one parent than another, or far from both? Smiling or expressionless? Looking away? Trying to avoid having his picture taken? Compare these frozen reactions to the chart above—they are further evidence of your child's body language, hence, style.

LOVING STYLES.   Finally, kids reveal their styles in the ways they show affection. The chart below lists examples of how children's styles are reflected in the ways they demonstrate love or appreciation.

STYLE	LOVING STYLE
Baby Bully	knocks you down with a hug
Kid Tyrant	volunteers to do organizational task (cleaning out the garage, for instance)
Loner	sends notes
Saint	frequent kisses, hugs, and compliments
Underdog	obsequious
Winner	spontaneous affection and words of endearment

Now you probably have a pretty good idea of what your child's style is. Keep in mind, however, that while styles can seem to change rapidly in childhood, even from moment to moment, each style nevertheless stems in part from a bedrock temperament. Your child may appear to "outgrow" a clingy personality, for instance, and become super cool and laid back. All the same, his or her basic style remains unchanged.

CHAPTER 4

CHILDREN'S STYLES

Now that you have a name for your child's style and a general idea of his or her behavior—the skeleton, if you will—let's put some flesh on the framework to get a fuller picture of how that style operates.

As a parent, you can use this information to help your child, whatever his style, to become more confident and less afraid, more generous and less angry, more collaborative and less lonely, without losing or diluting its essential and singularly rewarding worth.

When you understand and appreciate the assets that are unique to your child's style, you can help him become the best part of that style, and to be proud of how his strengths contribute to the lives of others.

Every style enriches the world in its own way. In the company of children, for example, there is always the need for the kid who will pick up a comrade who has fallen on the playing field (Underdog), the kid who organizes teams (Kid Tyrant), the kid who wants to belt out home runs (Baby Bully), the kid who is a cheerleader (Saint), the kid who wants to keep score (Loner), and the kid who wants to pull the team together in a united, common effort (Winner).

Within the family, your child's style can also make an enormous contribution; his assets can ameliorate the liabilities of other members of the family, and his different perspective can add a delicious variety to the lives of those with whom he lives.

Look for your own child, then, whatever his or her age, in the following detailed portraits of the six childhood styles. At the end of each description, we'll tell you the negotiating problems you may have with each style, and each style's negotiating strengths. Remember, these categories are guidelines—not pigeonholes—for negotiating with your child.

BABY BULLY

Baby Bullies have all the subtlety of a Roman candle. On the playground, they're the ones hollering at slow runners and barking at less assertive kids to chase down balls. At home they burst into a room rather than stroll, slam doors rather than close them gently, talk in exclamation points rather than chat casually.

Baby Bullies often get their own way because they are extraordinarily creative in planning an assault, against which many parents have trouble erecting barriers. Baby Bullies will use every maneuver available—force, flattery, cajoling, wheedling, lying, tantrums—to achieve their goals, and are nearly inexhaustible in their pursuit of an object, prize, favor, or gift. For them, everything is a contest. Often they will drop in their tracks, spent from their vigorous efforts, before they'll admit defeat.

Baby Bullies are seldom wrong; everyone else is. These kids don't get ulcers; they give them. Catch one with his hand in the cookie jar when he has been expressly forbidden from snacking between meals, and he will explosively take the offensive: "My teacher says you're starving me to death!" But they also have a wonderful sense of humor, which is disarming.

This style is a mind-boggling mix of opposites. Baby Bullies are a challenge because not only are they insatiably competitive, they are charming in the extreme—their ingratiation stands out in such stark relief from their incessant aggressiveness that it acquires a luster by default.

For example, your 6-year-old kid has broken a lamp, squeezed his little sister until she screamed, tormented the dog, kicked you in the shins, all in the span of an hour. Then, just as you are filling out an application to send him to military school, he pops up at your side, sunny-faced, with a bouquet of wilting wildflowers and a poem that would make Rod McKuen gag (Baby Bullies are geniuses at timing).

When they're in the mood, Baby Bullies are delightful to have around. They make you roar with laughter. You are spellbound by the creativity and ingenuity that mark the dramas they create in their lives, and yours. They have a unique way of doing things—you find yourself admiring their imagination, and their daring. As much as their moods drain your patience, they replenish it by being stimulating—never dull.

Peter, 4½, is a state-of-the-art Baby Bully. Says his mother:

I've never been able to stifle Peter's need for control. He gets what he wants by persisting—he nags and whines and makes me nuts. Let's say he wants to stay up late to watch television. Just as I'm getting to the end of my rope, he'll come into my room with a sweet smile, put his hands on my cheeks, pull my face close to his and say, "Mommy, please, I promise I'll go to bed right after this program." It makes me melt, and he gets his way.

What makes Baby Bullies so difficult to deal with, other than their unflagging energy and their inveterate charm, is that they can spot a weakness—yours—at 100 feet. It is this combination of qualities that makes them formidable.

And so sometimes it is hard to like them. Listen to this justification for misbehavior from David, 15, a classic Baby Bully:

My parents and I fight most about my doing wrong things and making up stories to cover up for them.

But they're not fair. They always crucify me. They've done it so many times in the past that it's no wonder that I make up stories when I get into trouble.

For example, the other day my friend and I bought some beer—I had fake ID, and since I'm tall, I look older than I am—and we got caught by his mom, who happened to be running errands that day right near the liquor store. You know what she did? She asked to look in the bag, and all this nonsense. She's insane!

Watch David's rationale very carefully: his parents are wrong in punishing him, that's why he lies; his friend's mother is wrong in finding out that he bought beer illegally, that's why she's crazy. Clever, yes? That's why negotiating with this kid requires stamina and concentration. But, as we will see, in some ways Baby Bullies are the easiest style to deal with precisely *because* they aren't subtle.

YOUR NEGOTIATING PROBLEM.   You never know when Baby Bullies are telling the truth because they will do anything to get what they want. These kids don't fight fair: they play on your guilt and pounce on any wavering in your resolve. Baby Bullies wreak havoc in the household and you find yourself dealing with the symptom— destructiveness or hyperactivity—rather than the cause, which is that they don't want you to see their vulnerability.

YOUR CHILD'S NEGOTIATING STRENGTH. When a Baby Bully is on your side, you have quite an ally. He can dispel the tension in an exchange with a joke or hilarious story. His energy and enthusiasm are infectious, inspiring you to stretch yourself—to try something new or, following his example, to take the initiative. If you tend to be passive and a procrastinator, your Baby Bully will help you to become more of a risk taker and to be a participant in, rather than merely a witness to, your family life.

KID TYRANT

Have you ever met a child who is so composed, so definite, so absolute, and so determined that you felt intimidated? Wondered whether or not he knew more than you, since he loves to correct your syntax or question your driving skills? Thought that, on a survival trip, you'd prefer to be with him over any adult you know because he's so annoyingly able? Made you think he's really a short adult rather than a kid?

This child is a Kid Tyrant. The Kid Tyrant has the endurance of a Baby Bully, but applies it to reasoning rather than to brute force; with magnificent logic, he plots the way to get you to turn over to him the keys to your new car and the deed to your house.

Here's how one mother describes her Kid Tyrant, a 6-year-old girl:

> When she grows up she'll go into sales, I know it. She's the most persistent person I know. If she wants candy, she'll start off by asking for two packs. If she can't get two packs, she'll ask for one pack. If she can't get one pack, she'll ask for a piece of penny candy. If I say, "You can't have *any* candy," she'll say, "Well, just say 'maybe.' " She won't give up until it gets to "Maybe."

Amy Moore, 4, is another Kid Tyrant. This child has Martha, her mother, in a perpetual state of high anxiety. Says Martha:

> Amy refuses to give up, no matter what the issue is. The other day she wanted some milk from the fridge. I was on the phone and told her to wait. She then brought me a cup and again asked for milk. I said, "Hold it, I'll be off in a minute." While I continued my telephone conversation, she quietly dragged a step stool over to the fridge and

climbed on it. I got off the phone fast, because I was afraid she'd fall, and I put her in her room as punishment for defying me.

The next day, I got a lock for the refrigerator. That evening—don't ask me how—she went back to the refrigerator and broke the lock.

The flip side of the very things that irritate you about Kid Tyrants are the things that make you proud of them: They are first-rate students, leaders, and achievers. They have an exquisite sense of how to use their time well, rather than waste it. Kid Tyrants are a boon in the family because of their dependability: you ask them to take care of a younger sibling, and they do it, including changing diapers. You present them with a problem and they sit down and try to solve it, making you feel infinitely less alone in the business of parenting or just getting through the day. And, because they are fascinated by the learning process, they are interesting—they are born teachers.

YOUR NEGOTIATING PROBLEM.   Subtlety does not work with Kid Tyrants because they see only black and white issues. You will almost never win an argument with them because they will doggedly debate you into a coma; for every point you make, they have a retort, possibly several. And if they can't get you to weaken, they'll try your spouse—Kid Tyrants are masters at playing parents against each other. Moreover, their know-it-all behavior can shatter your equanimity: whatever endeavor you undertake, they have fifteen criticisms and a plan for doing it better. When you are trying to figure out the new VCR, your Kid Tyrant will say, "I'll do it," even if he's only 7.

YOUR CHILD'S NEGOTIATING STRENGTH.   The fact is, the Kid Tyrant *can* figure out how to work the VCR. There are times when you treasure his persistence and ability to find solutions—as, say, when you have a logjam of chores and have to rush out of the house for an appointment. This child will help you set priorities and become more organized, motivating you to see issues clearly and helping you to feel less overwhelmed.

LONER

This child perpetually keeps you off balance, wondering "Was it something I said?" because of his unnerving taciturnity. If he speaks at all, it is in one-word sentences. When the late poet Phyllis McGinley wrote, "Silence breaks the heart," she must have had a Loner in mind.

The Loner *likes* to be alone, and is not to be confused with the bashful child who, given encouragement, opens like a flower. Loners don't want to open up.

On a brilliant, crisp day the kids in the neighborhood will all be outdoors playing, while the Loner will be glued to a computer or building a sailboat from a model kit. He is seldom idle; but he is active in seclusion. It is this voluntary solitude that can cause his parents to become concerned about his isolation, wishing he could be more social.

This child is not going to be your best friend. You could be weeping copiously over a dish that shattered on the floor, and he will be unmoved—by your emotion, that is. But he *will* whip out a tube of glue and try to fix it.

Some Loners are not only immune to you, but to their appearance as well. They are likely to wear unmatched shoes, or hastily pull on the nearest sweatshirt and jeans and neglect to comb their hair, because they cannot be bothered with such trivia as their image. Others are fastidious because they thrive on the order of things—including their clothing.

Although they don't reveal themselves outwardly, inwardly they often put tremendous pressure on themselves. These kids are often straight-A students because they are constantly competing against themselves, since they do not take anyone else terribly seriously, and they are perfectionists. As a result, their hard work at their studies and projects sometimes leads to exhaustion. Their ability to focus only on themselves and their own efforts is unmatched by any other style.

Loners are also extraordinarily dependable—if they commit to a project or task, not only will they complete it, but often before deadline, and with more thoroughness than other styles. They can be a joy at the end of the day when their parents, exhausted, come home, because they make very few demands. And when they do talk, it is the result of so much thought, you take them seriously.

You admire your Loner kid because he is so determined to be himself, and to do things his own way, without ever competing with you—he's not the jealous type. You can count on him to overlook your flaws and mistakes. And you treasure the fact that he is not a complainer.

When they do have friends—and these kids do have one or two friends, even if, by their unresponsiveness, they don't often keep them— Loners are extraordinarily loyal. They are also extremely trustworthy: Loners are nearly incapable of betrayal, because they seldom tell anyone anything, or dishonesty, because of their unshakable integrity. They keep secrets, and are more secretive than any other style.

The isolation of Loners is a matter of degree: some of them appear to be Loners at home, but their teachers remark on their verbal skills in the classroom. Others will talk at home—generally about themselves or the intricacies of a scientific experiment they are conducting in their bedrooms—and are silent in school.

Loners know they are "different"—many of them are artistic—and when they are young, are frequently the butt of a lot of teasing.

Rebecca Thompson, 15, is finally at home in her Loner style, but it took time. She says:

> I've always been a loner. I was an unathletic kid, never could throw, or catch, or run. Sports were a very big deal in grade school, and since I couldn't do them, it was just safer not to try.
>
> The kids in school thought I was a weirdo, especially because I like to write—artistic types are always considered weirdos. Back then the kids were certain that I had antennae and maybe even green scales.
>
> But before I started writing, I read a lot in my room. Once in a great while I'd have a friend over—which delighted my mother—but very rarely. After school, my time was my own. I liked it that way. It was hard for me to learn to make friends because I preferred my own company.

YOUR NEGOTIATING PROBLEM.   The biggest obstacle to dealing with Loners is that you lack information. If you press Loners for more conversation or news about their day, they will respond with either a fixed stare, grunts, or anger. You never know what Loners want, need, or feel, and that's how they want to keep it—they control their environment with silence. These are private kids, and you have the burden of figuring out the difference between invading their privacy and, if necessary, intervening. Their behavior says they don't require outside approval or interference—but sometimes they do: you may have no idea. It takes such a herculean effort for them to form attachments—and it seems to be at such cost—that they may take the fail-safe position of avoiding them altogether.

YOUR CHILD'S NEGOTIATING STRENGTH.   If you casually remark to a Loner that you'd give your soul to have a clean basement because you can't find anything in it, the next day you will discover that it miraculously got emptied of junk, and the floor was washed in the bargain. Your Loner won't tell you he did it; he'll just do it, alone, even if it takes until midnight, without complaint. Loners never give up, and this single-mindedness makes them a treasure of dependability.

SAINT

If your child frequently brings home stray dogs, hungry cats, birds with broken wings, and friends with broken hearts, you've got a Saint on your hands.

This child is often the teacher's favorite pupil. He or she eagerly volunteers to clean the erasers in class, or to rush to the office with a note, or to set up a movie projector. Saints are the first to offer to help you with the dishes, or notice your new blouse, or to give you a hug when you're blue. They'll rub your back when it hurts and bring you breakfast in bed. Adults adore these children: indeed, you probably have been told by your friends, "God, how did you do it? I wish my kid were like that."

Saints always have a lot of friends—they're often the most popular kids in class. Because they love to help people, are so cheerful and chatty, and are so good at feeding and entertaining guests, they have a genius for bringing together a variety of pals. They are the tireless campaign workers when their friends run for student government office. They have sleepover dates at friends' houses, or their own, at every opportunity, and every phone call to your house seems to be for them.

Sue Williams, 11, has numerous friends and, indeed, considers solitude a fate worse than, well, being with her younger brother. Says Sue:

> I always have to have people around. Sometimes I call somebody I don't even *like* just to talk to them on the phone.
>
> I go crazy if I'm down in the den by myself, watching TV. I can't stand it. I go up and talk to my mother, or father. Can you imagine how bored you have to be to want to talk to your *parents*? Worse is talking to my brother.

But I can get him to do what I want. I like to surprise my parents, and do things for them. The other day they went out for the afternoon, and I got him to help me cook dinner for them.

If you are not the parent of such a child, you probably reckon that he or she is perfect. But you might reckon wrong, because many Saints can manipulate your gold fillings right out of your head. This style keeps track of favors he or she has done with the same zeal that a pony player keeps track of racing odds. Saints are the most easily wounded style of all because they are always being "betrayed." A frequent lament is, "Do you believe what she did to me? After all I've done for her?" Saints *keep score,* and are miserable if you don't love them every bit as much as they love you. Because being loved is their first priority, they tend to neglect their own needs.

These kids are often underachievers in school. Their need for popularity is so great it eclipses their priorities and skews their sense of responsibility. Rather than competing for grades, they compete for the number of friends and social engagements they have.

But Saints do have a private side: if they keep things from you, often it isn't because they are trying to be covert; they give you small clues and want you to pull the information out of them. In a sense, the Saint has the core of a Loner; Saints want to know all about you, and collect as much information as possible so they can be persuasive with you—but they don't want to share their inner thoughts and vulnerability.

YOUR NEGOTIATING PROBLEM.   Saints sniff out your mood and change their behavior accordingly. If you criticize them, they retreat behind food, television, or efforts to make you feel guilty. Moreover, they collect information about you and use it to manipulate you—flattery requires awareness, after all. Their self-esteem can be in small supply because their confidence requires an audience—they get emotional nourishment and definition from others, rather than from within. Consequently, it's hard to know what they want for themselves, because they seldom give it much thought.

YOUR CHILD'S NEGOTIATING STRENGTH.   This is the style you relish having around when you're blue or exhausted. Even if you are short-tempered, the Saint will melt your irritability with a hug or a kind remark. If you're drowning in a sea of stress, he'll offer to help—even if he's only 3 years old. You are never lonely when there's a Saint in the family.

UNDERDOG

These kids are often called wimps by peers and, occasionally, by Jungle Fighter or Dictator parents (see Chapter 5), who have difficulty identifying with them. Underdogs can break your heart because they are so frightened—sometimes it seems as though everything scares them.

Underdogs can be manipulated more easily than any other style because rejection feels to them as though it were life threatening. And so they are bait for more assertive kids: Baby Bullies and Kid Tyrants seek out Underdogs to do their bidding.

These kids are frequently taken advantage of by others, so eager are they to avoid conflict. Often, they try to mediate when their parents argue with each other—they are undone by parental disagreements. Underdogs so devalue their own needs that they will willingly take on endless obligations—lending friends their clothes, helping kids with their homework, even letting other kids read their answers during tests—and consequently get overloaded. They do all the work and get no credit. Because they are virtually unable to say no to any request, they often are not able to honor all their obligations; so they don't follow through, which doubles their anxiety. So afraid are they of making a wrong choice, it is difficult for them to make decisions.

Underdogs are their own worst enemies either because they cannot ask for help, or because they wait until the last minute to do so, or because they undertake so much that they become paralyzed. They suffer in silence. Moreover, they anticipate the worst and so tend to set themselves up for failure.

This last trait is already evident in Jonathan, who is 4 years old. Says his mother:

> Jonathan has virtually no friends. He is very attached to his father and me, and doesn't like to go on play dates. Because he's passive, he is inclined to be intimidated by rougher kids. When they come near him on the playground—even if they haven't done anything to him—he starts to cry.

Timmy Ryan's need to be loved has skewed the 16-year-old's judgment and made him too trusting, another Underdog trait. He says:

When I was in the ninth grade, one of the guys in my class, Eric, was the prince of popularity. I wanted to be popular, too, and knowing Eric was my ticket to that. That's how I got introduced to drugs—Eric deals everything. I'd get high three times a day in the woods behind the school during study hall.

Then we took LSD, but I only took it once because it scared me. Next we tried mescaline—I heard it was safer, and over the summer I did that a lot. Cocaine too. I was spending all my money on drugs. Eric could get me to do anything. One morning I woke up sitting in my car, my head on the steering wheel, sweating as the sun poured in on me, not knowing how I'd gotten home. The night before I'd only smoked pot and I couldn't understand why I'd blacked out. I felt like shit and went into the house and took a forty-minute shower.

Later Eric called to tell me the pot was laced with PCP and he laughed. I haven't seen him since.

But Underdogs, because of their sensitivity and demeanor, are the style whose virtues often go unnoticed and unsung by all but their closest friends and their families. People who know Underdogs well cherish them: they will always give you a fair hearing if you have a disagreement with them, or with someone else. They offer a note of cheer and a comforting embrace when you most need it. They never forget your birthday, or fail to send a Valentine, Mother's, or Father's Day card. They love you through fair weather and foul.

YOUR NEGOTIATING PROBLEM. Underdogs tend to be overwhelmed by their feelings, and their behavior is a defense against their sometimes crippling insecurity. That behavior can put their parents in a bind: any criticism can be construed as a blow, and the lack of criticism can be interpreted as indifference. Underdogs are so needy that you feel sorry for and make excuses for them. Sometimes it seems as though they deliberately do things to annoy you—klutzy behavior, getting hurt, being crybabies. They invite domination. The result is that you have a backlog of unexpressed anger—so do their friends. Underdogs become scapegoats for people's impatience with them, which makes their incessant teariness a vicious cycle. So terrified are they of rejection that they will do almost anything to avoid it: their need for peace at any price can result in ulcers.

YOUR CHILD'S NEGOTIATING STRENGTH. Underdogs can keep a family disagreement from devolving into open combat, because they can always see each person's good side. Because of their peacekeeping abilities, they can prevent disagreements from escalating—as, say, by jollying a sibling out of a black mood. And when your other kids refuse to pitch in on a task, the Underdog will volunteer to take it on.

WINNER

Winners move into almost any situation with ease and confidence. They expect to be accepted and well-treated, and their demeanor reflects that expectation; when they are not, they usually realize that the problem is not theirs.

Not that they are indifferent to the feelings of others; it is just that they are comfortable with themselves, and do not anticipate trouble or rejection. Their quiet assurance often brings out the best in others, who are drawn to their steadiness and congeniality.

Because most children are not sufficiently seasoned to disguise their insecurities, less confident styles will tend to exhibit jealousy for Winners. At times, this will stymie Winners, who may be confused by that jealousy since they cannot see reasons for it. But their instincts are sound, and eventually they realize that there isn't a lot they can do about such reactions, other than to reassure, where they can.

Winners don't need to be defined by externals—the "in" crowd, money, trophies—and are comfortable with themselves either alone or in a group. They have the capacity to reach out for help when they need it, and to see options. Even when they have few material advantages, they are optimistic.

Steve Reynolds, 13, is such a Winner, which makes life easier for his mother, who is divorced and attempting to raise two children (she also has a 5-year-old daughter) on a secretary's salary. Says Steve:

> My mom sacrifices a lot for us. She rarely can find time for herself. So I try to help as much as I can with cleaning and stuff. It's hard, because I'm a very social person. But I'm not a jerk about it. I don't say, "No, Ma, my friends are waiting for me."
>
> Ever since last year, I've bought my own clothes—that's when I got a job at a lumber yard after school. Sometimes I get down about our not having any money. But then I think, "Wait a minute. We've got a cozy apartment, we've got a garden outside and we can grow our own vegetables, we've got each other. It could be a lot worse."

YOUR NEGOTIATING PROBLEM. This child seems too good to be true and so you are tempted to think he's withholding information, or bending the truth, or "on something." Occasionally his confidence will be shaken—for instance, when less secure and more envious styles take cheap shots at him—and you will need to reassure him that the fault is not his.

YOUR CHILD'S NEGOTIATING STRENGTH. Winner kids are born team players, and even the most fractious of family members will find a sense of belonging when this style is on hand. Winners know that their happiness rests on bringing out your best, so that you both retain your dignity and understanding and worth.

In knowing your children's styles, their strengths and weaknesses, you can bring about change by drawing on and profiting from their assets and by being aware of how their liabilities can hurt them and the family partnership. That knowledge makes it possible for you to have realistic expectations of your children, even to learn from them, and to convert your disappointment or despair or anger into pleasure, admiration, and hope.

CHAPTER 5

YOUR PARENTING STYLE

Betty and Larry Stein have been married for 14 years. They live in Illinois with their 11-year-old daughter, Carolyn, who attends a public school in their suburban community.

Betty sees herself as a "soft touch" with her daughter because she feels she must shield Carolyn from Larry's stricter, more exacting parental nature. She says:

> Larry and I don't fight about fundamentals, but we do fight about Carolyn—petty things, like his giving her a task at a time I think is inconvenient, say, in the morning when she's preparing to go to school. I'll intercede on little things, like whether or not her bed is made, and he and I will have a confrontation. I don't think those things are that important in character building or morality. Kids have so many demands on them, if you can make it a little easier in the inconsequential things, you should do it.
>
> But when I do, Larry says, "See, you're doing it again. You're stepping in. This is between her and me." He claims that Carolyn is a master manipulator, who will come to me when she thinks he'll say no to something. I'm not aware of that.

For his part, Larry views himself as an easygoing lug—quite different from Betty's picture of him—and portrays his wife as a compulsively neat, rigid parent who, in fact, "freaks out" if Carolyn's room is messy, or if she isn't presentable. He says:

> Betty wants things done her way, rather than a way that can be done. Carolyn will be dressed to go someplace, and she'll say to her, "Look

at you. You've got dirt on your face. You look like a slob.'' She'll get worked up and intense. I'll say to her, ''C'mon, lighten up. What the hell's it going to mean three weeks from now?''

We interviewed Carolyn separately to find out how *she* assesses her parents: is her mother really a mush, or is she persnickety? Is Larry a demanding ogre, or is he as laid back as he claims? How does Carolyn see them?

It's Mom who makes the rules in my house, not Dad. She is like a benevolent dictator. Dad gives in. It's like that saying, ''Pa's the boss as everyone knows/But what Ma says always goes.'' But when he gets into one of his moods, watch out—because the house will have to be neat as a pin. He is such a neatnik, it's disgusting. Mom doesn't get into those moods. She doesn't care how neat the house is, unless the cleaning lady's coming.

In this family, no one agrees on what Betty and Larry are *really* like. Somewhere in the mix of these three conflicting testimonies are two real people. But by whose account?

Parents see themselves—and, often, each other—in ways that are frequently at odds with how their kids see them, a human frailty common to almost all of us. That's why round-robin family interviews, such as those we conducted with the Stein family, illuminate how *Rashomon*-like parenting can be. The way we come across to our kids is often the antithesis of how we *think* we relate to them. We are seldom reliable witnesses, able to see ourselves as our children see us, or as we really are with them.

But in order to begin the process of loving negotiation within the family, parents need to be aware of their own style so they understand how it interacts with their children's.

WHAT'S YOUR STYLE?

The following chart outlines the six general styles of adult behavior, including the most frequently recurring assets, liabilities, and the ways each style tends to behave as a parent. Remember, nobody is purely one style—people usually are a combination of styles—but one style predominates.

STYLES	ASSETS	LIABILITIES	PARENTING BEHAVIOR
Jungle Fighter	extroverted bright tireless charming creative adventurous funny	overreacts must win goes for jugular breaks promises talks too much quick temper workaholic	great risk taker allows kids to risk batters kids' self-esteem with verbal abuse unpredictable heads off mutiny with gifts little respect for others' privacy publicly humiliates
Dictator	leader thinker articulate problem solver decisive organized clever	controlled intimidating perfectionist rigid critical doesn't listen opinionated	sets ground rules never satisfied demanding withholds praise applies pressure to perform eager to be known in public as a "good parent" debates
Silhouette	intellectual polite responsible tenacious dependable practical organized	ignores conflict denies feelings loner workaholic gives no feedback unemotional penurious	great confidante punishes with silence gives little support hides behind work lenient through indifference consistent withholding
Big Daddy/ Big Mamma	generous mentor nurturer sympathetic easy to talk to open-minded takes an interest	manipulates controlling encourages dependency wordy bossy smother love nosy	spends a lot of time with kids intrudes in kids' personal lives overprotective gives TLC punishes independence big in Scouts and PTA keeps score of favors done

STYLES	ASSETS	LIABILITIES	PARENTING BEHAVIOR
Soother	sees both sides understanding good friend kind affectionate creative generous	indecisive peace at any price conformist won't express opinions needy takes blame fearful	doormat for spouse and kids too emotional tries too hard inconsistent won't set limits unreliable nice to kids' friends
Win/Winner	interested in others helpful sees own limits takes calcu- lated risks empathetic reflective collaborative	none	balances work and home life helps develop self- esteem committed to kids resolves problems encourages kids to explore options sets limits patient

One way to get a handle on your style is to ask three people whom you trust—a friend, a colleague, and an intimate (spouse, lover, or relative)—to tell you what they think your assets and liabilities are, and to look for patterns in their responses. (Note: Most spouses don't like feedback from one another because it often feels like criticism. Don't use this exercise as an excuse for name-calling or accusations—both of you should use it as a means of gathering information.)

If all three people say, for example, "You always interrupt," and you've been unaware of it, you will discover that you have a blind spot about yourself.

When you have a hunch about what your style may be, fill in the blanks next to the following statements.

My assets are: _____   _____

                  _____   _____

                  _____   _____

My liabilities are: _____   _____

                  _____   _____

                  _____   _____

My blind spots are: _____   _____

_____   _____

_____   _____

Can you figure out what your style is? Probably not—you may need more information. The way we ascertained Betty's and Larry's styles (she is a Big Mamma, he is a Dictator) was to have them each fill out a parents' questionnaire, in which (among other things) they answered questions about themselves; we gave Carolyn a kid's questionnaire, which includes questions about parents; then we analyzed and compared the responses.

What follows are some of the questions on the parents' questionnaire. You might want to answer them yourself—later we'll provide a key to your responses that will tell you what your style may be.

1. Check off *five* things your child likes about *you*.

   a)_____ helpful

   b)_____ problem solver

   c)_____ take him/her seriously

   d)_____ respect his/her decisions

   e)_____ affectionate

   f)_____ sense of humor

   g)_____ share his/her interests

   h)_____ spontaneous

   i)_____ creative

   j)_____ open-minded

   k)_____ intelligent

   l)_____ responsible

   m)_____ dependable

   n)_____ I don't hassle him/her

   o)_____ generous with money

   p)_____ generous with time

q)_____ easy to talk to

r)_____ charming

s)_____ trustworthy

t)_____ organized

u)_____ keeps promises

v)_____ fair

w)_____ good listener

x)_____ forgiving

2. Check off *five* things your child *doesn't* like about you.

a)_____ impatient

b)_____ doormat for spouse

c)_____ unemotional

d)_____ critical

e)_____ don't keep promises

f)_____ bossy

g)_____ overreact

h)_____ talk too much

i)_____ don't listen

j)_____ won't talk

k)_____ scare him/her

l)_____ unpredictable

m)_____ workaholic

n)_____ apply pressure to get good grades

o)_____ quick temper

p)_____ try too hard

q)_____ expect too much

r)_____ don't spend enough time with him/her

s)_____ don't try to understand him/her

t)_____ indecisive

u)_____ on the phone too much

v)_____ too analytical

w)_____ hate confrontations

x)_____ don't like to be with people

3. When my child does something wrong, I . . . (Check off the *one* thing you *most often* do.)

a)_____ lose my temper

b)_____ engage in name-calling

c)_____ take something away from child

d)_____ ground child

e)_____ give silent treatment

f)_____ threaten

g)_____ lecture

h)_____ hit the child

i)_____ discuss it

j)_____ expect him/her to find solution

k)_____ interrogate him/her

l)_____ nothing (pretend he/she didn't do it)

4. When I don't get what I ask for from my child, I . . . (Check off the *one* thing you *most often* do.)

a)_____ persist

b)_____ give silent treatment

c)_____ lose my temper

d)_____ sulk and withdraw

e)_____ try to discuss it

f)_____ get into debate

g)_____ threaten

h)_____ flatter him/her

i)_____ buy gift

j)_____ try another tactic

k)_____ make tradeoffs

5. When my spouse (live-in, ex-spouse) and my child are arguing, I . . . (Check off the *one* thing that *most often* applies.)

    a)_____ interfere

    b)_____ take partner's side

    c)_____ protect child

    d)_____ solve problem

    e)_____ mediate

    f)_____ do nothing

6. I express love for my child by . . . (Check off *one* to indicate what you most often do when you feel loving toward your child.)

    a)_____ saying "I love you"

    b)_____ giving gifts

    c)_____ giving encouragement

    d)_____ being affectionate

    e)_____ praising him/her

    f)_____ spending more time with him/her

    g)_____ I have a hard time expressing love for my child

7. The one word that best describes me is: (Check off *one* word.)

    a)_____ cooperative

    b)_____ combative (like to argue)

    c)_____ aggressive

d)_____ passive

e)_____ silent

f)_____ wordy

Note: Before proceeding, keep in mind the following: Certain characteristics apply to more than one style. Take, for instance, the characteristic of helpfulness. The Big Daddy/Big Mamma is helpful to the point of suffocation; the Win/Winner is helpful when it is appropriate and/or when help is requested. It's a matter of degree. We are looking for your *typical* way of behaving. Also, for questions 3 and 4, we have selected the thing each style does most often, a person's predominant style; in parentheses we have indicated one other thing each style might also typically do.

If you answered 9 out of the 17 possible responses in each group below, you show a tendency toward that particular style.

KEY

JUNGLE FIGHTER	1. f, h, i, o, r
	2. a, g, k, l, m
	3. a (h)
	4. c (d)
	5. a
	6. b
	7. c
DICTATOR	1. b, k, l, m, t
	2. d, f, n, o, q
	3. k (f)
	4. f (a)
	5. d
	6. f
	7. b
SILHOUETTE	1. k, m, n, s, u
	2. c, j, r, v, x
	3. e (l)
	4. b (d)
	5. f
	6. g
	7. e

BIG DADDY/ BIG MAMMA	1. a, e, g, p, q 2. f, h, n, q, u 3. g (c) 4. h (f) 5. c 6. d 7. f
SOOTHER	1. a, o, r, v, x 2. b, e, p, t, w 3. l (j) 4. i (d) 5. b 6. e 7. d
WIN/WINNER	(Note: Win/Winners have as much range in their assets as anyone, but their liabilities are almost nonexistent. For that reason, we have eliminated a key for question 2.) 1. a, d, j, v, w 3. i (j) 4. e (j) 5. e 6. c 7. a

Now that you've had an opportunity to recognize your style, you can start to see how your style interacts with your kids' styles.

STYLE MIXTURES WITHIN THE FAMILY

Whether parent and child are different in style, or as alike as two people can be, there can be problems.

For example, less assertive parental styles, such as the Soother and the Big Daddy/Big Mamma, tend to envy the aggressiveness and outspokenness of Kid Tyrants, and so such parents sometimes give double messages: They *say* they want their kids to be more even-tempered and kind, but secretly they admire their Kid Tyrant, and they do not set enough limits to their child's aggressiveness. By their tacit approval, these parents may inadvertently stoke, rather than curtail, their children's liabilities.

Even when parents' styles echo in their children, disagreements can erupt. Kids' styles are mini versions of adults' styles, as this list illustrates:

KID'S STYLE	(becomes a)	PARENT'S STYLE
Baby Bully		Jungle Fighter
Kid Tyrant		Dictator
Loner		Silhouette
Saint		Big Daddy/Big Mamma
Underdog		Soother
Winner		Win/Winner

So if you are a Dictator, and your child is a Kid Tyrant, you may feel your turf is being threatened by an expert. It's hard to put a lid on your kid's liabilities when his very nature is provoking yours. But knowing adult styles gives you perspective on what your kids will be like when they are grown; if their liabilities are not modified, they can become, in adulthood, an amalgam of their worst stylistic characteristics.

Awareness of a mis-fit with your child—how you push each other's buttons—is the beginning of establishing or improving harmony within the family.

Here's a chart that illustrates how each childhood style interacts with each parental style, from the child's point of view:

CHILD–PARENT FIT-NESS CHART

	Jungle Fighter	Dictator	Silhouette	Big Daddy/Mamma	Soother	Win-Winner
Baby Bully	war zone	rebel vs. leader	punching a pillow	port in a storm	anarchy	learns limits
Kid Tyrant	battle of wills	talk it to death	actor/audience	parasitic	master/slave	learns give and take
Loner	stonewalls	impregnable	quiet desperation	empowered by silence	heartless to heartbroken	learns to communicate
Saint	kill with kindness	don't fence me in	running in place	not good enough	gets away with murder	learns to listen
Underdog	is annihilated	slave/master	dangling in the wind	emotionally crippled	lose/lose	learns to speak up
Winner	looks for another role model	indomitable	weighs words	lovingly independent	takes care of business	learns value of collaboration

If you are aware of the possible clashes between your style and your child's, you can limit your stylistic liabilities and monitor them in order to help him get a grip on his own.

More importantly, you understand that your children, especially if you are a mis-fit with one or more of them, may push you to the most negative part of your style. For instance, if a child pushes a Big Mamma too far, her authority is challenged, and so she issues orders without kindness, and expects the child to obey without discussion—her assets are eclipsed by the threat to her style.

Combine all the information you have gathered from the charts above, from your friend, colleague, and partner, and from the results of the exercise, and you will have a more clearly defined picture of your style, as well as a name for it. Now fill in the following blanks:

My style is: _____

How my style helps my kid: _____

_____

How my style hurts my kid: _____

_____

HOW STYLES EXPRESS THEMSELVES

Most of us have a fairly good idea of how our assets help our kids; but figuring out how our liabilities do harm is more difficult, because we may not be aware of how we come across to other people. Let's examine how styles express themselves.

Parents, like children, reveal their styles in the words they choose. Here's how each style might verbally respond to a problem that tends to unglue most parents: kids' messy rooms.

STYLE	VERBAL LANGUAGE
Jungle Fighter	"You're a slob."
Dictator	"You are incapable of responsibility of any sort."
Silhouette	"What messy room?"

Big Daddy/Big   "I'll help you clean it up."
Mamma

Soother   "You don't have to clean it up—it's not so
                     bad."

Win/Winner   "You are in charge of your room; but as
                     long as it's messy, keep the door closed."

These are the typical conversational patterns of each style:

- The aggressive (Jungle Fighter) parent insults first, talks second.
- The combative (Dictator) parent criticizes and debates.
- The silent (Silhouette) parent is monosyllabic or says nothing.
- The wordy (Big Daddy/Big Mamma) parent tells you more than you need to know.
- The passive (Soother) parent talks out of both sides of his or her mouth.
- The Win/Winner parent discusses in a nonjudgmental manner, conveying a desire to resolve issues with mutual help or feedback.

In the family, talk isn't cheap. Many of us can't recall what we said in a telephone conversation the day before, but we are haunted by things our parents said to us years ago when we were children. The memory of our mother's and father's casual, throwaway lines endures, remarks such as "I don't have to whisper—he knows I think he's stupid," or "You never were pretty," or "Why can't you be like your sister?" all linger in the scrapbooks of our minds.

When we remind ourselves of those lines, it's easier to evaluate what we say to our children, and how we say it.

Style also expresses itself in how we listen. Except for the Win/Winner style, each of the other five "hears" what it wants to hear and filters out, or uses as leverage for retaliation, that which it doesn't want to hear:

STYLE	WHAT IT HEARS
Jungle Fighter	listens for weakness
Dictator	listens for acquiescence
Silhouette	doesn't listen
Big Daddy/Big Mamma	listens for unalloyed loyalty
Soother	listens for endless love
Win/Winner	listens for honesty

Listening styles are mind-sets that can short-circuit good news and make it seem bad (as with the Jungle Fighter, who sees a contest in everything, or the Big Mamma/Big Daddy, who perceives independence as abandonment, or the Soother, who sees autonomy as rejection). They can also sabotage your child's ability to be open with you (as with a Dictator who always needs to have the last word), or block a signal of your child's unhappiness (Silhouette). These mind-sets make it difficult to pick up important information that your child is trying to convey.

Finally, style asserts itself in the way we *express love* for our children. In most relationships, how we want to be loved often is at odds with how others are best able to express love. Below are examples, culled from our interviews, of how each style expresses parental love:

STYLE	LOVING STYLE
Jungle Fighter	"Sure I love my kid—take a look at my bills!"
Dictator	"She knows I love her—I don't have to draw her a picture."
Silhouette	"We are not physically demonstrative in our family."
Big Mamma/ Big Daddy	"I give her everything she needs—when I think she needs it."
Soother	"I show my love by not hassling my kids."
Win/Winner	"We bring out the best in each other."

Children know when and why they are loved, depending on your loving style:

- If you are a Jungle Fighter, your children may equate love with money.
- If you are a Dictator, your children may know where they stand only when they're in trouble.
- If you are a Silhouette, no matter how much love you may feel, if your loving style does not convey it, your children won't know.
- If you are a Big Daddy/Big Mamma, your children may be confused by your spasms of effusiveness and, when you are wounded, the withholding of love.

- If you are a Soother, and loathe making waves, your children may feel either that they cannot count on you in a crisis or that they can easily take advantage of you.
- If you are a Win/Winner, your children know they are loved for themselves.

It may be necessary for you, then, to learn to stretch, or mute, the way you express love so that your child will receive it.

Put all these things together—verbal language and ways of listening and of loving, according to your style—and you have a pretty good idea of how you are perceived by your children.

HOW YOUR STYLE
HELPS YOUR KIDS

Style per se doesn't estrange people from one another—only its negative projection does. Its *positive* expression can make good allies of parents and children whose styles may be different, particularly when a parent's assets fall into areas where a child is weak. For instance, a Dictator parent can help an Underdog child see a project through to its completion. At the same time, if you and your child share the same style, you can help the child profit from your greater experience.

Each parental style has a side to it that can be extraordinarily helpful to children of all styles, motivating them to do things they want to do but didn't think they could, or to see another, useful perspective. The following chart illustrates how assets help our children, showing just one asset of each style:

STYLE	ASSET	KID'S RESPONSE
Jungle Fighter	adventurous	encouraged to explore the world, rather than to settle for the mundane
Dictator	decisive	learns to take a stand
Silhouette	responsible	knows promises will be kept

Big Daddy/ Big Mamma	open-minded	can talk about any-thing
Soother	generous	likes to have friends over
Win/Winner	respects others	values him-/herself

We talked to a number of parents of various styles whose assets have enriched the lives and experiences of their children.

Rachel is a sunny, artistic, 12-year-old Saint; her father, Harold, is a Dictator. Harold has built an extremely successful real estate business through hard work and bulldog tenacity. Although driven to succeed, he inspires his staff to do their best work through his leadership, clarity of thought, and genius for problem solving, all typical Dictator assets.

His assets have helped his daughter to apply her creativity in a practical way and to expand her intellectual horizons. When Rachel was little, she had (and still has) a playfulness that made her a joy to be around—so much so that she was categorized by the family as being the "cute" one, and her more subdued brother as "the brain."

Harold did not encourage Rachel's label, and when she would trot up to him and coyly say, "Betcha can't guess what happened today," he would reply, "A better way to put that is, 'I have some interesting information to convey.' " Although his criticism could be ranked with carping and nitpicking, she did not take it that way, because he did not try to intimidate her. The result: Rachel learned to evaluate the way she explores a subject and how she discusses it. Her father helped her to become more whole.

HOW LIABILITIES
HURT YOUR KIDS

Stylistic liabilities get played out with children in a variety of ways, as we also discovered in our interviews.

Martin Davis is an accountant, a profession perfectly suited to his Dictator style: he is extremely disciplined, logical, and controlled, and pays copious attention to detail. Those qualities are mirrored in his parenting behavior: he never misses a school play or parent–teacher conference, and constantly grills his children, providing a running commentary on everything they do.

According to Martin, Matthew, his 11-year-old Saint son, is "lazy" and "spoiled." Martin admits that he prefers his 13-year-old daughter, who is as much a perfectionist as he is. Martin says:

> I'm more critical of Matthew because he's illogical, and he's a quitter. He's not a realist. I tried to make him see that the other day when he said that the reason he had not performed well at a swimming meet was because he didn't like the coach. So I said, "Don't tell me you didn't swim well because of the coach. The reason you didn't swim well is that you don't have the talent for it."
>
> I have great expectations of Matthew. It's a dilemma for me because I'm a self-motivator, and he's not like me. He's more like his mother—supersensitive, moral, creative, but not analytical. So I have a quick temper with him. I've always had to struggle, ever since I was a kid, for everything I wanted—I had to work my way through college—and I try to turn disaster into success, something Matthew doesn't do.

Martin is disappointed in Matthew not because the boy is bad or without talent—but because they have a *clash of styles:* the more Martin pushes, the more defeated Matthew feels, as though he can never do anything well enough to please his father. Martin's expectations are based on his own controlling style, rather than an understanding and acceptance of his son's less assertive style.

So with his son, the liabilities of Martin's style dominate its assets: rather than using his capacity to solve problems—to act upon his awareness of the dilemma he has with his son—he exacerbates them through his rigidity.

Liabilities are rooted in feelings of insecurity. Most parent–child relationships are strained when external issues become smokescreens for our own unresolved emotional conflicts. What becomes an issue with our children often has more to do with those feelings than with the reality of what the child is doing. Our feelings not only intensify problems, they often *create* them. Parents cannot cope with their kids' styles if they haven't resolved their own feelings first.

Feelings tend to block the flow of healthy behavior, and when there is a pileup of emotions, we can't discriminate; issues become clouded, and, unable to discern them, we either overreact or underreact. Negotiations turn on our ability to discriminate, as we will see in later chapters.

You may have some unfinished emotional business with your parents that spills over into your relationships with your children; you may still feel like an insecure kid yourself.

Look back on your own childhood and ask yourself: Am I doing things that my parents did to me? What are the five things that hurt me most? Am I doing the same things with my child? Alternatively, what five things about my parents gave me the most joy? Am I giving my child good memories, as I was given?

How you responded to that early patterning depends on your self-esteem, as well as your style, and colors your relationship to your child:

- Are you afraid to speak up to your Baby Bully, because you were never allowed to voice an opinion as a child to a Jungle Fighter parent?
- Do you plead with your Kid Tyrant, because you were afraid, as a child, of being emotionally abandoned by a Dictator parent?
- Do you stifle your reaction to your Loner, because your Big Daddy/Big Mamma parent too often invaded your privacy?
- Do you have trouble setting limits with your Saint because you were given little affection as a child from a Silhouette parent?
- Do you push your Underdog too hard, because a Soother parent did not help you to develop self-control?

The feelings that stem from losses in your childhood will run in tandem with your style and have an impact on your relationship with your child. And so you may need to separate the real from the imagined or the remembered—and, perhaps, consult a therapist to help you resolve this often complicated, but extremely important, issue. When you can see your child as separate from you as you were when you were a child—or as separate from your parents in the feelings that are stirred up in you—you can change your parenting behavior. You may find, in your reflecting, that you've been too demanding, or unloving, or overcompensating with your child, and that the cause is, indeed, old, unfinished business.

When you can hold up a mirror to the child you once were who, emotionally, is still alive and well within you, you can help that "child" to grow up, and be less vulnerable to the liabilities that your own children can stoke merely by being themselves.

Parents who feel powerless with or threatened by their children often are unable to accept temperamental differences with them, largely because of their own insecurities.

*   *   *

Although it is not always easy to do, acknowledging the feelings behind the liabilities of our styles makes it possible for us to understand, if not cherish, our children's liabilities. Children, because of their youth and vulnerability, cannot be expected to be so understanding; their responses to parental liabilities stem from their limited experience.

STYLE	LIABILITY	KID'S RESPONSE
Jungle Fighter	quick temper	can't figure out when he'll be hugged and when he'll be spanked
Dictator	interrogator	lies or fibs or withholds information to get off the hot seat
Silhouette	punishes with silence	always off balance; feels abandoned
Big Daddy/ Big Mamma	talks too much	can't filter out important details; doesn't listen; withdraws
Soother	emotional doormat	feels guilty; can't count on parents for strength or reliability
Win/Winner	ideally, none	spontaneity

A difference of opinion or style or ability on your child's part is not a lack of love for you. When you can deal with how you really feel about yourself and your children, and recognize how your liabilities can hurt your child, parent–child conflicts become easier to resolve.

PART III

PREPARING THE NEGOTIATING SCRIPT

CHAPTER 6

THE LANGUAGE OF NEGOTIATION

Julia Patterson, a journalist who is the mother of a 12-year-old girl, works against perpetual deadlines. While in the homestretch of putting together a story, she and her daughter had an ugly fight, touched off by the child's launching a series of epithets that would make a dockworker faint.

Julia sat her daughter down to ferret out the cause of the seemingly unprovoked attack. After a half hour of her probing questions and of her daughter's invective, defensiveness, and angry tears, the eighth-grader finally blurted, "When you're on a deadline, you get *so cold!*"

Says Julia:

> Her comment stopped me dead in my tracks. I, who am so verbal, could think of nothing to say. So I mulled over her comment for a few minutes, sorting through all my projects, attempting to find out whether or not her observation had any merit. Finally I realized that she was absolutely right.
>
> I decided to level with her: "When I'm working on something," I said, "the reason I seem to be cold is that I'm scared I won't be able to finish it, and I'm scared that it won't be accepted. So I develop tunnel vision, and keep my feelings inside. I don't mean to close you out, but I see how it might look that way. I'm really sorry, and I'm very glad you let me know.
>
> "When you see me doing that, if you want my attention, I want you to grab me by the lapels and say '*I need you.*' I will stop whatever I am doing. And I'll try to be less compulsive about my work and more aware of your needs. But next time, I want you to find another way to tell me what's on your mind."

Julia deserves no medals for apologizing for her remoteness; but she does deserve credit for being willing to examine the way she communicates with her daughter, verbally and nonverbally. By her example, Julia was able to teach her daughter that there are alternatives to how she expresses her unhappiness. By accepting the truth, she let her daughter know she could tell the truth in an appropriate way.

It is tempting to assume that the people we live with can read our minds. Minimal explanatory language may characterize close friendships once they are beyond the getting-to-know-you stage. But verbal ''shorthand'' with children can be verbal carelessness or neglect.

As one woman put it, in recalling her own childhood, ''Whenever my mother got angry, she would seldom tell me why—instead, she'd say, 'You should be able to figure it out.' Even when I was 6. It frustrated the hell out of me. I always felt this amorphous wrongness— but I never knew why.''

Frequently, we do not tell our children enough about ourselves, our feelings, failures, and dreams—the way we automatically do in the building of friendships—and simply assume that they ''know'' us.

But Julia's daughter could not have known what her mother was thinking or even feeling, because her verbal messages were abrupt, and her nonverbal message said ''stay away.'' Only the most sophisticated and self-confident children are able to see beneath the brittle shell of parental anxiety.

At the same time, we often think we ''know'' our children; as the results of our survey make clear, often we don't. One of the pitfalls of that assumption is that the verbal abilities and gymnastics of our kids can sometimes lull us into believing they are more adult than they are.

The Saint child, for instance, who is so intent on being your benefactor, can cause you to forget that she does not have all the answers—that, in fact, she is not as capable of certain responsibilities as she would have you think. The Kid Tyrant who, at 2, tells you to ''just relax'' as you hurriedly put on his diaper (a story told us by the mother of such a child) may be verbally—perhaps even cognitively—precocious, but is not yet ready for Yale. The Loner computer wunderkind who reduces you to sobs while teaching you how to use his word processor is, nevertheless, still a kid.

When language is in disarray, negotiation has no place to begin. Children need to be taught how to use language that communicates, that states their problems, needs, and wants, without rhetorical mayhem.

The frustration of caring for an infant is that he lacks the language to tell us where it hurts. The child who talks early has real advantages over the child who does not, because he can express his needs and feelings. As one father put it, "My son could say such words as 'bottle,' and 'up,' when he was nine months old. So he didn't have the anger and confusion that other toddlers have, because he could ask for and get what he wanted. Now he's four, and he's incredibly articulate—and, God help us, still getting what he wants."

How children express themselves depends in large part on how parents characteristically convey their thoughts and wishes. When kids are unable to communicate appropriately—or at all—often it is because of two things: their style and the conversational climate at home. Baby Bullies and Kid Tyrants drown their views in a sea of words, for instance, while Loners are nearly mute. But style dictates children's use of language only to a point.

Children take their conversational cues from their parents. When parents are under stress or are impatient, they often use verbal and nonverbal language that reflects their liabilities, and nourishes their children's, deepening the spoken and unspoken differences between them.

The following sections will help you examine the verbal and nonverbal messages you send to your child.

VOICE TONE

Is it sarcastic or friendly? As a recent radio commercial illustrates, there are many ways to say "Oh, sure"—in a flat voice, as though cynically remarking on an empty promise, or with a rising inflection, as though in agreement or to express delight.

A recent study at Stanford Law School found that the tone of voice of judges when giving instructions to a jury has an impact on the verdict a jury will deliver: from his or her nonverbal messages—that is, tone of voice—a judge's negative or positive bias can be inferred by a jury, which itself can become subtly biased. How you say something has more impact, according to research, than *what* you say.

The pacing of your conversational style also subtly—or not so subtly—colors your speech. When you speak quickly or loudly, you imply a one-sided exchange or opinion; when you speak slowly, with occasional pauses, you invite a thoughtful response.

BODY LANGUAGE

While words convey thoughts and ideas, body language conveys feelings. If, for example, your child proudly shows you a painting he or she did in school and you say "Nice job" at the same time you are walking out of the room, you are nonverbally telling the child that you aren't all that impressed or interested—indeed, it is the body language, rather than your words, that the child will remember.

Do you avoid eye contact or do you appear to be open and interested? Nothing kills a conversation with a child faster than when the parent looks over the child's shoulder, or keeps his head down, or leafs through a magazine, or turns on the TV. Body language gives away the fact that you're only half listening, something parents often do, particularly with younger children, who frequently talk endlessly to hear the sounds of their own voices (the danger, of course, is that you may not tune back in—most parents, however, do have a sixth sense of when their kids are saying something important).

On the other hand, parents who sit with their arms at their sides rather than crossed in front of them, who maintain eye contact without staring, who sit next to their child rather than on the other side of the room, or who nod in agreement while the kid is talking rather than stifle a yawn, invite the child's openness, trust, and goodwill.

PHRASES

Do you ridicule or do you ask for clarification? Do the phrases you use cut off any chance for negotiation? Let's say your child brings home a report card that is riddled with C's and D's. Do you say, "What, again?" or do you say, "Tell me what's happening in school—maybe we can figure out how you can do better"?

Think of the phrases you routinely use—they are your conversational signature. If you can't think of any, ask your spouse or your kid to tell you—they *know*. Your speech may include some of the following phrases. You may be jolted, or pleased, to find that your child has picked up many of them from you.

POSITIVE PHRASES	NEGATIVE PHRASES
"Way to go."	"Butt out."
"That's neat."	"Get lost."
"Go for it."	"Don't ask *me*."
"Good for you."	"Forget it."
"Nice going."	"No way."

Sometimes children say things that seem to be fantastic or ridiculous. Your 4-year-old child may say he doesn't want to go to sleep because he's afraid of monsters in the closet. You may respond, "That's nonsense," but what sounds like nonsense to you makes perfect sense to the kid. Parents often forget the skewing of reality that is peculiar to childhood, the dreams that seem real, the possibility of sliding down the bathtub drain, the distortions of an adult's size relative to a child's. When children say seemingly ridiculous things, it is often productive to ask them for clarification so that you can get to the feelings behind the "nonsensical," but altogether revealing, things they say. The phrases you use can close conversational doors or open them.

CONVERSATION

The ablest negotiators are those who know how to strike a balance between speaking and silence. Either you are a talker, or you are a nontalker—either way, you already have certain negotiating advantages. The same applies to your children.

TALKERS. Baby Bullies, Kid Tyrants, and Saints are talkers. They know how to get their point of view across to you, to ask for and to get what they want—you don't have to dig for the information. Generally, they have fairly good social and conversational skills—depending on their age—and are not reticent about asking questions. As they mature, they become adept at concealing their private thoughts behind a screen of conversation. Saints, for example, can charm you with expressions of affection or by poking gentle fun at themselves, giving you the impression they are being revelatory. In fact, you've only been given a taste, and the Saint can then retreat behind the shelter of apparent openness, a distinct negotiating advantage.

But there are disadvantages to being a talker: talkers need an audience, and the feedback of a response, to bolster their self-esteem. Talkers are always "on." They tend not to be good listeners, so intent are they on impulsively getting in the last word. As a result, they often put too much distance between their words and their feelings; they don't spend enough time being reflective, and simply thinking.

NONTALKERS. Loners and some Underdogs are nontalkers—only seldom will they chat you up, or indulge in long, meandering conversations. But they have certain advantages over gabbier styles: nontalkers are observant, noticing small details in their surroundings and in your appearance or behavior. People love talking to nontalkers because of their silence, into which is read, rightly or wrongly, such character traits as trustworthiness and deep thinking. Nontalkers don't squander conversational energies; they speak only when it's important—and when they do, people *listen*.

But nontalkers, by playing their conversational cards close to the chest, rarely let you know what they are feeling, and so their needs, because they are unexpressed, often go unmet. Nontalkers keep people off guard—so only the most assertive styles are willing to tolerate that unease long enough to get to know these silent types.

Winners fall somewhere in between; they are a hybrid of the advantages of talkers and nontalkers, with few of the drawbacks of each.

As a parent, whether you are a talker or a nontalker, you need to think about how you converse with your children, keeping in mind their love or loathing of verbal exchanges. Do you lecture or do you share information? There's a wide difference between a monologue and a dialogue: a monologue gives information, but doesn't receive it—it's unilateral; a dialogue is the active involvement of two people who are giving and getting information.

Again using the example of, say, your child's mediocre report card, if you pontificate on the perils of laziness and the surefire, inexorable doom implied by crummy grades, nothing in your speech will motivate the child to improve. Indeed, the youngster will mentally check out, 30 seconds into your speech.

If, on the other hand, you say, for instance, "There was a time, when I was a kid, that I had trouble, too," and then share with your child how you felt and what you did about it, you are not condemning the child; rather, you are giving him the notion that no one is perfect, that there is always a next time, and that his worth cannot be reduced to a single letter on a report card. Moreover, you are doing so on his level—identifying with problems and pressures peculiar to his age and developmental context, rather than yours.

Here are examples of how stylistic liabilities are mirrored in the ways parents sometimes speak to their children (Win/Winners hardly have any, and so are excluded from this list):

PARENTAL STYLE	VERBAL LIABILITY
Jungle Fighter	"You dummy!" (aggressive)
Dictator	"A monkey could write a better paper than that." (combative)
Big Mamma/Daddy	"We're going to talk about this if it takes all night." (wordy)
Silhouette	"Not now." (curt)
Soother	"Of course you can't do it. Your teacher shouldn't assign so much homework— you're overworked." (passive)

Although such remarks may be momentarily satisfying, not unlike kicking the cat or passing the buck, they seldom produce the kinds of results that lead to problem solving. Children who are cowed by remarks that lead off with an assumption of wrongdoing, or who are discouraged from taking a measure of responsibility for their deeds, may be contrite or off the hook for the short haul, but have been given no reason to become autonomous, let alone collaborative.

Negotiating language helps *prevent* or lower the flash point of those situations in which parents lose their cool. But before it is employed, you must keep in mind the following:

- If your child is expecting a friend to come over to visit, that is not the time to ''have a talk.'' (Timing is one of the negotiating skills that we will discuss in Chapter 8.)
- The younger the child, the shorter his or her attention span. Be succinct. You can open and close an entire negotiation in a few minutes, if necessary.
- If you are not clear about what you want to say—if, for example, you are cranky with your child because you are still steaming over a fight you had with your spouse—you need time to sort out the purpose of a discussion before you begin it. Your uncertainty will

be reflected in the way you talk—generally, through overreaction and scattershot complaints—and as a result you will not be taken seriously by your child. Alternatively, you may frighten or confuse him. What seems like a big deal at one moment may not be at another.

- Be aware that your child's purpose may also be unclear. For instance, he may request a new baseball jacket, but the unstated issue—which he may not even be aware of—may be that he's trying to "belong" to a group from which he feels excluded. Once you sort out the child's need, rather than his want, the negotiation shifts from the jacket to ways to help him feel good about himself. This may include allowing him more opportunities for personal decision making at home so that he has a better sense of his own identity. Of course, he may simply want the jacket. Well-placed language will help you sort out the difference.
- Do not ask questions, such as "Did you have a good day?" that require a yes or no response, because in all likelihood that's all you'll get.
- Use language that your child can understand, rather than polysyllabic words that are mystifying. If he is under 12 years old, for example, use words such as "chip in," "help," "talk to us," rather than "contribution," "participation," and "deliberation." One man we talked to had been, in his childhood, frequently called impudent: "I knew from my mother's tone of voice that that was something bad—but I didn't know *what* it was that was bad, so I just figured I was cross-the-board rotten."
- The goal of using negotiating language is not simply to get results—it is also to exchange ideas and explore options.

The language of negotiation falls into four categories: words that open a negotiation, words that keep a negotiation going, words that stop a negotiation in its tracks, and nonverbal language.

LANGUAGE THAT OPENS A NEGOTIATION

When you want to open a negotiation with your child, you need to employ attention-getting language that will invite an honest and informative response. Some examples:

"I'd like to talk to you."

"Let's discuss the party you want to go to."

"Why don't we make an appointment to go over this—let's do it right after dinner."

"You may not want to discuss this today, but we'll need to by the end of the week. Do you want to do it Thursday or Friday?"

"We've tried to talk about this before, but now it's getting serious. Let's work on what we can do about it."

All of these openers convey a willingness on your part to hear your child's point of view; none of them, by their amiability, indicates that you are avoiding an issue. The way you set up a negotiation will contribute to its outcome, positive or negative. If you can keep in mind that the purpose of your discussion is to gather information and/or to solve a problem, your language will convey your intent.

For example, your child's teacher has called to tell you that your daughter has flunked three English quizzes in a row. A negotiating opener could be, "You must be upset by the grades you've been getting in English lately. Tell me what it is that you're having difficulty with, and we can figure out how you can do better."

By addressing your child's feelings—no kid deliberately does poor school work, nor is she immune to its consequences or to thinking she is stupid—you have defused what could have been a heated exchange, and instead invited her to examine what it is that stands in the way of her doing better work. If you address the issue with encouragement of her best efforts to improve, with your willingness to help, and with your belief that she is capable of learning, you engage her ability to deal with the issue rather than to feel blamed and isolated.

Such opening remarks may elicit information that you might need to help her. The problem may be a simple, mechanical one: she can't read the blackboard, and needs glasses, for instance. Or it could be a personality conflict with the teacher: your child is shy and sensitive, the teacher is belligerent and demanding.

Perhaps your child is over her head and needs a tutor; or maybe she simply hasn't developed the self-discipline to keep up with her work, and needs to have a structure that will enable her to do so. It could also be that she has other things on her mind, such as a death in the family, or a move to a new community.

By using openers that permit candor—even though what is said may be painful to hear—you can gather information that can help you both deal with the situation: in this case, to take the child for an eye examination, or to talk with her teacher or even to switch classes, or to monitor television watching and telephone time so that she doesn't fall behind, or to engage extra help in the form of a tutor, or simply for you to spend more time with her.

LANGUAGE THAT KEEPS A NEGOTIATION GOING

Getting your child to divulge the information you need can occasionally test your negotiating mettle. Some kids will become defensive, saying, "The teacher plays favorites!" or "You always blame me!" Or they play on your guilt: "I'd do better if you didn't have a job," or "You always liked my brother better." When your child tries to throw you off the track, you can say, "I know that bothers you—but that's not what we're talking about now. Let's stay on this subject, and we'll handle that later."

You can encourage children to continue talking by complimenting them, saying such things as "That's an interesting idea," or "I never thought of that," or "Tell me more." When children feel that what they have to say is important, they will continue talking.

You will also encourage your child to talk by your implicit respect of him. If he says, "You always interrupt," you can acknowledge the habit and apologize. If he disagrees with you, you can say, "You have a point—I'll have to think about that." Language that conveys respect will engender respect in return, and help maintain the focus of the discussion.

Children are most encouraged to continue a negotiation when you:

- Don't interrupt
- Don't become distracted by their defensiveness or "red herring" issues
- Don't let them push your guilt buttons
- Show respect

LANGUAGE THAT STOPS A NEGOTIATION

In response to our survey question, "What stops me from negotiating with my child is . . .", many parents wrote in comments. Some examples:

"She pouts and feels hurt and withdraws, rather than staying in an active dialogue."

"His lack of responsiveness, although I keep trying anyway."

"Her age—she's two and a half."

"It's very hard to make a three-year-old do what he doesn't want to do."

"He does not always view my position as authoritative."

Note that these responses really put the blame for failed negotiations on children. Said a mother we interviewed, "I believe that the burden of communication is on the parent. If I want to get my son to understand something, then I better make it clear so that he can get it, as opposed to expecting him to struggle to figure it out."

Children often try, even in early childhood, to avoid disclosure: they "crumble" in the face of criticism, and deflect your efforts at communication by seeming to be emotionally unable to continue a discussion; they tune you out; they retreat behind a facade of indifference, a neat trick pulled by most teenagers.

But even in the face of your child's avoidance or immaturity, you can still negotiate. Infants may be "too young" to talk, but even they are not too young to negotiate, as we will see in Part IV.

Negotiating cripplers come in a variety of forms:

NAME-CALLING. When parents refer to their kids as lazy slobs, crybabies, and the like, their words become weapons that call for a defense. You probably can recall having been saddled with such labels from time to time in your own childhood, and may have spent the rest of your life trying to prove them false, or worse, believed them, as though they were life sentences. Such terms go directly to the heart and circumvent the brain: rage, or sorrow, paralyzes the thinking process.

Alternatively, when your child calls you an ass or a wimp, or nosy, you can insist that such words are unacceptable, at the same time acknowledging the feelings that impelled them: "It sounds to me as though you are mad at me—but we can't have a conversation if you are insulting. Find another way to tell me what's on your mind." By retaining your composure—and not getting diverted into a tirade about bad language—and by requiring appropriate language, you encourage your child to harness his thoughts and avoid a shouting match, and to address the issue.

FATIGUE. Overwork, a logjam of stress at home, troubles with in-laws, and anxiety about money, all drain the stamina and the focus it takes to see a negotiation through and to recognize options. When we are physically and emotionally drained, all irritations—whether minor or monumental—take on equal weight. And so fatigue can cause us to say things we might not when we have reserves of energy to temper our language.

At such times, it's prudent to say, "I am too tired to go into this now. Let's talk about it tomorrow morning." You do not ignore the problem—you postpone it to a time when you can give it your full attention.

CRITICISM. The only person who ever feels good about a criticism is the person giving it. You could express concern about the way one of your children constantly teases another, for example, in either of these two ways:

"You have a cruel streak a mile long—you'll never have any friends if you keep this up."

"Let's talk about why you pick on your sister so much—is it because you think she's smarter than you? Or do you think that I prefer her to you?"

The first comment judges; the second looks for solutions. Criticism condemns; negotiation reassures.

But "criticism" works both ways—your child may take issue with something you have done or said; if you can point out your child's errant behavior, he or she should be able to make similar observations about you. Children who are taught to calmly articulate what troubles them about you, or about a friend, or about a teacher, without being called fresh, or irresponsible, or cruel, will not need to resort to inappropriate words and/or deeds to attract or to dodge your attention.

Using "I" statements can help each of you avoid attacking the other. When you say, "You're the most self-centered person I know," you only get your child's back up. When, instead, you say, "When you ignore me after I've told you I'm sick, it makes me feel that you don't care about me," you address the child's behavior, rather than condemn him as a person.

Again, you have to keep your goals in mind: if you want your children's behavior to change, you have to use words that will invite them to examine it and to explore the problem with you.

NOT LISTENING.   Good negotiators have a flair not only for words, but also for listening. Indeed, professional negotiators know that silence is as important as words in the negotiating process: when there is a conversational void, most people will try to fill it, and may say more than they had intended to.

But when most of us are in the heat of an emotional exchange, particularly with spouses and with children, we "listen" only long enough for the other person to pause so that we can get our licks in, not paying attention to content at all.

Moreover, many parents feel that they are abdicating their responsibility as adults by not providing a running text in the form of such comments as "That's brilliant!" or "You should have done it this way," or "Don't talk with your mouth full," or "That's a split infinitive," rather than simply permitting the child's words to flow unimpeded. By not listening, parents effectively muzzle their kids, and limit their ability to find solutions.

One woman we interviewed went into therapy because she and her son were always at loggerheads whenever she wanted to have a conversation with him. She discovered that when he was talking about his friends, she'd say "I like him," or "I can't stand her"; when he was talking about his teachers, she'd say "I wish I'd had someone so eloquent," or "The guy is only interested in grades." She had an opinion about every subject her son brought up—and as a result, made her son's experiences *her* experiences by constantly imposing her unsolicited views and injecting herself into the discussion. So he stopped telling her anything.

In conveying the idea that you don't have all the answers, you make it possible for your child to provide them or to admit that he doesn't, either. For example, if your child says something you don't understand, you can say, "I'm not getting it—could you put it another way?" or "Can you give me an example of that?" It may be that your child is puzzled about what he wants to say, and your questions will prompt him to clarify his thoughts.

In addition, by listening to your child, watching for signals that he hasn't finished saying what he has to say, you can gather information offered spontaneously that grilling seldom produces. The best journalists use this technique all the time—indeed, the next time you watch a television interviewer, pay attention to the questions that don't get answered because the interviewer couldn't shut up.

NOT CLEANING UP YOUR LANGUAGE. The next time you have dinner with your family, turn on a tape recorder. While at first everyone might feel self-conscious, in time you will forget that a machine is monitoring your speech. On playback, you can get a clear picture of how you use language with your family, how it changes from person to person, as well as how your children talk to you—information that will help you see the ways in which you might be using language ineffectively in a negotiation.

Another way to check your speech patterns is to ask your spouse to critique your negotiation with your child. One couple, in the process of trying to get their 5-year-old Underdog son to stop coming into their room at night, does just that: they each tell the other where their language goes awry, where they invite their child's dependency, and where they encourage his autonomy. They are learning not to get sidetracked, either by their emotions or by their son's, and they have become more effective in limiting his bedroom invasions.

The third and most obvious way to assess your negotiating language is to ask your children for feedback or to ask if they understand what you are saying.

Finally, we get a fix on how we talk from how our kids talk. One woman we interviewed admits that her normal, King's English quickly erodes into four-letter expletives when she is trapped on the highway in her car between 18-wheel trucks. When her 10-year-old son began using the same foul language, she said, "Don't expect me to do anything for you when you talk that way. Use real words."

A couple of weeks later, at the end of a grueling day, during which she'd asked her son several times to feed the dog, she finally yelled, "Get your ass down here and do it!" He strolled into the kitchen and serenely said, "*Ass* is not a real word. I won't do it unless you use another."

She has since cleaned up her language. At least when her son is around.

We do not mean that you should scrutinize every word you say to your children—your occasional irritability, periodic anxiety, and impatience are not going to irrevocably scar them. Indeed, when you use words to explain the emotions that caused the odd outburst, you give your children permission to feel angry or testy, and help to recognize what causes them to go over the verbal edge.

Teaching your children how to use well-thought-out and well-intentioned words gives them the tools for effective and loving communication with you and with others, and helps them avoid other methods—such as physical or verbal abuse—that mar their ability to communicate and to see and solve problems.

CHAPTER 7

THE SKILLS OF NEGOTIATION

Applying negotiating skills to the family may seem, initially, like learning a new tennis serve: at first it feels uncomfortable, even self-conscious. And even though your head tells you that a more effective stroke would immeasurably improve your game, you are annoyed not to be able to use your old serve, which, while awkward, was at least familiar.

Still, once you become accustomed to negotiating within the family—and once it becomes automatic—everyday issues are no longer everyday struggles, made incrementally more irksome by the weight of their repetition. You'll find that most disagreements will no longer escalate to squabbles. Moreover, dissension within the ranks will not only be minimized, but, when properly expressed, will also be useful, even creative. As you routinely utilize these skills, your children learn to use them as well.

Negotiation requires patience, and there is a payoff, even though it may seem unreasonably long-term. Most children at first will resist trying new ways of handling problems. They may pout, holler, deny. But the message is not lost. It's what psychologists call the Loop: we've all had those wondrous parenting moments when we hear our kid saying to a friend, verbatim, the very thing we told her 6 months ago. If your words are honest, and if you do not expect results this minute, they will eventually come back to you.

Before we outline negotiating skills, keep in mind the following guidelines:

- Negotiation takes time and practice. Don't give up if at first you feel discouraged. If, for instance, one of the skills we will discuss doesn't work, *try another*. You can practice your new negotiating "strokes" at work—reinforcing what you already know about negotiating in the business world—or with your partner or spouse, even with friends.

- Before beginning a negotiation with your child, hold off judgment about an issue until you've gotten all the facts, or you won't select the appropriate negotiating skill. Instead of saying "You left the milk out on the counter—*again*," ask, "Did you leave the milk out?" Your child may not have committed the infraction, or may have had a good reason for doing so, such as needing to answer the telephone. Or he may be bending the truth—you'll have to find out why that is so. Gathering information without an indictment will tell you whether or not a negotiation is even necessary, and if so, to what purpose.

- Assess the appropriateness of your complaint or request, and tailor your expectations accordingly. A 4-year-old cannot be expected to operate a washing machine, for instance; nor would a Loner be the best person to read a story to his little brother. Neither is up to the task, for different reasons, but may be capable of or willing to do other tasks.

- Remember that *you are in charge,* and you must make the judgment calls that determine the purpose, pace, and tenor of a negotiation. Is your child lying? Afraid? Tired? Merely rude? Do you know what's important to him? Is it the same as last year? Have you, due to stress or unresolved issues of your own, created or contributed to the problem?

- Give your child a chance to talk. Do not supply all the answers; you may be incorrect, or he may clam up.

- Keep it simple. There is a beginning, middle, and end to any negotiation. The beginning sets up the agenda; the middle allows you both to explore, discuss, persuade; the end is the time to recapitulate, restate the issue and its resolution, or to plan for another meeting. Make sure your child understands the purpose of the meeting.

- Be fair. Don't have a talk when you are pressed for time, or if you are overloaded with your own problems and unable to focus and to be judicious. Don't "dump" on your kid, either about all your woes or all his mistakes. Be aware that you have a goal—to resolve a problem or simply to discuss it.

- Do not drag in extraneous issues. If your concern is the size of your electric bill and the necessity of turning off lights, don't discuss your child's table manners.

- Pick your moment. The day your daughter was cut from the cheer-leading squad is not the day to discuss the nail polish she spilled on the rug.

NEGOTIATING SKILLS

GOAL SETTING. Do you want things done your way to accommodate your goals alone, or are you considering *both* your and your child's goals? Sometimes the former is your first priority, as in the instance of a toddler who runs out into the street, or who will not stop screaming in the supermarket: action (pulling the child back onto the sidewalk or taking the child outside), rather than reasoning, in these instances, is unilateral and requires no negotiation.

But in the family, most goals are negotiable: of paramount importance is the goal of improving and maintaining the relationship between you and your child, not to prove who is right and who is wrong at a given moment. Faultfinding and blame setting—looking for a villain—unravel any negotiation, let alone a family tie.

Many parents save up their arguments and spew them, all at once. If you want to talk to your child about his chronic tardiness, do not throw into the argumentative hopper his sloppiness, poor grades, insolence, and every other grievance you've had since his birth. To set a goal, you must first set priorities.

Your priority is the thing you want discussed or accomplished *now*. Not doing homework is less important than your child's forging your signature on a note excusing him from doing it. The issue here is not schoolwork—it's character.

By setting goals that match the situation and your child's age, you can alleviate tension and focus on manageable issues, one at a time.

AGENDA. An agenda outlines the items you want covered in a discussion with your child. Let's say you want to talk to him about a call you received from his teacher about his not having handed in several homework assignments. You prepare, either in your head or on paper, the problem you want to discuss, which includes, in this case, the following:

- The reason the teacher had to call you instead of the child telling you about the problem himself

- What caused the problem—his not understanding the work, or his lack of discipline, or his lack of time because he is overloaded, or his not feeling well
- What he, and you, are prepared to do to correct the problem

But let's say you aren't sure how to construct your agenda because you haven't clarified in your own mind what the problem is—you have a vague sense of unease, a feeling that something's amiss, but aren't sure what. Here's what to do:

Say to your child, "Listen, we've been doing a lot of bickering lately, and I'm not sure why. I want you to write down three things that I do that bug you, and I'll write down three things about you that bug me. Later we'll talk about it and compare our lists."

In this case, isolating and discussing these six items *is* your agenda. The purpose of an agenda is not simply to solve problems or to achieve a goal—often an agenda is made in order to examine the unhappy climate at home or the change in behavior that indicates that a problem exists, or to prevent a problem from escalating.

To get your agenda across, bear in mind the following:

- Anticipation of your child's characteristic response to a proposed agenda—he might roll his eyes heavenward, or say *"Another lecture?"*—is the key to its smooth course: if you can rehearse in your mind—even on paper—what the response is likely to be, *given your child's style,* you will not be rattled by the surprises that go with the territory of parenting.
- Ask your child to restate the agenda as you have outlined it; it may be that he doesn't understand what it is, and you will have to put it another way. For example, if the issue in your mind is his walking home alone at night from a friend's house, you can say, "I just want to be certain we're talking about the same thing. I'm concerned about your coming home after dark, not with which friend you're going to see."
- Pace your questions and answers to allow not only for his reactions, but also for his reaction *time*—some kids take longer than others to respond. Build into your agenda "thinking time," for you and your child.
- Monitor your child's grasp of the agenda, and each item on it. You can ask, "What are your thoughts about this situation?" or "How do you feel about that?" This includes him in the discussion, as well as making sure each agenda item has been thoroughly covered and understood.

▪ Volunteer, or ask your child to tell you, the ways you participate in creating a problem. If, for instance, he doesn't do his chores at the end of the day—such as helping clean up after dinner, taking his belongings to his room, and the like—it may be that you ask him to do too many things at once. Encourage him to give you feedback by saying: "I can't help you if I don't know what it is I'm doing wrong."

At first he may not trust your willingness to hear something negative— you may have a history of defensiveness with him, a litany of "How can you say that?" or "What are you talking about? I never did that." So you may have to get him going by saying, "Well, you may not be able to think of anything, but I can come up with at least one: I am very cranky in the evening, and I tend to bark orders at you instead of asking you nicely. Now it's your turn. Can you think of another thing I do?"

Having given him the example of your calm candor, you make it possible for him to look within and to suggest things he may do to make matters worse. If he can recognize his participation in a problem, he will be halfway to solving it. Remember, if he admits to deliberately smashing plates when he's emptying the dishwasher because he's angry, *do not retaliate* or punish. Stick to the agenda.

PRIMING.   Priming is getting your child ready for a future decision, task, or possible problem; it's like planting a seed.

Let's say your child tells you in the fall that he wants to go away to camp over the summer, and you aren't sure you'll have the money to send him. You prime him by saying, "Money is tight right now, and I'm not sure we'll be able to swing it." But, because of the time lag between fall and summer, you have to keep priming him, if your finances still are uncertain.

So you bring up the subject again periodically, saying such things as "I still can't tell you about camp because the situation is the same, and I don't want you to get your hopes up." By spring, you add, "It looks like we won't be able to afford camp; let's come up with some other, less expensive ideas about what you could do this summer."

The more sensitive the issue to be addressed with your child, the more notice he needs to think it over. It is important that you tell your child in advance what the subject for negotiation is, so that he can know exactly what you hope to accomplish in it, and so he can begin to think about the issue at hand.

Remember that priming is related to age: the younger the child, the less he grasps the concept of time. So if you have a toddler and you want to talk to him about his unwillingness, say, to put his toys away, you prime him five minutes—or less—before your discussion.

SHIFTING GEARS.   Be prepared to alter your negotiating agenda. Kids seldom have anything or anyone on their minds but themselves and how the world reacts to them. You want to discuss your child's leaving a trail of dirty dishes from the kitchen to his room, while he is stewing about an upcoming book report. Test his frame of mind before beginning a negotiation: there are times when it may be appropriate to let him ventilate first.

If your child can't tell you what is wrong, and you have a hunch about what it is, you may have to draw on his interests to unearth it, such as a television program that dealt with a similar subject, or a friend of his who had a corresponding problem. But if he still can't verbalize the problem—one as simple as taking a dollar from your wallet, or as urgent as child molestation—it may be that he's simply not ready to discuss it. Do not force the issue. Unless it is life threatening, or unless he exhibits signs of severe depression or anxiety, respect his privacy. Showing your concern demonstrates to him your willingness to discuss the issue calmly and with interest when he is ready. Raising questions today may produce answers tomorrow or 6 months from now.

ZEROING IN.   What may be an issue for you may not be for your child. If, for instance, he wants to stay out late, the curfew you set is your problem, not his—he sees nothing wrong with not coming home until dawn. You will have to zero in on the problem for him.

In this case, you can say that you expect your child home by a certain hour so that you don't worry about his safety, or because he needs his rest, and that members of the family have an obligation to let the others know where they are and to count on when they'll be home. The curfew is not necessarily negotiable, but the hour of the curfew could be.

On the other hand, the child may have a legitimate dilemma that you are unable to see. One high schooler we interviewed was still required to be home by 1:00 A.M. on Saturday nights in the spring of her senior year. Her father insisted on the curfew, until she gave him this argument: "I'll be leaving for college in three months. If you can't trust me now, if you won't let me use my own judgment, how can you expect me to do so when I leave home?" By defining the problem, she was able to persuade her father that he had to begin letting go. He removed the curfew.

Whether you are the parent or the child, sometimes a problem needs to be restated or defined more clearly. Ask your child for feedback so that he understands the reasons for your rule, or for your differing opinion. It may be that what seemed like a problem will no longer be one, or what appeared to be a gargantuan wedge between you is merely a minor disagreement.

FISHING.   This skill is the gathering of information to help resolve a specific difference, to clarify a goal, or to define a problem.

For example, you say to your child, "I got a note from your teacher saying he wants to have a meeting. Why do you suppose he wants to see us?" If he says he doesn't know why—and you sense he does—you'll have to fish for answers.

Fishing should not be a cross-examination, nor should it be lubricated with flattery when "making nice" is not the purpose of your meeting. Try not to answer your own questions—let your child do some of the work. And if your child responds with an insult or epithet, don't let him deflect your goal by provoking your anger. If he's that eager to change the subject, and to risk your wrath, you can bet the issue is not benign; kids are deft at getting you off the subject and in trying to outmaneuver you. You can respond by saying, "Sounds like you've wanted to say that for a long time—let's talk about it tomorrow. Right now we are discussing this problem."

FINDING COMMONALITIES.   The outcome of a negotiation is vastly improved if it begins by drawing on the things that you and your child have in common. Finding commonalities sets the tone—friendly, optimistic, agreeable. For example, "I know you like to stay up late watching movies—I'd love to be able to do that myself. But we'd both be wiped out the next day if we did that the night before a work- or schoolday." By finding mutual sources of pleasure, you acknowledge and share your child's interests and feelings, rather than admonishing him for having them. Once you establish mutuality, you can move on to the issue, in this case, the responsibility of getting enough sleep to meet one's obligations.

BRAINSTORMING.   This skill engages the child in problem solving, relieving you of the unspoken need to find all the solutions and merely guide him toward them. Let's say your child wants to go to a Little League game on Saturday, and you have to go to work. You can say, "Let's figure out how we can do it all—what do you suggest?" He might be able to get a friend's parent to drive him, or he may be stumped for a solution. The point is that you have asked his opinion, and given him the opportunity to participate in the resolution of the conflict.

This is a skill many parents overlook, and it is one that is crucial to helping your child develop self-esteem through decision making and through your respect for his opinion, no matter what his age.

TAKING YOUR PULSE. Parents have more trouble trusting their own instincts than almost anything else. You can tell in your gut whether or not what you are saying feels right. You know, viscerally, whether you are anxiously talking too much or angrily saying too little.

Check your intuition: Do I still have my child's attention? Is he really interested, or just trying to throw me off track with feigned boredom? Am I stating the problem in a way he understands? Am I asking too many questions, and not giving him a chance to respond? Are we still in sync?

At the office, when you are on the telephone, you know that you have probably lost your audience if you can hear papers being shuffled at the other end of the line—when that happens, you need to reevaluate what you are saying. Use the same intuition with your child.

TAKING A BEAT. Silence—yours—is an invaluable negotiating tool. If, for example, your child bursts into tears just as you are explaining to him the fine points of cleaning out the cat box, you need to stop and reflect on his reaction: you may have loaded on him one too many responsibilities, or he may be brooding about a playground cruelty he suffered earlier in the day, or he may be coming down with the flu. At such moments you do not press on; you take a beat to find out what's going on with your child.

Taking a beat buys time and allows you to weigh what your child is saying—or not saying; to go over in your mind any changes in his life that might explain his behavior; to determine if you are over- or underreacting; and to appraise whether or not the climate is too highly charged to continue a discussion. Sometimes a pause in the negotiation, or a postponement, is necessary: you won't know, if you don't take a beat.

OPTIONS. When you have options, you don't become paralyzed. Instead, you ask, "What else can we do?"

Said one woman we interviewed:

Ever since she was a baby, I've been trying to teach my daughter that life is full of alternatives. When she was an infant, I'd hold up two toys to let her pick one, so that she could not only make decisions, but see that there are always options. I am trying to teach her that any roadblock is simply a test to see how you can get over or around it. If you come to an impasse and see it as an insurmountable barrier, you will be scared all your life. But if you think, "Well, I can do this, or I can do that," you will find solutions.

By teaching your children that there are options, you get them thinking, and you plant the seeds of autonomy. The late child psychologist Haim Ginott illustrated this skill by using the ice cream scenario. You and your child go to an ice cream parlor that boasts 78 flavors. "I want *all* of them," shouts your 5-year-old. "Of course you do," you say, "they all look delicious. Tell you what. You can have *two*." If this is said with the appropriate enthusiasm, the kid will think he's getting 79.

If there is one secret to successful negotiation with kids (as with adults), it is to let them think that their decisions are their own, which, in part, they are. By giving them appropriate options from which to choose, they have a measure of control over their lives in a way that is suitable and which helps them to become independent and self-confident.

TRADE-OFFS. A trade-off is the thing you are willing to give up in order to get something in return. If, for example, your child wants you to drive him to a friend's house, and you are expecting company and so are short of time, you can make this trade-off: "I haven't time to both prepare for this dinner and take you across town. But if you'll peel the carrots and set the table, I'll be able to do it." You have traded off your time for his cooperation.

In making trade-offs, be aware that the concept of time means different things to different age groups. If you tell a 3-year-old, "I'll tell you a story tomorrow morning," he has little concept of time, and so will not be satisfied with your proposal, because he thinks you mean "never." A first-grader, on the other hand, may have just learned to tell time, and he will watch the clock minute by minute. So if you say, "At three o'clock, we'll do it," don't wait until four. He has to be able to count on your following through.

Make sure that the thing you are willing to trade off is of equal weight to the thing you are asking your child to give up. Fairness becomes exploitation if you say, "I'll scratch your back if you wash the car.'' At the same time, you can be exploited if you give up too much. When that's the case—when there's an imbalance—you will feel resentful.

Determining trade-offs requires weighing what is important to you and what is important to your child. Since you know, for instance, that tickets to a Sting concert are something he'd die for, you can say, ''I know this concert is important to you. Let's figure out a way you can pay for the tickets. I was planning to hire someone to put up the storm windows. Are you interested in the job?'' This is where knowing what's very important to your child—as we discussed in Chapter 3—pays off.

Perhaps you aren't sure what's important to your child, so you're uncertain about what he is willing to trade off. The way to find out is to ask him to list five things he most cares about at this moment. It may be to make the soccer team, or to learn to play the guitar, or to have a party, or to win a science fair prize. Your participation in helping him achieve these goals, either by car pooling to games, or in hiring a music teacher for him, or in giving permission to have a party, or in helping him with his project, has a potential price tag—his cooperation in terms of what's important to you.

Make your own list. Perhaps these things are very important to you: more time alone, getting your child to pick up after himself, having him vacuum his room and yours, having him prepare one dinner per week. If you show this list to your child, he will know what to trade off with you, and what's a fair exchange for your efforts to help him. Your child's cooperation increases in direct proportion to the importance of the thing he wants from you.

Trade-offs involve two people: you *and* your child both participate in the solution of a problem. If he wants something from you, and it is inconvenient for you to give it to him, he must think of a way he can achieve his goal and assist you in achieving yours.

But not everything that's important to your child, or every good deed you do for him, should be viewed merely as a way to score points. You do many things for him—and he for you—simply because you love each other.

TAKING STOCK.   Trading off is simple: it involves reciprocity. Taking stock, on the other hand, is more complex: it requires that you determine what is important in the family scheme of things—the big picture of your life and that of your partner and children.

Let's say your child wants to go to sleepaway camp, and you can't afford it. On the surface, the trade-off could be your taking on extra work—a free-lance project, for instance—in addition to your regular job.

Or it could mean working two jobs. The quid pro quo if you do so is the loss of enormous amounts of time with your child, with your spouse, and for yourself.

Or your adolescent wants to go to a private college, the tariff for which is $17,000 annually, which you aren't even close to having. Are your efforts better spent on helping him land a scholarship, or in seriously considering a state school, or is it really important to both of you that he attend the more expensive school, even though it means less time together as a family?

One man we talked to told us frankly that he had made the decision to make a big push in his career in order to make enough money to buy a summer home, a decision that keeps him traveling 6 months a year. But he has not yet examined the long-range cost to his family of his decision—he hasn't taken stock. Another man we talked to *did* take stock: he turned down a promotion that would require the same amount of travel because his kids are still small. "When they're older," he said, "that much time away from home will be less destructive to them. And my wife will be able to travel occasionally with me."

Teaching children to take stock is particularly difficult because they have little concept of the future ramifications of today's decisions. Nevertheless, they are seldom too young to begin learning how to weigh the importance of things. For example, your child wants to watch television every afternoon after school, but his grades are slipping. You can teach him the importance of weighing his decisions by saying, "I know it's fun to watch television—but you have to think about what that will mean in terms of your school work. How will you feel if you don't do well on your report card? Let's make up a schedule of study time and TV time, so you can do both."

These questions will help you take stock of trade-offs:

Is this something I can live with?
Is this unacceptable?
Is this something I can live with today, but not in the long run?

BACKUPS.   This is a way of doing something that is entirely different from your original plan. You want your child to clean up her room, and you tell her she has to do it within an hour. She gets a phone call from her grandmother, and so is unable to do the chore in the allotted time. You are not going to ask her to get off the phone—still, your expectation has not changed. So you use a contingency plan: "You have a reprieve until noon tomorrow,'' or ''That call was unavoidable—I'll help you finish up, this time.''

Let's say, however, that your request is deliberately ignored. You need to have a reasonable response to the misbehavior—grounding her for a year does not qualify. But saying, ''You didn't feel my request was important enough for you to do it, so I can't honor your request to take you shopping''—your fallback position if all else fails—does.

If you have a backup, you will not be caught off guard, vulnerable to overreaction or the compounding of routine misbehavior.

THE BOTTOM LINE. You've been negotiating endlessly in good faith, and still your kid won't budge in terms of your goal. You've *had* it. You're not going to give or negotiate one more thing: no more trade-offs, discussion, brainstorming. There is an invisible line in your mind about how far you'll allow your child to go, and he's just stomped over it.

Let's say he is persistently fresh, rude, and thoroughly obnoxious when you ask him to do something. Now, rather than negotiation, you want results: politeness.

So you say to him, ''This has been going on too long. But no more. I will not tolerate the way you speak to me anymore. This discussion is over. When you're ready to speak to me politely, then I'll talk to you.''

This is the hard part. Tears and stomachaches are the tools children use, often effectively, to get us to crumble in our resolve to build their character—in this case, teaching your child that there is a right way and a wrong way to talk to people, particularly those he cares about. But you must stand fast. Remember your anger at being mistreated—each time you relent in your resolve, your child will naturally assume that you'll cave in in other areas too. The time will come when you've been abused once too often. Hold to your bottom line.

Once you've won this particular battle—and bottom lines are not polite disagreements—you'll find it easier to settle future differences before they require one. It's like putting out small fires in order to prevent an inferno.

ERROR ANALYSIS. Now that you're at your bottom line, you need to examine what pushed you to ''I've *had* it!'' Error analysis is like walking backward to see where you've been. What happened? Who was involved? When did this all begin? What outside issues contributed to this? How did I get here?

Let us say that your child persists in doing the thing about which you have had several meetings: poor school work, or picking on his siblings, or waking you up early Saturday morning to ask the time, or not putting away his laundry. You and your child now need to address why the problem won't go away. And so you say, "Let's talk about why this continues to happen."

In the case of poor school work, it may be that the child doesn't have a quiet place in the house to study without interruption; or he may not know how to use a library and hasn't asked you for help with it; or his penmanship needs work; or you have done too much of the work for him.

When you help him figure out the cause of the problem, and when you carefully analyze what you have done to contribute to it—through error analysis—often this is enough to clear it up and to prevent its happening again.

TIE BREAKERS.   There will be times when a negotiation has stalled—your child will not talk, leaves the room, becomes intractable, digs in his heels. At such times your issue—say, wanting him to pick up his toys—has not changed, but the negotiation is deadlocked.

At these times you need to do something to break through the barrier. What you do is this: *try another approach.* This could include changing the time of your meetings with your child from morning to evening, or examining your tone of voice when you ask him to do something, or having a brief meeting when ordinarily your meetings take 20 minutes.

Think about what often happens within the family. You say, "Pick up your toys" quietly, then louder, and finally you are screaming, *"PICK UP YOUR TOYS THIS MINUTE!"*

Tie breakers involve finding options to the ways you routinely deal with your child. Try a new approach, and make sure your child knows you mean it. Kids *always* know when you mean it. Even the most permissive parent will reach the point at which his or her tone of voice leaves little room for conjecture on the part of the child. Think about those moments and remember them—they are triggers to help you change your behavior, and, in turn, to change your child's.

To summarize negotiating skills, and to illustrate how negotiating language expresses them, a sample discussion between a parent and a child, giving the parent's side of the dialogue, follows. The subject for our theoretical negotiation is the desire of a parent to carve out some special time with his child:

SKILLS	LANGUAGE
Goal setting	"I'd like to spend more time with you; I have the feeling you'd like that, too."
Agenda	"Let's talk about doing something together, just the two of us."
Priming	"It's been a long time since we went camping."
Shifting gears	"I didn't know you don't like camping anymore—how about sailing?"
Zeroing in	"I've been thinking about how we can do that, and I realized that I don't know enough about what you like to do when we're together."
Fishing	"How do you feel about our spending more time together?"
Finding commonalities	"Let's go to our favorite pizza joint and discuss what we'd both like to do."
Brainstorming	"We could leave Friday after school or wait until Saturday morning—what do you think?"
Taking your pulse	(To yourself) "Something tells me that he's getting impatient—I'd better keep this short."
Taking a beat	"Let's eat first, and talk about it over dessert."
Options	"We could go to the lake, or sail on the river. Which would you prefer?"
Trade-offs	"I'll shop for the food while you get the equipment together."
Taking stock	"These chores can wait—it's more important for us to have this weekend together."

Backups	"If it rains, we'll go next weekend."
The bottom line	"You've put me off three weeks in a row—I guess you'd rather not take time alone together just now."
Error analysis	"What do you think happened to our relationship? My mistake was not noticing that you're not a baby anymore. When do you think we got off track?"
Tie breakers	"Everything I've suggested, you've vetoed. What *are* you willing to do?"

With any of these negotiating skills, as you may know from the business world, there's a time to prepare for your meeting psychologically, emotionally, even physically, especially if it's a matter of grave concern to you. Sometimes it's not possible to prepare as thoroughly as you would like—you may not have had the time to gather more information, or it may be a matter that can't wait.

Nevertheless, to maximize the effectiveness of these skills, try to do the following:

- Keep the appointment. Give it as much importance as you would a business meeting.
- Be on time—don't oversleep, or arrive home late from work.
- Plan a time for the meeting that is convenient for both you and your child.
- Think about what you want to say and where you are going to say it—the car is often a great place to have a talk because the child isn't distracted by TV and the phone and can't get away.

You may approach a negotiation with your child with a roiling stomach, anticipating defensiveness, insults, excuses, and rationalizations, only to discover that your meeting is over in ten seconds:

YOU: Listen, I'd like to talk about why you don't want to go away this weekend.

CHILD: Gee, I'm sorry, I forgot to tell you—I've been invited to a party. Let's go next weekend.

At the same time, all this will seem less daunting if you know that your child has a skill that is built into his style. The following chart illustrates the skill–style connection:

STYLE	SKILL
Baby Bully	Bottom line
Kid Tyrant	Formulating agendas
Loner	Taking a beat
Saint	Taking your pulse
Underdog	Tie breakers (these kids are the peacemakers)
Winner	Options, trade-offs (Winners use all 17 skills, but are particularly effective at these two)

Not all issues are of equal weight, nor are the discussions to examine them; indeed, most of the time you may need to utilize only one or two of the skills we have outlined here. By dealing with issues as they occur, you prevent the need for full-scale meetings that may pull on *all* your negotiating skills.

Still, there may be times when you do need all of them, problems of such urgency that they tap the full extent of your negotiating resources: your child refuses to go to school, or gets drunk, or has been arrested. The greater the problem, the more intricate the solution. These skills will cover almost any issue, including crises—and will keep you focused on finding a resolution.

Negotiating skills keep you from panicking because, in the final analysis, they continually beg the question: "What can we do next?"

CHAPTER 8

THE STRATEGIES
OF NEGOTIATION

$\mathbf{T}$he purpose of negotiating within the family is to give parents a vehicle for intervening with their children to help them stop behaving negatively and instead become the best parts of their styles: that vehicle is your negotiating strategy.

Strategy includes an awareness not only of your children's liabilities, but also of their assets, because you want to encourage them, and because they are a barometer as to how well your strategy is proceeding. And so, while the issues we will discuss in this chapter center on things about your children that may trouble you, be aware that those assets are there—they will encourage *you* to carry out your strategy.

The one thing for which parents most often formulate strategies is their children's college education. Indeed, that planning often begins when the child is in utero and parents are selecting the "right" nursery school; it continues through elementary and high school, often aided by college counselors, in the selection of the "right" courses, activities, and grade point average to increase the odds of getting kids into the "right" colleges.

But in nearly every other area of their children's futures, parents often do not use the same kind of foresight, because they get caught up in the day-to-day wrangles and minutiae of child rearing.

When, for example, your child refuses to eat his lunch, and 10 minutes later, in the car, wails about hunger pangs, it's hard to think about 6-month, or 5-year, projections, and quite easy to consider saying, "I *told* you so!"

Nevertheless, it is because emotions run high in the family that the virtues of strategic planning for your children begin to make sense.

When you have some emotional distance, it's easier to be more patient with your child and yourself, and to begin the incremental strategic steps that lead to your goals, long- and short-term.

Before discussing strategies—what "works" for a Kid Tyrant, and what "works" for a Saint, for example, as well as what doesn't and *why*, which we'll explore in the next chapter—here are some terms we will use to help you outline and implement strategies within the family:

LOGICAL CONSEQUENCES

As we mentioned earlier, you will notice that we will not use the word *punishment* when discussing strategies with your children; we *do* use psychiatrist Rudolf Dreikurs's phrase, *logical consequences*. Although on the face of it there may seem to be very little difference between the two, the differences are vast indeed.

Here's how "punishment" works: your child fails to put the grape juice in the refrigerator, and when he accidentally knocks it over, it puddles vividly onto the dining room carpet. You send the errant child to his room with the admonishments, "No TV, no phone calls, and no dessert." What has your child learned?

- A lot about the inside of his room and how to amuse himself in it
- A great deal about how to get someone else to clean up after his mistakes
- A surefire way to get attention

But he hasn't learned anything about taking responsibility for his actions and being motivated to change them.

Here's how logical consequences works: same scenario, but with a new ending. Instead of banishing the kid to his room, you ask him to mop up the juice and add, "When you don't put the juice away and it stains the carpet, we have to have it professionally cleaned. It'll cost about twenty-five dollars. How do you plan to pay for it? With your allowance, or by earning the money at a job?"

The kid may clutch his chest in horror, weep wretchedly, accuse you of child abuse, say that he's just a kid and that he will reach retirement age before he can pay off so princely a sum. But if you do not waffle on your calm enunciation of the *consequence* of his behavior, he will begin to see that he has a stake in becoming more responsible. In this case, you can negotiate the consequence: apportion a percentage of his allowance to the payment for the cleaning bill, so that the kid isn't penniless, thereby becoming too dispirited to clear up the debt.

When you use reward and punishment, you underscore misbehavior, rather than engineer a cure for it. But when you use logical consequences, you *set limits*, and you let the child decide whether or not to adhere to them, and then permit the child to experience the consequences—joy or regret—of his decision. Logical consequences differ from reward and punishment because the child has been given a *choice*, and has had to be responsible for that choice. And you have been a leader, rather than a warden.

Kids who are constantly bailed out, punished, or indulged by their parents learn that there is an external payoff for good, and bad, behavior—the payoff is your attention, rather than learning how to develop healthy coping skills from within.

For example, Amy, 10, has a book report due tomorrow. But she wants to watch a special television program. Her mother says, "If you watch the program, you won't have time to complete the report."

"No problem," says Amy. "I'll do it *after* the program."

"Your decision," says Mom.

At 6:00 the following morning, Amy, in tears, wakes her mother and hands her a crumpled, illegible wad of papers. "*Please* will you type this for me? I was up all night and didn't have time to write it over neatly."

Mom says sympathetically, "I know how tired you must be. But you made a choice, and you can't ask me to do work you chose not to do."

This is "natural and logical consequences." Amy can holler and scream and weep—but the problem is out of her mother's hands; it's in Amy's. Amy's teacher, and not her mother, will provide the consequences. Ultimately, so will Amy, who will be less willing to have this problem reoccur. Bonus: Mom, because she wouldn't be manipulated, is not involved in a power struggle. Dividend: Mom has throughout demonstrated respect for Amy's decision by not doing the work for her.

This tidy story includes a postscript: it was years before Amy's mother was able to stick to her word, to stonewall her child's urgent and nerve-wracking demands, and to refuse to give in to them. Says the mother, "I was proud of that exchange about typing the paper. But let me tell you, the whole time my fingernails were digging into my palms, and I had to force myself not to help her. This, from a grownup."

Sometimes, "logical consequences" are not as clear-cut as this one was—when, for instance, your child constantly interrupts you during a conversation with your spouse or with a friend. At such times, you have to invent a logical consequence, in this case, by saying, "It seems to me that you don't want to listen to our conversation, because you keep interrupting, so I think you should go into another room. If you feel like hearing what we're talking about, you can come back when you're ready to listen quietly."

The consequence of your child's not letting you have a conversation is that he cannot hear it, because he doesn't let it proceed. You have not attacked him personally—you have let him know what it means to him if he keeps interrupting. And you have given him a choice, as well as a second chance.

Sometimes, a logical consequence may not come to mind, or the situation may not immediately call for one. In that case, a negotiation with the child may do the trick: "I'm not happy with the way we've been getting along—let's talk about it."

By applying logical consequences, parents withdraw from potential battles of wills and do not get caught up in angry exchanges.

It is not simply that using logical consequences works—it is that punishment, abuse, and nagging do not. Kids who do not learn that behavior has consequences tend to grow up to be adults who feel either that they do not have options, or that they cannot control their own destinies. You can guide your child toward figuring out how to modify his own behavior, and how to control his destiny in a positive way.

TIMING, TIME LINES, AND READINESS

TIMING. Timing in implementing a strategy with children is crucial: you wouldn't begin on a day when you are overtired, or when your child is sick, for example—you'd wait for a more auspicious time. But your child's style—when he is most likely to respond to a strategic negotiation—is also an element in your timing.

Here's how to pick your moment with your child, by style:

Baby Bullies are expert at throwing you curves: just as you try to implement a strategy, they'll jackknife into cloying charm or they'll suddenly manufacture a crisis. They are also impatient, and can't wait for anything. Your job is staying the course, rather than being distracted from pursuing your strategy. It's easy to get sucked into the urgent Baby Bullies' ploys, impatience, and/or pleas. So your timing with them is to implement the beginnings of your strategy on the spot. You can't be subtle.

Kid Tyrants and *Loners* get deeply involved in their interests and take pride in giving them their full attention. Their concentration is so great and they become so engrossed that you feel as though you need a bullhorn to get their attention. With these children, you need to make an appointment to begin to implement a strategy.

Saints also need advance notice because they too are focused, generally on their elaborate social lives. They nourish their self-confidence by keeping five social balls in the air, just to be able to count on one, and are always behind schedule because they take on too much.

The result is that they avoid becoming involved in family activities, or taking on household responsibilities. Be careful not to give Saints too much latitude in selecting a time for a talk with you, because they will almost always respond, "In a second," or "I can't until the prom decorations are finished," or "I *promised* Julie I'd fix her jacket." Saints tend to put their parents on perpetual "hold." There's a point at which you need to say to your Saint, *"Now."*

Underdogs will tempt you to make an exception regarding any strategy because of their pathos and inertia—they are the style most likely to take forever to do something because they get buried in an avalanche of deadlines that were ignored. It feels as though any strategy is a bit crass, so terribly sensitive are they and so outside the "rules" of routine child rearing. Such thinking is a mistake because Underdogs require a structure to prevent or to reverse their habitual nature of being a victim. You don't want to overwhelm them, but at the same time you don't want to prolong their dependency upon you, or to fuel the power of their powerlessness. Your strategy may include a gentler, even slower, approach than with other styles, but that doesn't mean tabling it.

TIME LINES. Time lines are the time within which you want your child's behavior to change, or a deadline for accomplishing the goal of a strategy.

Let's say it's now December. Your 11-year-old Underdog has asked to go on vacation with his friend's family during the summer, and you have agreed to let him do so—you have until June to get your normally shy and reclusive child emotionally ready. Perhaps, however, you've had a previous experience with this child *begging* to visit someone, only to call you a day later begging to come home. He couldn't go the distance because you did not have a strategy for helping him become more independent.

So your strategy is to build into your calendar small ways to make your child become more autonomous—to learn to express his feelings without bursting into tears, to take on small responsibilities and challenges in order to build up his self-esteem. If he does take his trip, and you know he will be well treated, you want to help him to achieve the goal he has set for himself.

You use time lines to structure the pace and scope of your strategy. When strategizing with children, you don't want a given negative behavior to evolve into a habit, when it's harder to change. The kid who hits you when he's 2 could break your jaw when he's 14, if you haven't put a time limit on his behavior.

In establishing time lines, you have the luxury of long-range planning within which to map out your friendly persuasion. You also have the time to take a very long beat, when you can calmly think about how to alter your own behavior in order to help your child modify his.

Time lines are as important for the parent as they are for the child. Many parents, because they want to avoid confronting an issue with their child, will say, "Oh, it's just a phase," or "He'll outgrow it." This latter is exactly what the mother of a 3-year-old says about the kid's biting. "It's just a stage," she adds. He may indeed outgrow it, but it would be far better for him, and for his victims, if his parents didn't wait that long.

Both passive and aggressive parents may tend to avoid time lines— the former out of fear, the latter out of insensitivity or impatience. The reasons may differ, but the result—tacit approval of misbehavior through inertia or anger—is the same.

READINESS.   In setting up a strategy for your child, it is extremely important to keep in mind his readiness. Readiness includes a host of items that may not fit the "norm": walking, talking, starting first grade, joining a club, inviting a friend over to play, having a boyfriend or girlfriend, concentrating on studies, getting a driver's license, leaving for college. In all these situations, sometimes kids need a year or two beyond the norm to "jell" before taking on the next developmental task, but rarely is their delay abnormal. You cannot force a child to do something he isn't ready for—and if you do, the child will almost certainly fail or in some way sabotage the task.

Remember, the younger the child, the shorter his or her attention span, even within his timetable. If you give him too short a deadline, he may not succeed.

ENCOURAGEMENT

When you want your child to do or accomplish something, you build encouragement into your strategy. That encouragement might include, at times, a motivating gift, as in promising a toddler new fancy panties if he or she learns to use the toilet; but you draw the line in, say, paying for good grades, or "encouraging" a reluctant teenager to get his driver's license with the promise of buying him a car. You want the child to mature for himself, not just for you or your largesse.

Encouragement is not the same thing as praise, as Dr. Dreikurs also pointed out. When you praise, you make a judgment that one thing is better than another, and your judgment is of the person being praised. When you encourage, you applaud a deed. "I love the way you set up that meeting, because it was convenient for everyone," are words of encouragement for an action, not appraisal of a person. You imply your faith in your child's ability to improve, but you do not demand perfection: that is the difference between encouragement and praise.

When giving encouragement, it is important to remember that the child is not what he was, nor is he what he will become—he is *changing*. If you concentrate on his negative behavior, even if only in your own mind, rather than on his efforts to gain control of himself and his decisions, it will seep into the way you interact with him, however much you try to conceal it.

It is important not to make comparisons. When you compare your child to other children, you imply that there is only one yardstick for success or approval. To encourage your child, you must respect his individuality. Do not compare him to a sibling, or a friend of his, or you ("When I was your age . . ."), except in terms of understanding his feelings.

IMPROVING THE ODDS

While you may give your children choices to help them learn decision making, you would not make those choices inappropriate. For a Loner, these two choices are inappropriate: "Tell you what—you can either call your aunt to wish her a happy birthday, or you can go over to her house to tell her in person." Neither of these choices suits his style, and so he is set up for failure. More appropriate choices would be these: "You can either write her a note, or we'll buy a birthday card."

You will achieve your goal more readily if your suggestion is commensurate with things he does well or easily, rather than things that fill him with loathing. Your goal does not change—the options for reaching it, however, do.

HUDDLES

Huddles are periodic family meetings that have this goal: to provide an arena for discussion and for problem solving. They are a way to check whether or not your strategy is working. But huddles are not simply forums for sorting out conflicts—they are also opportunities to celebrate victories and to be supportive when someone's had a defeat or setback.

Negotiating within the family is *family business*, and that business cannot be conducted in a vacuum; everyone must participate. If one member of the family refuses to participate, the rest of the family can use its collective persuasiveness to get him to reconsider. But if all else fails, you can't empower the negative member by letting him sabotage the system. So you may have to tell him that he'll be excluding himself from the family in a meaningful way.

Keep in mind, if you have very young children, that their attention span is short—you might want to make a huddle in which they are included with older children brief; or you might want to huddle with them alone and save longer huddles for the rest of the family.

GROUND RULES.   Here's how to structure a huddle. Unless there is a crisis, try to begin the huddle on a positive note: each person can provide kudos for the kindness or special efforts of other members of the family. For example, expressions of gratitude such as "Thanks for picking me up at football practice," "I appreciated your patience while I was on the phone," and the like, set the tone for the huddle.

After the thank-you's have been made, for the next 5 minutes, each family member, whether the meeting is between two people or the whole clan, discusses *one* grievance. State what the problem is and how you feel about it. This section of the meeting is not a dumping session; it is an open forum for allowing everyone to ask for help. Moreover, if the same problem keeps getting raised about one person in the family, that person will eventually "hear" the problem. Use the family as allies in clarifying problems, as well as in arriving at solutions.

Let us say that you want to call a huddle to discuss a redistribution of family labor, because Mom wants to go to graduate school or to take a job, or because Dad is out of work, or because the children are older.

The parent or parents should arrive at the meeting with a detailed list, written out on a large piece of paper, of what it takes to keep the family running: carpool schedules, errands to be run (groceries, dry cleaning, car servicing), doctors' appointments, household chores, *everything*. The purpose of this list is for the family to share its execution; the motivation for doing so is that the family will have more time to relax with one another, and/or to pursue outside interests.

From this list, your children can select one task they want to do that week. The chores should be age-appropriate. Four-year-olds can empty waste baskets; 10-year-olds can unpack groceries; 12-year-olds can vacuum; 14-year-olds can cook one meal; 16-year-old licensed drivers can run certain errands. Mom and Dad can take care of the larger responsibilities, such as scheduling appointments with doctors or teachers, providing lunch money, getting the dog to the vet, and the like.

Try to make the chores *style*-appropriate. Kids who hate to be alone may be more eager to help do the dishes; kids who like to be alone may not mind cleaning up the bathroom.

Chores should be rotated and reevaluated in family huddles. It may be that one child is given too much to do, or hates what he or she is asked to do. You can ask the kids to list on a piece of paper the things they are willing to do and the things they absolutely hate to do. Then they can negotiate among themselves, or with you, trading off one onerous task for another, perhaps less repellent, task.

Even if you have only one child, you can still plan the distribution of chores in this way, but you will have to take a greater role in sharing them, given the smaller pool of labor.

Huddles can be called for large reasons or small, and any member of the family has the right to request such a meeting. But what about children who are less assertive—who cannot summon the nerve to speak up at a huddle, let alone call one? You can put a "Suggestion/Grievance" box in the kitchen, into which anyone can place an anonymous comment; at the next huddle, you can say, "Someone has raised this point. What do you think? How do you all feel about it?"

Many of the families we interviewed have casual huddles from time to time—usually at dinner—yet very few formally schedule them. Not everything, however, requires a huddle—only those things that either require a family consensus or which seem to call for your intervention.

THE SECOND STRING

In order to implement a strategy, sometimes you need to call in reinforcements: you need to enlist the help of others to carry out your plan.

Let's say you're trying to get your child, who skips lunch at school each day because she's afraid no one will sit with her, to form a strategy for resolving her quandary. You want her, perhaps, to learn to ask friends in advance to sit with her each day, thereby circumventing the awful moment of standing, unnoticed, in the cafeteria line.

Tell her teacher your plan, so that the teacher can encourage the child's efforts and/or monitor its progress and report back to you. In addition, you might want to talk to the guidance counselor with a view to starting a club that would be of particular interest to your child, and to children who are like her.

Sometimes you need to educate teachers, coaches, and significant others in your child's life because they have been bamboozled by your child's style as much as you may have been, and you don't want them unwittingly to undo your good negotiating work.

Says the father of Carl, a 10-year-old Kid Tyrant:

> Even when he was in nursery school, he could talk his way out of anything. The teacher would say, "Carl, you shouldn't have done that," and would look at his composed face and listen to his mature arguments, and she would let him get away with it. So it's not only been me giving in, but the teachers too, all along.

Another way to corral support is with your child's siblings. Let's say the conversational efforts of your Underdog child are constantly crushed by her Baby Bully older sister, who can't shut up. You don't tell the Baby Bully your strategy—which is to help the Underdog to open up—because she'll use that information to tease or torment her less resilient sibling. Instead, simply say to the Baby Bully, "Keep quiet. When your sister is finished talking, then you can talk." Part of your strategy is to get the Baby Bully to restrain her liabilities.

Siblings can help each other in a variety of ways—helping younger brothers and sisters with their homework, or giving advice on clothes or how to behave on a date; younger siblings often are able to cheer up older siblings who are in the dumps.

You do not want to sully this often touching sibling connection by making comparisons, or by exaggerating each child's style with such comments as "He's the quiet one," or "She's the school clown," which could create resentment between them.

By enlisting the support of others, you make it possible for your children to be encouraged to help themselves.

In the next chapter, we'll show you how to integrate these strategies, as well as negotiating skills, into your family relationships.

CHAPTER 9

STRATEGY WITH STYLE

In formulating strategies that are tailored to your children's styles, you set into motion the achievement of your long-range parental goals for them—their good character and their increased or more positive involvement with the family so that you all become closer. The purpose of your strategies is to nurture the best qualities of your children so that they will grow up to feel valued and valuable in their working and loving relationships, and so that they will be able to bring out the best in others, and in themselves.

What follows is the game plan for strategizing with each of the six styles of childhood. While there are built-in variables, such as age, in general these strategies apply no matter how old the child.

For each strategy, there is a double strategy—one for you, one for the child. Your strategy for *yourself* is to monitor your liabilities and your tendency either to weaken or to overpower your child when he or she exasperates or confuses you. Your strategy for your *child* is your plan to help him achieve his goals, enhance his assets, or overcome his liabilities. Following each strategy, we will provide a list of questions to help you evaluate how well your strategy was implemented.

BABY BULLY

Many parents feel helpless when it comes to curbing the larger-than-life behavior of this style, especially if it has been allowed to spiral for some time, unchecked. Says Susan Katz, the mother of Samantha, a 13-year-old Baby Bully:

I don't like my kid very much, and she doesn't like herself, either. She's been thrown out of five schools in the last five years, even though she's very bright. She's disruptive in class, talks too much, and is the class clown.

When she was in the first grade, she became violent—she'd pick up a chair and throw it at me. Another time she took a screwdriver and went after her sister.

Nothing works with her, not hitting her, or sending her to her room. She just browbeats everyone in the family. The thing is, she's wonderful with adults, with old people, and with little children, but she has no friends her own age. I just don't know what to do with her.

Samantha did not emerge from the womb with all the worst characteristics of her style in full sway. When she was 2, she became desperately ill with a kidney infection, and for a period of 3 months her parents gave in to her every request, so relieved were they that she was still alive. It was after that illness, says Susan, that Samantha became "incredibly demanding."

For 11 years, Susan has been making excuses for Samantha's behavior, thereby encouraging it, because she has chosen the line of least resistance; she has been unable to confront her own insecurities, which include an inability to set limits with her daughter. At the same time, by her passivity she has enraged Samantha by effectively shutting her out of joint decision making and a healthy sense of control over her own life: Samantha is allowed to be out of control.

Compounding the problem is her husband's perfectionism, and his impatience with the time-consuming subtleties of curbing his daughter's behavior. Susan overlooks her husband's impatience by denying it to herself and to her daughter.

Samantha alone is not responsible for the tension within her family— and the only way to modify her behavior is for the whole family to examine how they contribute to it, and how they can get beyond their impotence, or anger, to change it.

Even when a Baby Bully has reached the outer edge of her violent behavior—which begs for limits—she can still be turned around. The strategy for handling Samantha, and for motivating her to learn self-control in spite of her long, destructive track record, is this:

1. Susan needs to be aware of the ways in which she rewards Samantha's negative behavior. She explains her reticence by saying, "If Samantha doesn't want to do something, and you force her to do it, she makes your life so miserable that it's not worth it."

Moreover, she has not negotiated with her husband in formulating a strategy for setting limits for their daughter that they could enforce jointly (see the following chapter).

Susan is too intent on pleasing the two demanding members of her family and has undermined any structure within which to help her daughter.

2. Samantha needs to be given options, rather than to be "forced" or ignored. Baby Bullies can develop controls only if they are given the chance to exercise them appropriately. For example, once Susan and her family took a summer vacation to Vermont, and Samantha did not want to go. Her parents insisted, and so, says Susan, "She ruined it for us." Instead, she could have given her daughter this choice: "You can come with us, and behave, or you can go to your grandmother's house for the week we are away, or you can go to camp. Which would you like to do?" If Samantha said, "None of them," Susan could say, "If you can't decide, then I will. You're going to your grandmother's."

Sometimes you run out of options to offer your child and you have to exercise one of your own. In this case, the residue of rage everyone in this family feels may have so depleted any resources they have to correct the situation that a more drastic measure is necessary, for everyone's sake. That option, because Susan and her husband can afford it, is boarding school. While this sounds like cruel exile, there are times, albeit rare ones, when the domestic scene is so heated and parents are so frazzled, or anxious, or defeated, that everyone needs a break—even a dramatic one—from the tension. There are first-rate schools that will firmly and lovingly help children like Samantha, settings where old buttons can't be pushed, and which provide kids with opportunities to succeed in ways they cannot at home.

3. Samantha needs an outlet for her energy and her creativity. One way to siphon off her anger and frustration would be to get her involved in an acting class and with school plays. Creativity will out, either in positive or in negative ways. By giving Samantha the chance to channel her creative energies, she can express her zealous anger, or joy, through the positive structure of a creative endeavor.

Baby Bullies are often exempted from logical consequences and limit setting because they are so persuasive in their excuse making: "I didn't hear you," "She did it," "I forgot," or "I was too tired," said with sufficient urgency, can be utterly convincing, especially because parents tend to be worn down long before this style runs out of its considerable energy and tenacity. Baby Bullies do not feel there is a price for their behavior, because they are so often let off the hook.

You cannot postpone action with a Baby Bully: You must set firm limits immediately, and you must be consistent, not allowing the child to throw you off course. One 8-year-old Baby Bully, when asked by her mother to pick up her books, charmingly said, "I can't, my arms hurt." Her mother replied, "If they aren't 'cured' by four o'clock, your books will be in a shopping bag in the basement. If you can't put them away, I'll have to put them someplace else where no one can trip over them." The strategy worked.

If you can apply these rubrics when your Baby Bully is small, his or her liabilities will not erupt, as they have with Samantha, with such force later on. Be consistent and firm, and your Baby Bully's negative behavior will not escalate to terrifying proportions.

STRATEGY EVALUATION

- Have I used logical consequences? (This skill is extremely important not only with Baby Bullies, but with Loners and Underdogs as well.)
- Have I been direct?
- Have I reacted quickly?
- Have I been consistent?
- Have I stuck to my strategy?

OR

- Have I considered the child's behavior a "phase" and done nothing?
- Have I allowed myself to be charmed too much?
- Have I allowed myself to be pushed into using physical violence?

KID TYRANT

Kid Tyrants do not need a lid on their temper, they need a lid on their lips. Born litigators, they can, by virtue of their extraordinarily logical minds, find an answer for everything, and will have you on the proverbial ropes if you engage in a verbal contest. As one woman put it about her 5-year-old Kid Tyrant, "If it makes sense, I give it to him. It *always* makes sense."

This style requires two strategies: The first is to teach the child to learn how to share control; the second is to nourish the youngster's emotional life. Because Kid Tyrants are so able, and so often in leadership roles, it's hard for them to develop humility or sensitivity toward others. You'll have to help them do so.

It isn't always easy.

Brenda Mullin, 37, is a runner, logging 5 to 10 miles every day. Running seems to be a metaphor for her life as a mother and wife—her kid "runs me ragged"; her husband, Matt, a Jungle Fighter, "can run rings around me in an argument."

Their 3-year-old Kid Tyrant daughter, Jessie, simultaneously awes and mystifies Brenda. Jessie didn't talk until she was 2, and then one day recited the entire alphabet. And, according to Brenda, the child has a will that is enviable. Says Brenda:

> When she wants to go for a walk, and I say "not today," she will go over to the door and try to reach the lock. But since she's small, she's figured out that she has to drag a chair to the door and climb on it, in order to undo the lock. The first time she did that I thought it was adorable, and I burst out laughing.
>
> I realize it's not appropriate for a 3-year-old to leave the house alone, but it was so cute. I know—I was giving her a mixed message. But I admire her for being a free spirit, because I wasn't like that. Part of me is still locked up, and I haven't found the key. I don't want that to happen to her.

It's not too likely that it will. Brenda tends to plead with Jessie to cooperate, and to acquiesce to the child's every request. Jessie often gets to stay up past her bedtime because, says Brenda, "When I let her, she snuggles with me, and I can't resist it."

Kid Tyrants have only one goal: To be in charge. When they are not, they retaliate. Even toddlers. Says Brenda, "I've been trying to get Jessie toilet trained, because she's supposed to start nursery school in the fall. So far, it hasn't worked. She just withholds, even though it gives her cramps."

Your strategy with a Kid Tyrant is to arrange experiences for her where she is not in charge, and in which she must share decision making. Let's say she wants to slice some bread, and you don't want her to use a knife. You can say, "Why don't you get out the bread and a cutting board, and hold the end of the bread while I slice it. Then we can make something together to put on the bread. Do you want tuna or egg salad?" You've let the child participate, but not be in charge.

Changing the behavior of a Kid Tyrant does not require breaking her spirit—rather, it calls for a strategy that will encourage both her intellectual abilities and her emotional awareness. Because this style excels in school work, and since that is a socially laudable accomplishment, parents may forget to stress the importance of informing one's academic success with compassion.

Let us say that your Kid Tyrant always monopolizes conversation at the dinner table, verbally running roughshod over her less assertive siblings. You can say to her, "How do you feel if no one gives you a chance to talk in class? You feel rotten. No one likes to feel rotten." You have not admonished her for that which she does best—logical discourse; you *have* pointed out how she would feel if she weren't given the opportunity to display it.

Such children have trouble getting in touch with their feelings. They are achievers, but if limits are not set on their admirable, but coercive, mental gymnastics, their emotional lives may be neglected; they run the risk of becoming morally and/or emotionally neutral in adulthood.

In carrying out your strategy, avoid at all costs getting into a Great Debate with a Kid Tyrant. These children love verbal combat, and will redouble their efforts the more you resist. There may be times when you have to jolt them off their cerebral thrones.

Kid Tyrants love to issue orders, such as, "Bring my lunch to school," "Iron my shirt," "Get me a cookie," or "Go to the library for me." Indeed, they make demands with so much authority that you find yourself either springing to the task or apologizing for why you cannot.

Try this: When a Kid Tyrant next gives you a directive, *ignore it.* Nothing rattles this style more than silence or deliberate inaction. When he asks you why you won't take care of his request, keep your responses brief: "I don't like the way you order me around; in the future I will not listen to your demands," or "I'm interested in hearing a request, but not a demand," or "If I'm unable to do what you ask, I don't expect you to harass me." He will pepper you with arguments as to why you should think otherwise; do not relent.

If you stick to your strategy, in time he will learn to take his own lunch to school, wear a shirt that doesn't require pressing, ask the school librarian for help. Your response throws him off guard and forces him to be aware of your feelings and to solve his own problems. By not adhering to his demands, you take inappropriate control away from him.

Brevity of speech and in the time between his request and your strategic response is crucial with Kid Tyrants. If you don't engage in a long, drawn-out argument, debate, or apology, he'll have to look within for a more productive way to reach you. You may have to sit on your hands, or bite the inside of your mouth, in order to maintain your resolve—but your consistency will pay off. Not achieving his goal—which is to be in charge—he'll find other goals, including collaboration.

And although it's hard for him to do so, the time may nevertheless come when he wants to talk about feeling unloved, for example, or guilty, or lonely—then you can encourage his sensitivity by demonstrating your understanding of his feelings and help him to work on them in a tension-free talk. And if you have trouble expressing your feelings to him because of your own style, or anger, work on it—you'll have to be his emotional role model.

STRATEGY EVALUATION

- Do I keep my comments short and to the point?
- Have I encouraged him to share decision making and control?
- Have I avoided debates that don't lead to resolution?
- Have I focused on getting him to express his feelings?
- Do I routinely express my feelings to him?

OR

- Have I given up too much control to this child? Have I given him too much responsibility because he's so good at handling it?
- Do I jump at his commands?
- Do I talk too much?

LONER

Loners may behave as though they want to be let alone, but they do not want to be abandoned. You have to make it safe for them to come out of their shells so that they can learn to live and interact with other people, whether in the classroom, in the home or, when they are older, in an office or in a marriage.

Loners can passively push their parents to the limits of their patience and, at times, their sanity. Ruth Arnold describes her relationship with her 10-year-old Loner son, Larry, this way:

> Larry spends a great deal of time in his room, mostly drawing or making things, sometimes listening to records, or daydreaming. He's very strong minded, and has no compassion for teachers who are inept or at all weak. He does his least good school work when it's very routine,

when the teacher just drills it in and wants him to regurgitate facts. But if it's a project he likes, he'll dig in and won't stop until it's finished.

It isn't easy living with Larry. He ignores every request I make as though he were deaf. In order for me to get him to do something, I have to get extremely angry, often so angry that I end up feeling quite frazzled and on the edge of guilt about it, usually when I think I've been abusive in my anger. I save it up and explode. Larry sometimes feels bad for the way he behaves, but he never apologizes.

Loners are mavericks who, given their creative head when they are adults, will find innovative solutions to corporate conundrums or medical and industrial breakthroughs that more conforming personalities can't come up with. But it takes a particularly inspired employer to sanction the offbeat working styles of these different drummers.

You must respect Loners' privacy, and not attempt to engage them in long, heart-to-heart conversations. If you want Loners to do something, your strategy is this: put up a bulletin board and leave them notes, or write them short letters.

When you do have conversations, keep them brief, and get right to the point. You can tell them how frustrating it is for you not to know anything about their life, and just let them think about it; then you can give them options to help them express their feelings.

That's exactly what was suggested to one father when his 12-year-old Loner son asked to be brought home from camp midsummer, but wouldn't say why:

1. The parents' goal was to find out why the kid was so unhappy at camp.

2. When the child refused to tell them, his father could say, "I have the feeling that something happened to hurt you. We can talk about it now, or tomorrow, after you've thought about it."

3. The next day, if the child says, "Nothing happened. I just wanted to come home," his father can reply, "If you don't want to talk about it, how about sending me a note at the office, or you can leave it on the kitchen table." If the child still doesn't communicate his camp experience, his father can say, "Why don't you write about what happened on your computer [or a friend's computer, or on one at school]. Next week you can print it out and give us a copy."

4. If the child still refuses to talk, or to write, the parents can set up a meeting with the camp director, the camp counselor who was in the boy's cabin, and the boy.

Loners hate being estranged—even though they prefer to be alone—yet they don't know what to do about it. By giving them several options about how to reveal themselves that show respect for their covert style, you can help them find a way to "talk" that is comfortable for them.

When you strategize with Loners, remember to be quick, brief, and specific, and to repeat the strategy as often as necessary. Eventually they'll meet you halfway, providing they do not feel forced, and if you make it easy for them to do so in their own fashion.

STRATEGY EVALUATION
- Do I give him advance notice when I want him to do something?
- Have I given him options, other than verbal, for expression?
- Have I used logical consequences?
  OR
- Do I talk too much to fill in the silences when I'm with him?
- Do I forget he's around and exclude him from family discussions or meetings?
- Have I permitted his remoteness to push me to yelling?
- Have I been tempted to give up on this kid because he's so taciturn?

SAINT

When you strategize with Saints, you need to build into your plan more time for change than is required for other styles. The reason: Saints' lives are loaded with activities, deadlines, friends, obligations, and social responsibilities, all of which they take very seriously.

For your part, it's time-consuming to find out what's on your Saint's mind. It isn't necessarily that he's lying or withholding information; it's that he's so good at manipulation, at putting you into a generous or forgiving frame of mind, and at being "popular," that it's difficult to steer him to the heart of the matter. Negotiating with a Saint is like panning for gold—you may have to dismember a mountain of palaver to come up with a nugget of hard fact.

Many parents find it hard to set limits with Saints because they are so engaging and affectionate. Says the mother of a 3-year-old Saint:

> He began talking when he was six months old, and he hasn't stopped. From the minute he wakes up, his mouth is going. He thinks he

can cajole me because he's so sweet and cute. Once I was having an argument with my husband for coming home late from work, and my son said, "Mommy, don't yell at Daddy, he has to work. He doesn't mean to come home so late."

When you tell him not to do something and why, he says, "Okay, Mom, but can I do it just one more time?" And I usually say "Yes." Often that's enough for him and he'll stop, but sometimes he keeps pushing, and I have to yell at him. He gets very emotional—he doesn't like to be yelled at—and he'll apologize. He needs a lot of attention. Only once did yelling really work with him. We were in a restaurant, and he started acting up, being demanding, having a tantrum. A waiter came over and said to him, "Shut up!" My son was so aghast that he just sat there silently for the rest of the meal. The waiter was more effective than I am.

As the Saint gets older, he tends to become overwhelmed by activities, and one of your strategies may be to help him learn to set priorities and to meet them. Part of your strategy is to refuse to bail him out when he's in a jam. He'll ask you to write a note to the teacher excusing him from turning in his homework because he was up late fashioning posters for an upcoming football game. He'll beguile you into calling his piano teacher to cancel a lesson because he has to catch up on his homework.

Don't do it. Logical consequences will force this child to pare down his activities. It won't be easy, because for him, everything is a tragedy: A Saint is more likely to cry wolf than any other style. But if he gets into trouble enough times for not meeting his commitments at school, or with friends, he will decide that the better part of wisdom is pleasing some of the people some of the time, instead of attempting to please everyone all of the time and, naturally, failing. And he'll even learn the difference between an irritation and a crisis.

You can say, "Let's make a calendar, and write down all your deadlines. We'll make a list of how long each task will take. Then you'll put your deadlines in order of importance. The things at the bottom of the list you may have to cross off, and get someone else to do them. That way you'll do very well at the things that are still on the list, because you'll have more time to do them."

Discussion with Saints must be brief and succinct, because they love to talk and tend to be all over the conversational map. When you have a huddle with a Saint, let him know up front that the meeting will be exactly 10 minutes, and that he should keep his comments to the point. By abbreviating the time, you force him to say only that which is important and germane to the subject. You also shut out the possibility of being manipulated, since your agenda does not include enough time for cajolery. At the end of 10 minutes, if you still haven't covered your agenda, nor he his, you can say, "Time's up. Let's try again tomorrow." If the Saint wants your time and attention—which, indeed, he craves—he'll have to learn to play by your rules.

Engage your Saint in problem solving; it makes him feel important (feeling unimportant is part of why he creates problems, such as overscheduling) and he'll see it as a loving game. But your strategy needs to include fishing, and information gathering. Saints need to solve some problems themselves (logical consequences); you can help them solve others.

The point is that your strategy—setting priorities, applying logical consequences, and having brief huddles—will help him help himself. These three negotiating tools will be the framework in which he can succeed at what's important to him, and are the barriers against your having to nag.

STRATEGY EVALUATION
- Do I remember that this is my child, and not my pal?
- Do I build into my child's weekly agenda time for him to be inactive or to reflect?
- Am I encouraging my child to pare down his commitments by helping him weigh their importance?

OR

- Have I overrated my child's sense of responsibility, misreading his promises to take on certain chores, when I know that they are not likely to get done because he seldom keeps promises?
- Do I frequently overlook or excuse my child's being overextended?
- Do I allow this child to plan my life by saying such things as, "You know, you really ought to join a gym—it's good for you"?

UNDERDOG

Underdogs have a great talent for getting you to reinforce their helplessness. You don't expect them to excel, or to be popular, or to follow through, because they have you entirely convinced of their emotional fragility.

If you are the parent of such a child, you have probably become so exasperated by his constant teariness that you are tempted to blurt angrily, "Okay—turn on the faucet." Then you feel so guilty for breaking his heart—it's happened so often, you wonder if it has zippers—that you redouble your efforts to make excuses for him and to treat him with kid gloves.

These children will only remain frightened of everything if you reward the fear, not only by your low expectations, but also by making their decisions for them. Underdogs will not exhibit their considerable strengths if you make it easy for them to conceal them—nothing succeeds like eternal victimization.

Underdogs want you to tell them what to do: what to wear, what TV show to watch, which friend to play with. Since they are the most malleable of all children's styles, and since many parents often feel unimportant to their more independent children, the Underdog's neediness can be an insidious breath of spring: you *love* feeling so indispensable, for a change.

Do not be seduced by their insecurities. This is the style that *most* needs to learn how to be autonomous, because it is the most likely to be encouraged to remain dependent.

It helps when Underdogs are lucky enough to have a parent who is a loving Dictator. Martin Somers is such a parent to Mary Ann, a 10-year-old Underdog:

> I don't see Mary Ann as weak—I see her as incredibly strong. When she was little, she was standoffish and scared of new situations. Over the years she's become braver, but she's still not close in terms of confiding. She has a lot of trouble with that.
>
> Mary Ann's afraid of not being liked; she has a terrible fear of doing something wrong or of getting punished. But at home she manages not to get into real serious trouble because she just takes care of business. She's a straight-A student and, since her mom's a neatnik, she makes her bed every day.
>
> She's extremely cunning that way. She also knows how to be heard in our family. Our older daughter's a nonstop talker, a kid who talks about everything and says nothing. Mary Ann's a kid who talks about nothing and says everything: when she does talk, people listen.

Underdogs flourish if you give them the opportunity to be in charge, and encourage them to take on leadership roles, however minor. Your goal is to help them learn to make decisions, so you have to give them chances to solve problems. Start small, and work up to larger challenges.

For example, if you are rearranging your living room, you can say, "I don't know where to put this lamp. What do you think?" If your Underdog doesn't answer, just leave the lamp where it is, and say "I can't decide—when you figure it out, would you put it where you think it looks best? I really could use some help on this one," and walk away.

Do not praise this style: if you pay Underdogs a compliment, they may feel that you have an expectation that they can't possibly meet, or that you have expressed love, rather than seeing the larger lesson of their accomplishment. Instead, encourage. If, say, you are shopping in a supermarket, and you ask the Underdog to pick out all the vegetables for that night's salad, and he does it, you can follow up by saying, "Thanks, that really saved me time. In fact, we've got ten extra minutes before we have to go home. What would you like to do—get ice cream or go to the record store?" It looks like you're giving a reward, but you're really presenting him with another decision, one that, either way, is appealing.

You might ask the child to set up a huddle, canvasing each family member as to the time that would be most convenient for everyone. After your Underdog has carried out this mission, you can say, "I like the way you handled that. It's important that everyone be in a good mood when we meet, and you got them to agree to a time."

The one strategy not to use with an Underdog is surprise. Underdogs are mullers, and need structure and predictability so they have time to work up psychologically to new situations. For instance, if your Underdog is about to enter first grade and the school has planned a bus trip to help the children become familiar with the transportation and the school layout, you may need to go along. But follow up one more way: take the child to school yourself *before* the bus trip, so that he won't be daunted by first impressions ganging up on him. Instead, he'll be an authority before the bus trip and have an advantage over the other children. He may find that he doesn't need you to accompany him on the bus after all.

The secret to strategy with Underdogs is to provide a series of little victories. Set deadlines for even the smallest effort. You do not need to feel sorry for them—you need to encourage their strengths.

It is imperative that you do not give these children an opportunity to fail—keep after them, subtly, gently, and withhold your excuses if, at first, they don't cotton to decision making. If you believe in Underdogs, in spite of their best and most effective means of undermining your high hopes (or underscoring your low ones), eventually they'll begin to believe in themselves.

STRATEGY EVALUATION

- Have I created situations for the child to build self-esteem and autonomy?
- Do I prepare him for new situations?
- Do I encourage him whenever I can?

OR

- Have I lowered my expectations for this child too much?
- Am I always impatient with his lack of follow-through or tenacity?
- Do I foster this child's dependency by doing everything for him?
- Do I feel alternately resentful and guilty about this child's helplessness?

WINNER

Don't be misled by Winners. You're doing a great deal that's helped them to be the way they are, but you nevertheless must employ a strategy to encourage their style. As they get older, they'll have experiences that may jar their belief in the benefits of being a Winner. This is particularly true in highly competitive schools wherein "winning" means having the best grades or being first in any race.

Your strategy with Winners is to continue to give them opportunities to take reasonable risks, to give them greater challenges as they grow up, to stimulate their faith in themselves. Encourage in particular their wonderful sense of fair play, because they may live in a community in which fairness is less important than achievement.

STRATEGY EVALUATION

- Do I have the self-confidence to appreciate and learn from him?

OR

- Do I hold him up to my other children as the ideal against which they must compare themselves?
- Because he is such a "winner," do I sometimes expect too much of him?
- Do I neglect him, thinking my parenting and time with him are somehow redundant or not needed?
- Do I sometimes compare myself to this child, and feel inadequate in comparison?

Change is rarely easy, and you may have a child who, like calcification on a broken limb that was never properly set, has become what seems to be the irresolute amalgam of his liabilities. The older the child, the more patient you must be in your strategy to help him change and to succeed within his style.

Still, children, even the most apparently intractable ones, are much easier to guide than adults. Your job is to structure a strategy that makes it more appealing for them to change than it is to remain the same.

And so, be patient. Remember the Loop (see page 106). Remember also that strategy is long-range, and may take dozens of negotiations to put into place. You must be consistent in applying your strategy, but bear in mind that as your child grows, your strategy needs minor adjustments. The child who needs constant attention and direction at 2 will not need such a tight rein at 4. You'll have to think up new challenges for him within your strategy. Monitor your strategy as he becomes more mature and more able to set his own limits.

At the same time, monitor your expectations of your child. Try not to think about how far he has to go—think, instead, about how far he's come.

CHAPTER 10

WHEN
PARENTING
STYLES DIFFER

Many couples have radically differing parenting styles—one of you is laissez-faire, the other is exacting and demanding; one of you tends to overlook your children's misbehavior, the other believes that the children's characters will be forfeited by such laxness; one of you encourages the kids' scholastic efforts, saying "I know you did your best," the other says, "So how come it was an A minus instead of an A?"

And one of you doesn't like it.

Your partner may be doing things to your child that make you uncomfortable—being verbally abusive, or grunting a greeting from behind a pile of paperwork; being too lenient, or spoiling your child— and you are torn about how to handle it. There is a delicate balance between siding with your child and remaining loyal to your partner.

The dynamics of any partnership are such that disputes are relatively easy to recognize and sort out because they are confined to only two points of view. But as soon as a couple have children, the equation is thrown off. When there are three (or more) people involved, often one parent will be in an uneasy minority position. It may be that in your relationship with your partner there are snags between you that haven't been sorted out, or somehow lacked urgency until you had children.

The issue here—and the core of this chapter—is that your partner's liabilities may be damaging your child, and you can no longer avoid examining those liabilities. Any serious clashes between you, if they are not addressed, are likely to spill over into the parent–child relationship and do considerable harm to the child. Where you were unable—or chose not to address—those liabilities before, you can begin to do so now. The vehicle for doing so with a minimum of marital mayhem is negotiation.

Sandra and Gene Harrison have one child, a 12-year-old daughter, Beth. Gene and his daughter are at loggerheads much of the time because each stokes the other's liabilities—Gene's Dictator temper and Beth's nonstop Kid Tyrant debating are like gasoline and heat; explosions are inevitable.

Here's how Gene explains his relationship with his daughter:

Beth is very anxious to be right, or to make sure that everyone else is wrong. She tries to humiliate me. She won't let anyone else get in a word at the dinner table. She can talk you to death, and either I send her to her room or I leave. For about three months I refused to talk to her at all, because I was tired of her negative behavior and didn't want to reward it by listening to her.

I try to challenge her. For this whole year she's been annoyed with me because I kept telling her that her grades wouldn't go up, and they did. I challenged her and it worked. Beth has said she's scared of me, but that's baloney—it's just another way to get everyone on her side, ganging up on me.

Beth describes her relationship with her father this way:

I know I talk too much—I do it out of nervousness, happiness, anger—I just talk. It's my solution to everything, but it doesn't help.

Dad overreacts. A few weeks ago he told me to turn my stereo down. I should have turned it down, but I didn't. He came charging into my room and yelled, "Either turn that thing off or I'll smash it to pieces." I was furious, and I yelled, "Don't you dare, that's my property." He walked over to my stereo, picked it up, and threw it on the floor. I ran out of the house and Mom followed me. She was upset, but she doesn't want to take sides or get caught in the middle. She supported me as objectively as she could; she said, "Nobody has a right to take someone else's things and destroy them, no matter what."

Dad never apologized. He never apologizes. How does peace get restored in our house? No one talks about it. It's like it never happened.

Sandra, caught in a three-way stretch, is trying to walk a fine line between loyalty to her husband and love for her daughter. She says:

When I defend Beth, it's hard for Gene to take, because he sees it as totally undermining him as a parent. So now I won't talk privately to Beth anymore—I insist that Gene be present. It's funny, because whenever the three of us have a conversation, Beth is always looking at Gene. I guess she needs her father's approval.

I've pointed out to Gene his tendency to fly off the handle, but he gets defensive about it. Gene can zero in better than anyone else—he can really get your goat. He can win any argument, even though he's totally wrong. He has to be right; he's much more unreasonable than Beth.

But Beth also has to be right. I told them both that my definition of hell is the two of them being in one room for the rest of their lives.

If their relationship improves, it'll be because Gene is working on it, not because I'm more assertive with Gene. I'm afraid of confrontations. I don't like having fights, so I avoid them by being real nice.

Sandra's a Soother with her husband and, increasingly, a Silhouette with her daughter, her solution to keeping her marriage intact. Because she has difficulty being forceful with Gene—no easy matter, given his aggressiveness—it's hard for her to declare or act on her perceptions of his treatment of Beth.

When there is a clash of parenting styles like this one, what's a parent to do? Sandra can begin by understanding that she cannot change her husband—she can only change how she reacts to him, and how she allows him to dominate both her and Beth.

Sandra's dread of intimidation could be reduced by taking stock: what does she know about her husband's style? Her child's? Her own? How long will she be willing to put up with her husband's treatment of Beth—what's her time limit? What strategy can she employ to help each member of the family, including herself, learn to negotiate their differences?

Ask yourself the same questions, and this one: how can you help your children become their best selves without jeopardizing your marriage?

As a rule, parents are better able to provide stability for their children, and are less vulnerable to their children's manipulation, when they have a consensus about how to raise their kids, when they are consistent, and when they do not undermine each other's decisions.

This is not to say that mothers and fathers need to be joined at the parenting hip. Sometimes it isn't possible for them to discuss an issue about the kids that requires a decision—Dad might give permission to his son to go on a trip with the Scouts, which, it turns out, isn't okay with Mom, because she has plans for the family about which she hasn't yet told her husband. Occasional disparities are not going to permanently confuse your child, or undo your routine, joint approach to such matters.

Moreover, if Mom buys a new blouse and says to her child, "Don't tell your father," her maternal authority will not be permanently destroyed. Nor will it if Dad occasionally sighs to his child, "Sometimes your mother confuses the hell out of me." Acknowledging individual styles and learning to live with them is part of what family is all about.

Parents do not always have to agree about consistency and have a concert of opinion. But when parental differences become *chronic,* even if there is a "united front" with the children, they inevitably filter into the parent–child relationship because of the tension those differences create in you—then the children *do* become confused.

In our survey, we asked parents "Do you and your spouse fight more about the children than anything else?" to which 17 percent replied "Yes." But in following up that general question in separate interviews with mothers and fathers, we discovered that one reason some of the remaining 83 percent checked off "No" is that sometimes parents do not address their differences or, having tried and failed, have allowed one partner to dominate.

These differences are not lost on the kids.

We spoke to a man who has given up trying to get his wife to curb her terror that something awful will happen to their son. She is aware of how her fears are being imparted to her child, but is unable to bridle her hysteria. Says her husband:

> She's deathly afraid of insects. We've even canceled family vacation plans because she's afraid of terrorists hijacking the plane. And she's afraid of our son being kidnapped.
>
> For instance, the walk to his school bus stop requires going past a long stretch of woods where there are no houses. She thinks that somebody in a car will bang him over the head, shove him into the car, and he'll be gone before anything could be done. So I have to drive him to the bus stop.

In talking to another couple, we learned from the wife that she cannot bear her husband's constant teasing of their children. She says:

> When I tell him it's cruel, he says "You have no sense of humor." But he doesn't see that the teasing backfires, and makes them hate him. Once he took our 6-year-old daughter on a walk and hid behind a bush to scare her. She was panicked, but he said it was "just a joke." Other

times he kids her about her chubbiness. He says that's his way of being affectionate and that it's all in good fun—but his "kidding" goes too far.

Recognizing that your partner is damaging your child can be anguishing, particularly in a shaky marriage. It is one thing to point out to your children the ways in which they create trouble in the family, but it's quite another to say to your spouse, "I think you need to look at what your temper [or perfectionism, or passivity, or overprotection] is doing to the kids." You cannot be sure of how that observation will be received.

When you describe to your partner the ways in which his or her blind spots exacerbate animosity with or insecurity in your child, the risk is that your partner will become defensive and angry, or teary and overwhelmed.

No one likes being criticized—and the older people get, the harder it becomes to hear criticism. It will be particularly difficult for your partner if he or she has put in a long day at the office, or is concerned about the new management at work, or has fallen behind on the bills, or has other issues that have created marital tension. The last thing your partner wants to hear is, "You're screwing up with the kids."

Nevertheless, there are times when the cumulative effects of your partner's liabilities will engulf your children and begin to take too great a toll to ignore. Sometimes it takes a jolt—a child's attempt at suicide, for instance—to galvanize one parent into recognizing that he or she has contributed to that toll by not doing anything to prevent it. You can preclude such "jolts" by risking the real or imagined wrath of your partner in order to deal with the burden those liabilities are placing on your child.

Many parents are afraid to confront those differences, because it feels as though they may inevitably lead to the divorce court; and so, in the name of the greater marital good, they keep the confrontation at bay by trying to explain to the children mommy's or daddy's behavior.

Other parents believe that they are confronting those differences, but that confrontation doesn't go far enough. Said one woman:

> My husband can be very dictatorial, and often he's right, but he expresses it too harshly. Recently he and my daughter had an argument, and she ran up to her room. I went up to talk to her, and she was crying. I said, "Oh, Daddy gets angry." I did not tell her that she was right, even though she was. I just let her have her thoughts about her father,

but I didn't soothe her. I let her air her feelings a little bit. I have rarely told her I thought her father was wrong, because I didn't want to be disloyal.

This is probably the stickiest of family wickets: telling your partner when and how he or she is off base as a parent is an immediate guilt giver; at the same time, as the above example illustrates, not doing so begs the question of your fudging the truth with your child. There are times, as we will discuss later in this chapter, when you have to take a stand and risk "disloyalty"—perhaps even divorce—for the sake of your child.

But for most routine parental disagreements where the couple is committed to their marriage and family, instead of criticism, we prefer to call observations of a spouse's negative behavior toward a child "positive feedback." And it is in that spirit that negotiation with your partner can address those issues without necessarily resulting in marital disarray.

Before we show you how to negotiate with your partner, ask yourself these questions:

1. What am I doing to fuel the animosity between my partner and my kids?
2. Have I the courage to take a hard look at how my partner and I set priorities within the family?

Let's look at these questions one at a time.

HOW YOU MAY BE ENCOURAGING THE ANIMOSITY OR DISTANCE BETWEEN YOUR PARTNER AND YOUR KIDS

Before you can point the finger of parental blame at your partner, you need to take stock of what you are doing to create problems between your partner and your child, and how you may be setting up your partner for failure as a parent.

Most parents do not consciously or deliberately try to pit their kids and their partners against each other, but often they behave in a way that inevitably leads to that result. There are several causes of that unconscious motivation.

DENIAL. Most parents are acutely aware of the stress children feel and how it manifests itself—drug and alcohol abuse, depression, anorexia, suicide—but they tend to recognize it in *other* families, rather than in their own. According to a 1986 *Better Homes and Gardens* survey of 30,000 readers, virtually all of whom are parents, 88 percent of the respondents believe that they are good parents. But a whopping 75 percent think that *other* parents do not spend enough time with their kids, and nearly half believe that, as a rule, parents are shirking their parental responsibilities. It is not possible that 12 percent (who did not give themselves as high marks as parents) can be doing 75 percent of the damage to all American children. No one likes to believe that he or his partner is the one who is at fault. Still, many sensitive parents know in the long night of their souls when and if they avoid stepping in on behalf of their children. "I know I should speak up more," said one father of his inertia about his wife's harsh, disciplinarian treatment of their children. "I just don't do it—it's not worth the hassle."

For many parents, it's simpler to ignore the problem than to tackle this potentially volatile, and always painful, issue.

DIVIDE AND CONQUER. This device works in two ways: First, among families in which one of the parents is an alcoholic, there is the "scapegoat" dynamic—when the alcoholic begins to recover, the alcoholic's spouse may subconsciously wish to sabotage that recovery, because without a "bad guy" to blame for all the family's ills, it may become apparent that the nondrinking spouse is also contributing to family strife.

So it is in some families wherein drinking is not a problem, but relegating "bad guy" status to one of the parents is. As one woman told us, "I learned in therapy that as long as my husband behaved like a beast with the kids, I had reasons to leave him—even though it took me years to do it—and I could look good by comparison. The kids felt sorry for me, and let me know that they preferred me to him—they were on my side."

The other way dividing and conquering operates is this: you do not want to address your differences with your children, so you get your partner to do it. For example, you tattle: "Do you know that your daughter has been using your razor?'' or ''Your son hasn't taken out the garbage in three days—he's impossible.'' By firing up your partner to be the ''heavy,'' you can sit back and be the innocent, particularly if you know that he or she is not likely to sidestep the complaint.

DADDY DOESN'T DO IT AS WELL AS I DO. This behavioral pattern often occurs among women who do not feel that they have any other vehicle through which they can feel powerful—women who do not have careers, for instance, or who are unable to address ''power'' issues with their spouses. Instead, they become the parenting ''power'' by subtly not allowing their husbands to have parental authority or input. These women exert control in a socially acceptable way—by being ''the good mommy''—sometimes with their husbands' tacit approval.

One woman we interviewed, Helen Post, corrected that unconscious habit by accident. Her husband, Aaron, is an attorney who spends very little time with their 4-year-old daughter, Susan, and of the time that he does, he says to Helen, ''Listen, I see so little of her, don't ask me to be the villain—you do the disciplining.''

Helen works full time as well, but has always felt that child rearing was her responsibility alone. One evening after a particularly frantic day, she said to Aaron, ''Please give Susan a bath—I'm trying to get dinner going.'' He replied, ''I don't think I'd better, I've never done it before. You're so good with her, you do it.'' Says Helen:

> My first thought was, all right, damnit, I'll do it. Then I thought, ''This is stupid. Short of holding Susan's head under the water, nothing will happen to her if he gives her a bath.''
>
> I told him I just couldn't leave what I was doing, that he had to do it. He did, and she didn't drown. It was fine.

You have to make it possible for your partner to do some of the parenting, which spouses sometimes undermine by saying, ''She'll get it wrong,'' or ''My child is used to me, not her father,'' and the like, in the same way that many parents will not allow their children to do a chore or assignment because the kids won't do it as well as Mom or Dad. If you don't let your partner try, he'll never learn how, and ultimately may give up.

Sometimes one parent feels left out of the parenting process and is jealous of the attention lavished on the kids, because the other parent has not given him or her enough attention and reassurance. It's not enough for you to be annoyed by your partner's insecurity—you have to deal with it in order for him or her to want to become more involved in the parenting process.

Women can ask themselves these questions:

- Have I asked my partner to pitch in, and in what manner?
- Have I assumed all the burdens by not dividing them up? Have I given my partner a task, and then done half of it for him?
- Have I given him the opportunity to help, or have I instead valiantly pushed on alone, suffering in silence?
- Have I stood my ground?
- Have I neglected my partner's needs in the name of "loving" my child?

DEPENDENCY NEEDS. Many parents are more terrified by the possibility of being single than by a painful status quo, wherein they see damage done to their kids but do not try to intervene with their spouse on their children's behalf. And so they invent elaborate excuses for their inaction with statements such as "I don't want to put my kids through a divorce," or "It could be worse."

Indeed, sometimes divorce is the only solution. As a psychologist we know said, "Don't stay together for the kids—they'll never thank you." There may be times that the problems within your family are so severe and the harm done to your kids by domestic hostility, whether overt or passive, is so great that a divorce is the sole option.

Sometimes being alone, with its crushing financial and emotional fallout, is preferable to continuing a destructive marriage. (See Chapters 17 and 18 for negotiating through a divorce and negotiating with stepfamilies.)

But more often negotiation between parents will solve the problems— negotiation that could stem the flow of bad blood, or lead to greater self-esteem, and which could prevent the buildup of rage and emotional bruising from which there is no recovery. In most cases, there are dozens of options and strategies that can be employed in a marriage that can prevent it from reaching the wrenching bottom line of divorce.

For these reasons, many parents contribute to the parenting failures of their spouses. It's important to remember that when you postpone a resolution of parenting clashes, your children become the repository of those clashes, which may in the long term result in their being emotional time bombs or unable to trust a loving relationship.

RESOLVING DIFFERENCES. Sorting out your parenting differences begins with understanding your partner's style, and helping your
child to understand it as well. One couple we interviewed has done
exactly that, in large measure because of the wife's perceptiveness and
negotiating acumen. Says April, her 16-year-old daughter:

> My mom knows when to step in with my dad. He's a workaholic,
> and he's also a worrier, especially about my sisters and me. Sometimes
> Mom will say to him, "Chuck, will you do something about these kids?
> They're driving me crazy," and he'll say, "Okay, you're grounded for a
> month." Mom will say, "I asked you to do a simple thing, not to be
> ridiculous. Do you know what you just did?" He'll laugh and say,
> "Yeah, forget it. Erase what I just said." He knows when he's being off
> the wall. She'll side with me if she thinks he's wrong, and he'll side
> with me when he thinks she's wrong.
>
> I've learned to stand up for myself because of my mom. I never saw
> her bow down to my father. Never. And if they get into a fight, I never
> think divorce is around the corner, because he knows he married some-
> one strong willed, like himself.
>
> Mom has taught us how to get along with him. She says, "This is
> how you get your way with him—you bring it up slowly." So if he says,
> "I don't want you to do it," I know it's not the same thing as his saying
> flat out, "No, that's it, you can't."
>
> Dad isn't a talker. He doesn't like to say what's bothering him. So
> sometimes Mom says to him, "If you don't want to say what it is, that's
> fine, but don't take it out on us." He may not say much, but he shows
> us how he feels. When we were small, he was real affectionate, giving
> us piggyback rides. Once a week he'd take us to the Dairy Queen—
> we'd all pile into the station wagon, and we kids would bicker all the
> way. Four kids are tough—but he never complained. I know he loves
> us—he just shows it differently from how my mom does.

In this case, the wife's understanding of her husband's style enabled
her to help him to become aware of his short fuse, and to show her
children how to deal with it, rather than excusing it. April's Win/Winner
mother confronts her husband's Silhouette liabilities, rather than ignoring them, in the spirit of love and sensitivity, thereby encouraging his
assets.

The same cannot be said of Harriet Norman's mother, a Soother,
who apologizes to her children for her Jungle Fighter husband's harsh-
ness, but who doesn't know how to intervene with him on her

children's—or her own—behalf. By permitting her husband to intimidate everyone in the family, she has done substantial harm to Harriet, who feels emotionally stranded. Says Harriet:

> I love my mom a lot, but she's unbelievably compulsive, because she knows my dad hates clutter. She does everything for him and for the whole family. Her life is everyone else's life—I can't remember the last time she did anything for herself.
>
> My dad's a crazy workaholic, more than any person I know. He says he works so hard for us, to give us vacations, nice clothes, a private school education. Then he takes out his tension on me. He'll get very angry with me and say, "You don't realize how important it is to have a three-five average," and I already have a three-three.
>
> He doesn't see how hard I'm working. A few times this year I was taken to the hospital because they thought I had mono. It was overwork. If I were one of his clients, Jesus, he'd do *anything* for me.
>
> Dad makes me cry more than anyone, he's so harsh. He slaps me sometimes, and when I was little, he hit me a lot. When I'm real unhappy, I keep it inside—I cry and get angry. I've thought of suicide a few times. . . .

The issue with these two families is not that Daddy is a workaholic—both fathers are—nor that Mom is unloving—both mothers are extremely affectionate to their children. The issue is that in the first family, the mother intervenes on behalf of the children; in the second family, the mother does not—she is not acknowledging the fact that her denial of her husband's cruelty may destroy their child, and that she should seriously consider separation or divorce if he does not let up on his intimidation of everyone in the family.

Before you start your negotiation, be aware of your bottom line: even if you can't get your partner to change, assuming that he is not completely destructive, at least you can make it easier for your child. Given sufficient goodwill on your partner's part, as well as your negotiating skills, you may never have to reach that bottom line.

HOW YOU OR YOUR PARTNER MAY BE SETTING INAPPROPRIATE PRIORITIES WITHIN THE FAMILY

Sociological studies regarding the long-range mental health of children of working parents pile up on both sides of this question: are children harmed when both parents work?

There is no authoritative consensus on the dual career question. Ultimately only your instinct and gut feeling can guide you in determining how your child is being affected by your or your partner's extra-family obligations. It may be that what your child needs is a greater *quantity* of *quality* time from one or both of you.

Setting priorities in terms of one's family does not mean jettisoning your career—it means rearranging your work schedules in order to allow for more time for your kids, and negotiating within the family for more time together as a family.

The importance of parents reevaluating their priorities within the family was revealed in some of the comments of the children we polled in our survey. In describing how they would like their relationship with their parents to change, not a single child wrote that they wanted to have more money, more toys, or more clothes. Rather, *nearly half of them said they wanted more time with their parents.* We were surprised to discover how many adolescents, who developmentally might be expected to have had a bellyfull of familial togetherness, were, in fact, just as needy of time, approval, affection, and acceptance from their parents as younger kids.

Said a 17-year-old boy:

There's too much yelling in our house. There isn't time for discussion, especially with my mother because she's always exhausted when she gets home from work or rushing out the door to get someplace. Discussion takes too much time, so it's just easier for her to scream at us as she gets into the car.

She can never remember my friends' names—I guess it's just not really important to her. I've told her how I feel, and she's aware of it and we try to spend time together on weekends. But there are just so many hours in the day, and she has so many obligations at work and in the community and places she has to be.

Absentee and ambitious fathers who are on stress overload are not new. What has changed is that over half of mothers of minor children are in the work force, and many of them are not around enough to ameliorate the damage done by such absenteeism and ambition, or to be a buffer between it and their children, as they traditionally have done. Because many of them are also on a career track, women frequently are, if anything, more exhausted than their husbands. Many mothers are doing triple duty: achieving in the marketplace, running homes, and raising their kids, frequently alone or with little or no help from their partners.

But the same can be said, we found, of a number of mothers who do not work outside the home but who nevertheless are workaholics, if not in the conventional sense: their calendars are jammed with appointments for exercise class, volunteer activities, social engagements. Among the children we sampled, nearly 20 percent complained that their mothers are "always on the phone." The problem, then, is not simply that women work; it is that many of today's parents—mothers *and* fathers—have placed their children lower on their list of priorities than they were placed when they were growing up.

But it also costs considerably more to raise children today than it did 20 years ago. And so we are not recommending that parents not have careers or not try to be successful. Most parents must work to support themselves and their families. What we are saying is that your child may be having trouble, and you can examine how your priorities contribute to that. And if one parent is unable to recognize that contribution, it's the responsibility of the other parent to do so.

There are some meetings or business trips or professional dinners that parents can give up without jeopardizing their jobs. Says Bill Honig, Commissioner of Education for the state of California, "I know a lot of CEO's who do not neglect their children, who make time for their kids."

Many parents don't know how to set priorities at home. But they can learn to evaluate their professional or community obligations in terms of their impact on the family. They can learn to rearrange their priorities, rather than get locked into them; for example, if their child is going through a needy time, they can postpone, delegate, or drop certain obligations.

One father we interviewed turned down a lucrative job offer in another city because it would be too destructive to his children to uproot them. And several women we talked to have taken sabbaticals from their careers, or taken part-time jobs, or done free-lance work in their homes, in order to be with their young children.

You can weigh your priorities by examining them in terms of whether or not the child exhibits symptoms of stress, which we outlined in Chapter 1 (see section entitled "What Do We Mean by Intervention?"). If your child exhibits any of these symptoms, it may be time for you to take a stand and say to your child, "You are not being fairly treated, and I realize it's time we did something about it." If you have not already done so, that is the moment at which you need to begin negotiating in earnest with your partner in order to rearrange family priorities.

NEGOTIATING WITH YOUR PARTNER ON YOUR CHILD'S BEHALF

All the negotiating language, skills, and strategies you use with your children can be employed in negotiating with your partner. Remember that your goal is your child's welfare, not yours. For many people, going to bat for someone else makes it easier to negotiate and keeps the boiling point high. So keep your eye on your goal. Once you acknowledge that your partner is behaving toward your children in a way that distresses you, then you can address that issue with him or her in the following ways:

1. *Prepare.* Rehearse in your mind—or, better yet, on paper—what it is you want to say, and the issue as you see it. Remember, you want to help your child, not "get" your partner.

2. *Pick your moment.* Timing with your partner is more crucial than it is with your child because adults are more sophisticated and have had many more years of using such escape hatches as defensiveness, offensiveness, fatigue, and the like. By paying attention to the patterns in his or her behavior, you'll be able to figure out the best time to negotiate with your partner.

Said one woman we interviewed, "I know that the wrong time to ask my husband for something is in the morning on the way to work. On the way home or at the end of the day, the answer is likely to be yes. He's happy that the work day is over, home is relaxation for him, and everything is a plus then.''

Sometimes dinner at a restaurant is the best time and climate for bringing up your concerns—away from the house and the phone and the kids. Such a setting also requires a degree of civility, and it's less likely that your partner will lose his temper in public, even if he is inclined to do so in private.

3. *State your concern about both your and your partner's relationships with your child.* Use yourself as the bridge between your observations and your desire to improve the situation. You can say, ''I have contributed to the tension and unhappiness at home by not discussing it sooner with you, and I'm trying to correct that situation by having a talk now. I've been afraid to say anything. But our kid's in trouble, and we have to do something about it.''

Most parents both want the best for their children, and for a variety of reasons may have failed in the past to speak up on their behalf. If that is true of you, don't beat yourself up for it—the point is that you're ready to do something about it now.

Here's how one woman, who, like her husband, was brought up in Europe with old-world values, has learned to handle differences with her husband. She says:

> My husband is very difficult because he thinks things have to be only his way. The fact that he's head of the family has gone to his head. I had to educate him. He was shocked the first time I said, ''We all have to bend toward what you want, but you aren't willing to bend for us—it isn't fair.'' It just never dawned on him. Now I say, ''There comes a time when if we all feel you are wrong, you have to listen to us.'' And we sit down as a family and discuss it. It's hard for him to digest, still. But he's learning.

4. *Don't get sidetracked.* Prior to your negotiation, you can keep an anecdotal diary of the things your partner does that disturb you, so that if he or she says, ''What are you talking about?'' you will have the information. Try not to become emotional or defensive—simply describe the occasions that gave you pause.

5. *Bring in outside information.* If your partner still resists your interpretation, give him or her a list of what other adults in your child's life have said or observed: a teacher's comment about the child's disruptiveness or unhappiness can sometimes shock a parent into action.

6. *Discuss areas of unresolved issues in your marriage that may be spilling over to your relationship with your child.* You can say, for example, "I know I create problems between us by not telling you how I feel—instead I punish you by being miserable and trying to make you feel guilty. How do you think you create problems?" Your partner may be relieved to have an opportunity to discuss items about which he or she has been silent.

The risk, of course, is that your partner will dump on you. If that occurs, you can say, "I don't think blaming each other is going to help. This is a chance for both of us to try to deal with how we are hurting the children. Let's try to focus only on that issue."

If your partner insists on denying any and all difficulties, or on trying to saddle you alone with their resolution, at least he or she will know that you will from now on separate marital problems from child-rearing ones, and further that you will attempt to intervene on behalf of your child—in the interest of trying to improve the domestic climate—when it seems necessary.

7. *Make sure you are not overreacting to wounds suffered in your own childhood.* One man we talked to said, "My parents always treated me like an uninvited guest. I was determined not to let that happen to my child. But I went too far—my daughter became spoiled and manipulative because I was so intent on being the benevolent father I never had. I had to learn how to set boundaries, rather than trying to 'woo' my child."

Perhaps you, too, have overcompensated with your child. You can mention that to your partner, thereby inviting him to examine the ways his childhood haunts his current relationship with your child.

8. *Point out to your spouse that it is possible to turn a mis-fit with your child into a fit.*

Neither you nor your spouse needs to abandon your values in the process of raising your child. While it is true that each child has his or her own style that may not fit your or your partner's style, that does not preclude a middle ground of shared family values and interests.

If, say, it's important to you both that your family make a contribution in some way to the community, you can achieve your goal even though it may have to be tailored to everyone's style. One family we know cooks once a month for Meals on Wheels. The 9-year-old son was always disruptive when the meals were delivered, a 4-hour task. Finally his parents decided to let the boy get the meals ready—wrapping them with foil in individual portions—before they left, rather than accompanying them on the delivery. He wasn't temperamentally prepared for several hours in the car, but he could tolerate the hour it took to *get* ready, once the meals were cooked. In his own way, he was able to participate and to cooperate with an obligation that was important to his parents.

9. *Be prepared to hear criticism and to think about it.* Once you have invited your partner to a session in which he or she is to be made aware of the ways in which your child is suffering from a less than optimum parent–child relationship, the invitation becomes bilateral. You may hear things that cause you pain or embarrassment; try to avoid a defensive or "victim" mentality, and give the positive feedback serious thought. It may help you, just as you are trying to help your partner. You can ask your partner to point out ways in which you err with your child, and you both might come up with a signal to use in your child's presence to indicate when it is occurring.

10. *Know your partner's style.* We discussed at length in Chapter 5 the ways stylistic parental liabilities may have a negative impact on your child, particularly when there is a conflict of styles between parent and child, and it would be useful to review this material.

Once you know what your partner's style is, you can negotiate accordingly. Keep your expectations realistic—you can only get what each style is capable of giving.

NEGOTIATION WITH YOUR PARTNER— BY STYLE

What follows is a road map for negotiating with the six adult styles. Note that although we use the pronoun *he*, these guidelines apply to women as well.

JUNGLE FIGHTER. When you see him constantly criticizing your child, you can say, "I am no longer willing to allow you to ridicule our child about his school work. I see the damage it's doing to him. This has to stop—he needs your help. You may want to discuss the problem with his teacher, or pay for a tutor, or you might want to stop making negative comments for a month and see if he improves." Make sure there is no "maybe" in your voice. Don't ask the Jungle Fighter to sit down and go over your child's homework—give him a larger responsibility. He likes the challenge of solving problems, and hates details; he is bored unless he gets challenged by the Big Stuff. Appeal to his need to win. Say "Our child needs your influence."

Caution: Stick to the issues, and make them clear; don't think about your feelings of resentment. Remember, Jungle Fighters are not good at guilt. Make sure your tone of voice reflects your determination to intervene and to insist on change—he won't get it unless you do. Do not discuss the issues at a restaurant, where he might become sidetracked by chats with the waiter or a friend you've run into.

DICTATOR. When you see him demanding perfection from your child in the execution of his chores to such an extent that the child has no time for extracurricular activities, you can list the facts on a piece of paper. Show him a flow chart that illustrates the jam-up of responsibilities in a column labeled "child." Then say, "The family can no longer operate like this because our child has no time for his own needs." Use every persuasive word you can think up to show him the consequences of his tyrannical nature. Don't threaten—point out the losses if he doesn't help, such as your child's exhaustion, resentment, neglect, or physical illness. Appeal to his logic.

Caution: Don't allow your negotiation to turn into a debate. Make sure your observations are on paper, and if he starts to interrogate you, you can reply, "It's all in my report." Watch out for his intimidating side: don't give in to fear, or he won't listen. *Stick to the facts.*

SILHOUETTE. When you see him refusing to give your child an allowance, or any money at all, you can say, "Our kid has to work after school to get any spending money. He has no friends. Friendship may not be important to you, but it's crucial for our child." The Silhouette hates to talk, so put in writing a list of what the kid is missing—sports, school activities, study time. Ask him to briefly tell you what he is willing to do to remove the burden he has placed on his child—say, letting the child work an hour every other day to earn money around the house. You'll have to educate the Silhouette about the consequences of his behavior that he may not have considered, such as loss of friendship, because that isn't important to him.

Caution: Silhouettes hate intimacy, conversation, and spending money. Don't sit too close to him. Keep your discussion brief. Write down your goals and make sure he reads them.

BIG DADDY/BIG MAMMA. When you see him failing to set limits, or doing your child's homework, or interrogating the child about her friends and feelings, and generally making the kid a basket case by his hovering, you can say, "Our child is an insecure baby because of your anxiousness. Let's write down the things you now do to 'help' her. Which of those things are you willing to let go of? We have to give her experiences that let her do things on her own. What should they be?"

You have to help this style see how he is suffocating his child. He will protest his good intentions, and seem to be mortally wounded by your comments. Don't be seduced by his righteous indignation. Instead, say, "I know you want to help our child learn self-reliance—how do you plan to do that?"

Caution: Engage him in the process and do not become distracted by his flattery, or the list of needs you brought to your meeting will double by the time it is over.

SOOTHER. When you see him making promises to your child but never keeping them, and letting your child off the hook by making you the heavy, you can say, "I resent your making me do all the disciplining. You have to learn how to say no."

He is the classic passive–aggressive, unable to state his real feelings, but showing them instead by his inability to keep promises or to set limits with your child. He'll agree to shape up just to shut you up, and then do nothing. Give him time limits and deadlines, and don't overload him with tasks. Help him by rehearsing with him the ways he can say no, either to requests he won't honor anyhow or to your child's misbehavior.

Caution: He hates confrontations because he needs to be reassured constantly, and will tell you exactly what you want to hear, but won't follow through. Make certain you persist—gently but firmly.

WIN/WINNER.   When you see him getting so involved in his work that he has missed a lot of time with your family, all you have to do is point it out directly: "We've missed your company. Our child says she wishes she could see more of you. Would you talk to her?"

Don't try to manipulate or charm him because he doesn't respect such treatment. You don't have to tell him how to help—you have to state your feelings, to which he'll respond.

Caution: He does what he says he will do, so if you change your mind, you will need to renegotiate.

Although all these negotiations may smack of manipulation, they are not: to manipulate is to try to gain an advantage by clever or unfair means. But negotiation means *mutual* advantage—that is, collaboration—where both sides win. If you understand your partner's style and you speak to that style, you are simply showing respect for individual differences and sensibilities.

Notice that none of these negotiating tactics involves name calling, disloyalty, or blame; instead they provide the arena in which parents can discuss together how to bring out the best in each other and in their child.

TEACHING YOUR CHILD TO NEGOTIATE WITH YOUR PARTNER

If your partner is unwilling to modify his or her behavior with your child, you can nevertheless help your child to have faith in himself, rather than to feel that he is to blame for unreasonable or unkind treatment of him. Mental health requires the belief that you have a right to your own thoughts and feelings—so even if your partner can't be brought around, at least your child can learn to believe in the sanctity of his anger or sorrow at being mistreated.

Here's how you can teach your child to calmly express his or her feelings to your partner, and the words he might use:

- A child who is verbally abused by a Jungle Fighter can say, "That scares me. When you do that it makes me not want to have fun with you even when you're not yelling at me."
- A child who is constantly criticized by a Dictator can say, "I feel you don't like me very much. What do you like about me?"
- A child who is routinely ignored by a Silhouette can say, "You never seem to want to talk to me, and I don't know what to do—can you help?"
- A child who is overprotected by a Big Daddy/Big Mama can say, "I need to have you trust me more. What are you willing to let me do?"
- A child who is frequently let down by a Soother's broken promises or absences can say, "It's too hard for me to believe you now. Just tell me what you are really going to do."

You can teach younger children to say the same things, but in short phrases, such as, "That scares me," "How come you don't like me?" "I miss you," "I can do it myself," or "I don't believe you."

Children who can verbalize their feelings in these ways, even if their comments are dismissed, at least are in touch with their feelings, rather than thinking they deserve the treatment that provokes them. This is a concept that is particularly difficult for children—especially when they are very young—who, by definition, are egocentric: when their world collapses, they believe that they are at fault.

You can show them that they are not, and that they can try to do something about it in a mature way. Even if the attempt fails, they have had the courage to try, a lesson that will encourage them not to ignore their own feelings and instincts in future relationships.

Children all want and need a relationship with both parents—witness those children who continue to have loving connections with both their mother and their father after they divorce—even when there is a mis-fit. Your children may be rebellious, defiant, childish, or adultlike—but they still want to have a sense of belonging in the family. That is only possible when both you and your partner can periodically take stock of what you are doing to help, or to hurt, your children.

The only "united front" that has any meaning in the family is one that has depth, not one that is superficially erected and pasted together. Children are best able to please their parents if both of you are just and affectionate and honest and courageous, and if they can count on one of you to come to their aid if the other is temporarily out of kilter. You can do the latter without the child's thinking that such "off" days are a prelude to divorce. This is marital partnership at its best.

When you can negotiate with your partner on your child's, and each other's, behalf, your kids will want to be with you both in a loving, joyous way, and you will feel more loving and joyous with them, and with each other.

PART IV

SCENARIOS: NEGOTIATING WITH YOUNGSTERS (PRESCHOOL AND ELEMENTARY SCHOOL AGE)

CHAPTER 11

NEGOTIATING WITH PRESCHOOLERS

On a crisp, freezing winter afternoon, Peter, age 3, is marketing in a vegetable store with his mother. Barely able to bend his arms, which are swollen by his snowsuit, Peter totes a plastic shopping basket that is nearly as big as he is.

From farther down the narrow aisle, his mother calls, "Peter, please pick out three tomatoes—we're going to eat them at dinner tonight." Peter somberly observes the cartons of goods at his feet, reaches into one, clutches an orange, and holds it aloft.

"No, not those, the red ones," his mother says. "Tomatoes are bright red and squishy. Make sure they don't have any cuts or bruises." At last, Peter finds the requisite carton, carefully studies its contents, and places four perfect tomatoes into his basket.

"*Very* good job," his mother says, smiling. "Are you sure you have three?" Peter peers into his basket and with one stubby finger points to the tomatoes, one at a time. He removes the redundant tomato and returns it to the carton. His mother says, "Now pick out anything you want—you decide." Peter surveys the produce around him, selects a pint of strawberries, and cautiously places it into the basket.

Oblivious to the legs of other shoppers into which he and his cumbersome bundle careen, Peter staggers down the aisle to join his mother and, heaving a sigh from his exertion, hands his basket up to her. "Thank you," she says. "That was such a help."

Notice that in carrying out his assignment, Peter never said a word. But he understood everything his mother said to him, and, thanks to her patience and confidence in him, was able to carry out a fairly complex task, one that involved responsibility, arithmetic, discrimination, and choice. And his mother demonstrated these negotiating skills: she gave her child options, set a goal, and, no doubt, took several beats herself as her son inexpertly, but diligently, carried out his mission.

Clearly, Peter has had considerable experience with decision making, even though he's only 3. His mother has boosted his self-esteem by making him a participant in the rituals—in this case, food shopping—of family business. She has begun teaching him the rudiments of effective negotiation.

GETTING STARTED: THE IMPORTANCE OF RITUALS

If you are the parent of a newborn or very young child, you are in a fortunate position indeed: planting the seeds of negotiation in your child's first years gives you, and your child, an early advantage, because by developing certain habits and establishing certain rituals, you can prevent future parent–child problems.

Family rituals are the benchmarks of your child's day that connect him with you according to your routine activities together, and are the context of your negotiations. These rituals include who wakes him up in the morning or after a nap, when he eats his meals, and with whom, when Daddy and/or Mommy come home and what they do with him, who tucks him in bed at night and whether or not a story is read to him.

Mastery in early childhood is rooted in family rituals, and without them, the structure of negotiation cannot work. With them, your child learns how to negotiate, to develop people skills, and to control himself and his environment in a healthy way. Moreover, his feelings of mastery, through problem solving and decision making, carry over to those situations when you are not there—say, in day care, or at a friend's house, or in preschool—rather like a long and friendly parental shadow.

But if you are part of a two-career couple, or if you are a single parent, the idea of establishing rituals may seem utopian. Some mornings—as you try to get yourself primed for the work day, make lunches, pray your kid doesn't have a cold, race for a train or bus—the idea of rituals may seem like a cruel joke. And at the end of the day, you may be exhausted, perhaps worrying about cutbacks at the office or dealing with problems raised by the baby-sitter or in day care.

Nevertheless, even with a paucity of time together—whether or not you work full time—it is important to build rituals into the family scheme of things. Rituals help you to be consistent with your child, and help him to feel that he can rely on loving structure, the basis for his emotional security. That structure makes it possible to learn how to negotiate together, even in limited time, because it establishes trust and a bond between you.

RITUALS AND FEELINGS.   Parents of young children often say that discipline is the single greatest issue they have with their kids: how to get their kids to learn self-control, to take responsibility for their actions, to learn how to pitch in when everyone in the family has varying obligations, to stop engaging you in a test of wills—in short, to give you a break.

But as you will see in this chapter, the issue is almost never discipline, but the feelings behind a lack of it. If, for instance, your child gives you a hard time about going to bed, you find yourself nagging, then yelling, then screaming, then spanking, and then feeling out of control. All this can be prevented by looking at what's behind the bedtime mania—it could be that your child doesn't feel a sense of continuity, because bedtime is never at the same hour each night. Or perhaps he feels you are rushing him off to bed, when his style requires a certain amount of preamble. Perhaps his is a fearful style—the Underdog, for instance—and you haven't found a way of subduing the nighttime monsters that haunt him.

By paying attention to these feelings, as well as their stylistic expression, you can negotiate the ritual of bedtime so that it becomes a pleasant routine.

As we discuss the issues for negotiation with little kids, remember that by addressing your child's feelings first, and acknowledging them, your negotiations (and the issues that necessitate them) become much easier to anticipate. It is not enough to supply the Band-Aids of how-to's without this attention to feelings.

Notice also that the negotiating skills we present here will be different for this age group—birth to 5—from those that may apply when your child is older. Negotiations change as your child develops. Certain skills are paramount for little kids, and are repeated over and over. Once they are mastered, other skills come into play, as we will see in the next two chapters. The main goal with preschoolers is to help your child begin to be an indispensable partner in the family.

INFANCY:
PLANTING THE
SEEDS OF
NEGOTIATION

Children are astounding creatures, so much so that parents may sometimes underestimate how much information their child can process, even in infancy. Most mothers and fathers have a sense of their infant's temperament—the "easy" child versus the "difficult" one, the baby who coos contentedly in your embrace and the one who grimaces when being held. But beyond these wriggling hints of personality, it's hard to judge just how much kids who do not yet talk actually *know*.

According to recent research, infants know quite a lot, and behave accordingly. Babies as young as 3 days will imitate your facial expression; 4-month-olds can distinguish the person speaking to them and will turn toward that person; and 6-month-olds can tell the difference between a vowel and a consonant and understand simple words and instructions. Infants can also demonstrate assertiveness by, say, averting their eyes or engaging your attention, as with a squeal of delight.

But just because infants are smart, this does not mean that they are savvy enough to invent ways to bamboozle you. Crying infants are usually unhappy for a reason, and it is a mistake either to assume they are capable of pulling your strings by wailing or to ignore their cries. Their urgent needs, which they cannot describe to you, outweigh any "knowledge" they may have, so you do not want to confuse the two, or to think infants are more precocious than they are. As the late child psychoanalyst Selma H. Fraiberg put it in *The Magic Years,* your infant is not "a cunning fellow who plots the overthrow of his parents behind the bars of his crib. . . ."

Nevertheless, while infants are all urge and almost no control, they often do respond, for instance, to differences in their parents' routine treatment of them. One man we interviewed noticed that his 8-week-old infant is more fretful after an afternoon with her mother—who, unable to tolerate any crying, holds the baby for hours—than after several hours with him, because he does not pick up the child every time she murmurs. When the baby is with her father, she has become accustomed to gurgling contentedly in her bassinet from time to time. The mother does not allow the baby (or herself) to develop any frustration tolerance. And so the baby is collecting information about how to negotiate with each parent—one is "easy," the other is "tough."

This inconsistent behavior may carry over to the caretaker, if any, in your child's life; it's a good idea to discuss with baby-sitters, full-time housekeepers, or other child care helpers your child's behavioral patterns and your requirements for handling the infant, as well as your older children. You can train these caretakers to implement your strategies in your absence, and to follow through on them.

Once children reach 6 months or so, they can begin to tolerate longer periods of isolation or discomfort—as, say, when you are preparing dinner or attempting to quickly do some household chores. By now you probably know which of your child's cries are for hunger, which for fatigue, which for loneliness or pain. If you don't jump at each sound (other than those that are clearly urgent), you may discover that they are for their own sake alone, or simply for your constant attention, and that they will quickly subside. In this instance, the skill of taking a beat pays off handsomely.

We are reminded of a couple who, when their child was 10 months old, finally acted on what they knew to be the difference between crying for companionship and tears from hunger or pain. Their son was waking them on and off every night, which left them aching with fatigue. Finally they decided they had to hold the line and let him yowl—in other words, they had to begin to employ negotiating skills, in this case, shifting gears.

Says the father:

It took every ounce of determination on our parts. After tucking him in, we sat at the bottom of the stairs, cringing like kids, huddled together, for a full two hours while our son bawled. Each of us had to keep the other from running to his room. But finally he went to sleep. It was the longest night of our lives, but it worked—the kid stopped crying for nighttime entertainment.

And so, for older infants, where there is manipulation, there is knowledge; where there is knowledge, there is choice; and where there is choice, there is the possibility for negotiation, even without verbal language on the baby's part.

Much of the interaction between parent and preschool child depends on your experience, parenting style, and the child's basic nature. It is your instinct that will best determine what the child needs, and what he merely wants. And you can consider your own needs and begin, even before his first birthday, to help your child become part of the family and to adopt certain negotiating patterns that will keep you from being run ragged by the blessed event.

During the first year a great deal of time is spent gathering information—your child about you, and you about your child. Give yourself time to get to know him and to watch the patterns in his behavior.

At the same time, you may be introducing a new sibling to a child you already have. Perhaps the new arrival has defied all your parenting assumptions, based on your previous experience. As a result, you may inevitably compare him to your first child.

Try to remember that children are from birth temperamentally different from one another and that God is not punishing you by sending you a "difficult" baby after first giving you a "good" one. It will take you both time to adjust to one another; that's a negotiation, too.

Most of the effort will be yours in the beginning, either to figure out what the child wants or to begin to set some low-level limits, as in small amounts of frustration when that seems appropriate, or simply learning enough about your child to figure out his or her style. If you think you know what your child's style is, you can begin encouraging your child's stylistic strengths, even when he or she is very young—but be prepared to shift gears, in case you've guessed incorrectly.

You will recall the woman we discussed earlier, who from her child's birth gave her choices between toys, holding up two of different colors, or different shapes, to begin making the child aware of options.

She also knew in her child's infancy that the baby was, as she puts it, "independent and strong-willed, which I encouraged. If, when she sat on my lap, she pushed against me, I would hold my hand under her foot to give her something to push against even harder. She got strong fast."

Whether or not you have identified your child's style yet, be aware that *not* meeting his urgent needs in the early months, or assuming that he is, in fact, out to get you, will lay the groundwork for his future insecurities and stoke the liabilities of his style. But if you can give equal doses of love, limit setting, and your good sense, the partnership between you will become loving and balanced, rather than a contest for control.

BEYOND INFANCY: NEGOTIATING WITH 2- TO 5-YEAR-OLDS

The years between 2 and 5 are full of meteoric changes in your child. But they are also filled with your expectations of what kids "should" be doing by a certain age. Some kids defy what you have read about "normal" development—the child who walks and/or talks at a year may be developmentally on a par with many 2-year-olds. What is important about your child is what he is able to do, and not when he does it (although, obviously, great lags in certain motor and cognitive abilities may require medical or psychological attention). So when we talk about this age group, we are talking as much about behavior age as about chronological age.

It is important to know not only that your child is going through changes, but also that they are in tandem with the relinquishing of certain dependencies and the trying on of new challenges. So parenting means paying attention to a triple track of development, as, for example, in the case of locomotion: what's fading (creeping), what's currently occurring (walking), and what is emerging (climbing). Readiness is a trinity of behavior; if you can think of it that way, your expectations will be commensurate with that readiness, and your negotiations and strategies will shift accordingly as the child gets older.

Negotiation with preschoolers begins in earnest as the child approaches the double threat of walking and talking. Many of the parents we interviewed said that these two events resulted in radical changes in their children, many of whom, until they were verbal and ambulatory, were fairly easy kids. Once they begin to control their environments, kids can become handfuls. By this time, when your child is 2 or 3, you may have a pretty good idea of what his style is.

Although the degree may vary, these are the issues that most concern parents of preschool children and are the major arenas for potential difficulty, and for negotiation:

bedtime
meals and food
manners (tantrums, sharing, etc.)
cleanup
toilet training

Each of these issues reflects style. And because the issues may vary from style to style, so will the negotiating skills used to address them. And so we will include in descriptions of these issues—pegged to style—the negotiating skill or skills on which you will need to draw.

As we discuss these issues, be aware also of their parallels to other issues—cleanup relates to cooperation with chores and respect for people's belongings; manners encompasses temper tantrums and empathy for others; bedtime involves separation; meals are allied to hygiene and health; toilet training is one example of self-control. The Big Five have infinite spin-offs, and the negotiations we will outline for them have myriad other applications.

BEDTIME

Getting enough rest at night is one of those childhood issues that is nonnegotiable. If your child was allowed to stay up until 3 A.M. and sleep all day, which Baby Bullies and Saints would dearly love to do, no one in the family could function.

Bedtime is also one of the most important childhood rituals, giving your child a sense of security in good times, and helping to bridge the bad times (as in the case of a divorce—see Chapter 17). It may be the only time during the day when you and your child can have a few moments alone together. You will not always be able to enforce exactly the same bedtime—for instance, if you have a party, or if there is a holiday get-together with relatives. But try to keep bedtime fairly consistent, moving it back as the child gets older, but keeping it constant during the plateau times.

For little kids, bedtime means separation from you, and some styles are able to tolerate this better than others. Nighttime can have its own sorcery; young children who have recurring anxiety dreams, for instance, do not know that they are dreaming, and so bedtime can be filled with dread because it is a prelude to imagined horrors that seem real. The more creative (Baby Bully) and fearful (Underdog) styles may require more reassurance than the more independent styles (Loner and Kid Tyrant), and so nighttime rituals—tucking in your child, perhaps reading a story, having a quiet, intimate chat, or giving the youngster a backrub— will take a little longer for the former than the latter.

At the same time, bedtime is "alone time" for children, something that the more gregarious styles have trouble with. If your child is beginning to give up naps, for instance, you can still teach him the benefits of "alone time" in this way: tell your child that this is, indeed, time for him to be by himself and to do whatever (within reason) he wants with it in his room. Say to him, "I'll have my 'alone' time in the next room for 15 minutes, while you have yours. I'll come back soon to play with you." If your child protests, ask, "What are the things you can do with your 'alone time'?" Children learn how to be contentedly alone when they are in the vicinity of an adult; they can run back and forth, from their room to yours, lengthening their time by themselves, and in time will be comfortable with periods of solitude.

If you build solitude into your child's day, he will begin to respect your privacy, and to appreciate his own. Moreover, separation from you, either in the form of nursery school or time with a sitter, will lose some of its sting, because you have helped encourage the child's self-esteem and independence.

Here's how to negotiate bedtime with children, by style:

> *Baby Bullies* may fight bedtime because separation from you is anathema to them—without someone's response, they aren't convinced they exist. And so they will argue with you about being alone, finding endless excuses to prevent sleep, even if they are faint from exhaustion (this style is less likely to require a lot of sleep than other styles). "I want a glass of water," "Turn the light on," "Turn the light off," "I have to go to the bathroom," "Read me a longer story," "I want *another* glass of water," and similar delaying tactics can turn the bedtime ritual into a nightmare. Baby Bullies' demands make you angry, not only because they need their rest, but because you need *yours*.

> Baby Bullies are very likely to throw tantrums if they aren't allowed to have their way. Of all styles, this one is most in need of limits and consistency—*you must do what you say you'll do*.

> You need to be gentle but firm about enforcing bedtime routines with your Baby Bully, and the sooner you begin to do so, the better.

OPTIONS
ZEROING
IN

Give your child several options for what he can do at bedtime: look at a book or play with a toy in bed, or just relax with the light on. But no TV, radio, or records, all of which will be too stimulating for him to sleep. Your child has options about what to do in his bed; he has no options about being there. If he says he doesn't want any of them, you can say, "I can see that you don't want to do those things. So perhaps we should turn off the light right now. You can try again tomorrow." Narrowing his choices in this way, and establishing a logical consequence for his not making a decision, will inevitably result in his taking the more inviting of them. But in no case do his options include your staying indefinitely in his room with him.

BOTTOM LINE   Your time with your partner is important: tell your Baby Bully that his bedtime is your " 'alone time' with mom/dad"—time apart from him.

Unless you establish early your need for privacy, your Baby Bully will get the idea that he can monopolize you. Betsy and Marvin Hawley learned this the hard way. Jeremy, their 2½-year-old, would continuously get out of bed after being tucked in and come into their bedroom at night, demanding their attention. One night it finally became too much for the parents. In desperation, they locked themselves into their bedroom for a half hour's respite from their child. Jeremy banged against the door, screaming, and they told him to go back to bed. Still screaming, the child went to the end of the hall, hunched his shoulders, and, like a cannonball, ran headlong into their bedroom door, trying to force it open.

By this time the child was in hysterics, screaming to his parents through the door, "Let me in! Let me in!" Marvin replied, "Stop crying first so you can hear me. When you stop crying, I'll open the door." At last the child quieted down and his parents opened the door, took him to his room, tucked him in, and said, "We love you and know you're unhappy. But it's bedtime. You will not get up again. We'll see you in the morning." It took several sessions of gentle but firm bedtime ritual, but finally the child got the message.

Kid Tyrants who, as you know, become immersed in their projects and activities, will view bedtime as an unwelcome interruption. Because routine is particularly important to them—they like any measure of control over themselves and others—you will need to give them notice that the hour

PRIMING of bedtime is approaching. While young children have little concept of time, you can give them the general idea with such phrases as "when this television program is over." Or you can put on a record and say, "When the music stops, it's bedtime." Whatever method of time setting you use, Kid Tyrants can begin to disengage, if only in their minds, from their activities and wind down toward the sleeping hour.

Kid Tyrants are supremely gifted at logical defiance and love engaging in wars of words. If this verbal sparring is allowed to continue at bedtime, the ritual becomes a contest.

Kid Tyrants will generally go to bed if you keep the hour or two before bedtime relatively stress free and if you follow your bedtime ritual faithfully. But that isn't always easy. Says a mother we interviewed:

> When I am patient and calm, and when it's time for bed, my son watches a TV show, then I read him a story, and he goes to sleep without a peep. But if I'm busy and I don't do all that, bedtime becomes a battle. And it's made worse by my husband, who, when he comes home after working late, overrules me by saying, "Aw, let him stay up a little longer." So my son has learned to manipulate us.

Kid Tyrants cooperate most freely when they are given loving structure. Don't engage in a drawn out debate or acquiesce to a growing checklist of your child's demands at bedtime. Tuck your Kid Tyrant in, do the things you normally do for a set amount of time—say, 15 minutes—and then say good night. If you child gives you an argument, **BOTTOM** say "Lights out." Be aware that Kid Tyrants have a tre-**LINE** mendous sense of pride, and you don't want to humiliate them. Give your child a chance to pull himself together after stating your bottom line, and an opportunity to recover and to reform. But do not have a question mark in your voice: set firm limits on debate.

Loners are fairly easy about bedtime and look forward to being alone. It is because of their potential social isolation that you might want to use this time for a brief chat, because you want to help your Loner learn to verbalize his or her feelings and thoughts. You can make conversation a gentle bedtime routine and get the child used to a few minutes of intimate talk at the end of the day.

Saints, no matter how exhausted, will insist that they are not tired, so much do they fear missing out on the action, and because they believe that your business is *their* business. They are extremely social, and even very young Saints often prefer talking to people to playing with their toys.

Saints have a huge arsenal of stalling tactics at bedtime—wanting to help you clean up, to perform a dance for you, to chat with your guests. One 4-year-old Saint we know interrupted her mother nine times (by the mother's count) in 35 minutes for water, another trip to the bathroom, complaints of a stomachache, and loneliness.

OPTIONS

Because of your Saint's charm and persuasiveness, you must be resolute in your limit setting, at the same time making as inviting as possible the child's "alone time" in his room. Give the child the same choices as the Baby Bully about what he or she can do in bed. This youngster might enjoy having as an option drawing a picture for you; the picture represents a connection with you in your absence.

ZEROING IN

The Saint may wake you at night because he wants to be cuddled. Take him back to his room, tuck him back in, but do not sit down. Reassure him quietly by saying, "I know you want to stay up and talk to us, but it's time to go to sleep," and then go back to bed. The reward for waking you will be so slight that he'll soon give up the habit.

Underdogs often are fretful at bedtime because they tend to be afraid of the dark. There is no harm in letting these children keep the light on. Most children can fall asleep whether or not the light is on; you might want to wean the child from a table lamp to a nightlight, and from that to leaving his door open so he can see a light from the hall. He can still have a light—you can negotiate which one. Do not underscore the Underdog's fears by being so solicitous at bedtime that he thinks there's something to be afraid of.

One parent we interviewed handled her Underdog daughter's nighttime terrors—in this case, a monster—this way: her 4-year-old slept on the bottom tier of a bunk bed.

One night the mother crawled onto the top bunk and whispered words her daughter could not hear. Then she climbed down, sat on her daughter's bed, and said, "I've just had a long talk with the monster, and he says he really doesn't want to hurt you. He just wants to get some rest. He says he can't sleep because of all the fuss you're making."

But more than the dark, the Underdog is fearful of separation from you. This style needs most of all to learn about "alone time" during the day. At night, you can use the child's anxiety as a springboard for getting in touch with his feelings. This can be done by reading him a story and asking him

FISHING   questions along the way: "What do you think the bird is feeling? Where do you think he went? Do you ever wish you were a bird?" This drawing out of Underdogs gets them used to thinking about and expressing their feelings, whether happy or sad, rather than burying them behind a wall of silent suffering.

For Underdogs, the issue isn't bedtime—the issue is their feelings about bedtime; problems in that department can be cleared up if their fears are addressed and reassurance is forthcoming.

MEALS AND FOOD

Suppertime is the witching hour in Sylvia Shefler's house. That's when she sits down with her 2½-year-old son and places a roll of paper towels on the table. Says Sylvia:

I put the plate down. He picks up the food and throws it across the room. I get up, clean up the mess, and put more food on his plate. He picks up that food and throws it on the floor. Then I make him something else to eat. Mind you, I'm a psychologist, and an expert on behavior modification. But who is modifying whom?

Manipulation through food is one of your child's most effective controlling mechanisms, because you want him or her to be healthy. Guilt about your child's incipient malnutrition, or fear that you are a dreadful parent because of the child's horrible eating habits, can turn mealtime into a food fight. Moreover, the use of food for reward and punishment can endow food with properties beyond nutrition—as in saying, "If you are a good boy, I'll give you a cookie." Equating food with love can lead to obesity and other eating disorders.

But you too can be manipulated through food. When, for example, your child is sick and confined to bed, if you are constantly bringing him meals, or snacks, or drinks, he will come to enjoy the benefits of being unwell. Don't make sickness pay off: say to your child, "I'll get whatever you want now—but for two hours, I'm off duty."

Food is food, not love, not a toy, and the eating of it needs to follow the same kinds of patterns that bedtime rituals do. At the same time, food involves more than just eating—it is a vehicle for family sociability, and it requires thought and preparation in which you can involve your children.

Many American families have gotten into the habit, however, of eating TV dinners, or some other instant meal, in front of the television, shutting out any conversation. Mealtime, especially dinner, should be a family ritual and not a mechanism for the avoidance of fellowship.

With that in mind, there should not be a division of labor wherein Mom does all the work pertaining to meals, and has her own dinner interrupted by repeated requests from her kids and her spouse to wait on them. You can negotiate with your spouse and even with very young children to contribute to cooking, eating, fetching, and cleanup; the amount of extra time children's "help" takes will be more than repaid to you later on.

Make the menu, however, nonnegotiable. You are not a short-order cook: if you have planned the family meal with your child's tastes in mind, and your child doesn't like what you are serving, he does not get a substitute menu. Do not force your child to eat—but do not make him a sandwich an hour later either.

Despite all your best efforts, meals can be hectic or a sometime thing, rather than a family ritual. Because of dual-career marriages, as well as earlier eating schedules for young children, sometimes it's not possible for the whole family to eat together. Many couples seldom eat dinner with their children because the husband comes home late—say, 9:00 P.M.—and his wife feels obliged to wait to eat with him.

If you can't have dinners together, what do you do? Perhaps you need to rearrange your priorities and plan your weekly agenda to include mealtime with your children. Instead of dinner, it could be breakfast. If that's not possible, try to have at least one meal a week that is sacred to the family, perhaps Sunday evening—with the TV set off—so that children can get used to seeing you in a pleasant way and to talking about the events of their, and your, day.

As we have said, if you do not know your child, you cannot negotiate with him. Mealtime may be the only time during the day when you have an opportunity to learn more about him, his experiences, friends, and preferences. Do not use mealtime for complaints and criticism or as open season for arguments.

Teaching children to make mealtime pleasant involves negotiation. How kids behave during meals, and how they respond to and try to manipulate you with food, depends on their style:

> *Baby Bullies* tend to treat a plate full of food as though it were a playground; they build tunnels through mashed potatoes, pile rolls into fortresses, improve their eye–hand coordination with the accurate projection of a grape onto the wall from across the room. Among other things, these activities prove that they probably haven't much appetite, or that they don't mind pushing you into a contest about getting them to eat.
>
> You feel as though you are in a culinary tug-of-war with the Baby Bully because you appreciate his creativity and his verbal acuity, and don't want to squelch them when he demonstrates both with his food; at the same time, you want him to behave appropriately at mealtime.
>
> Part of Baby Bullies' creativity is their ability to camouflage issues. Robert, 3, becomes a screamer at mealtime to avoid having arguments about the food he is, or isn't, eating, and the mess he makes. His parents' concern, then, is his screaming, and they don't get to the havoc created by the food he spills, nor to its being cleaned up. They exacerbate the problem by threatening to take him to his room, and then not following through.
>
> Baby Bullies can make mealtime a horror, ruining for everyone the one time of the day when the entire family may be together. Says the mother of a 3-year-old Baby Bully:
>
>> I let him get away with his tantrums and his acting up at dinner because he just keeps badgering me, and by the end of the day I'm bushed and I give in to him.
>
> Baby Bullies tap into their parents' end-of-the-day exhaustion, as well as their guilt, at suppertime. One father we

interviewed said that Pam, his 5-year-old daughter, competes with her sister for her parents' attention and, in addition, is a fussy eater. The two tendencies collided at dinner one night when he began answering, in great detail, a question posed by the older daughter. Says the father:

> While I was talking, Pam got up and went over to the piano and began noodling. As soon as I finished my response to her sister's question, Pam came back to the table and continued to eat dinner. If the conversation drifted away from her for more than two minutes, she'd get up again. Needless to say, that broke up our conversation. She absolutely must have a certain amount of attention, and won't eat without it.

Baby Bullies need to know not only that there are limits on their misbehavior, but also that there are consequences for making everyone miserable or angry.

TIE BREAKER ZEROING IN

If your Baby Bully uses the dinner table as a target range, you will need to use a tie breaker to avoid a test of wills. The Baby Bully requires your swift response. Say to him, "I guess you aren't very hungry," and remove him from the table. Then tell him he must pick up the food from the floor (wall, lamp, rug) because it belongs on a plate, or in the garbage.

If he throws a tantrum, wait out his screams and hand him a paper towel. If he refuses to clean up the mess, tell him, "I see that you don't want to be with us when we're eating. Go into the living room. When you're ready to clean up the floor and join us for dinner, you can come back."

Here's how one family taught their 2-year-old Baby Bully to behave at mealtime. Like most small children, their son had a short attention span, and once he was finished eating, wanted to get out of his chair to play. But rather than go to his toy box, he insisted on crawling onto his mother's lap and interrupting her dinner. And so she set firm limits on his interruptions:

GOAL SETTING

I said, "You can go into the living room and play while Daddy and I finish eating." I knew he could see us from the other room, so he wasn't totally alone. But he immediately tried crawling onto my lap. I put him down and told him again to go into the living room to play. He proceeded to scream and to have a tantrum, which we ignored. When he calmed down, I said, "I know you are angry; you can cry all you want. But you cannot come onto my lap while I am eating. When I'm finished, I'll play with you." He finally got the message, because I was determined not to give in.

TAKING A BEAT

BOTTOM LINE

ERROR ANALYSIS

Perhaps you've never set limits before with your Baby Bully and he punches you for sending him away or removing his plate. Now you want to get beyond your past parenting mistakes and the unbridled patterns of his destructive behavior. Get down to eye level with him and, while holding his arms against his sides, say to him, "That is not okay. Tell me what you feel or want, but you can never hit me or anyone else. Never."

BRAIN-STORMING

FINDING COMMON-ALITIES

The way to avoid mealtime hassles with your Baby Bully is to make him part of the whole mealtime process—menu planning, shopping, setting the table, cooking, cleanup. From this he will learn cause and effect, decision making, and how to find commonalities. In other words, you tap into his strengths to bring out his negotiating best. When he discovers that food doesn't appear by magic—and his is the style that is most prone to take it for granted—he will help come up with interesting food combinations, and his creativity will be channeled in a healthy way. At the same time, if he decides he wants farina and mushrooms, and then refuses to eat it, you can say, "That's what you chose, and there are no substitutes. If you don't want it, you don't get anything else."

Losing your temper or caving in with Baby Bullies will not change their behavior, because by your loss of control, you reward the behavior. The logical consequence of the child's acting up at the dinner table is to be excluded from the family during mealtime. As with any logical consequence, impose this one firmly, but calmly: you need to be an authority figure—but a measured one.

Kid Tyrants use mealtime as the venue for issuing demands about food: "This is icky, I want something else."

"Get me an apple." "I want pancakes." One 3-year-old we know makes it nearly impossible for her mother to sit at the dinner table for more than 10 minutes, because of the kid's insatiable thirst: "Get me juice" is a command that is repeated throughout the meal.

OPTIONS   We suggested to the child's mother this negotiation: tell the child that she can have two small glasses of juice, or a big one now and another one at the end of the meal. But no more jumping up by Mom for more juice. The parents gave their Kid Tyrant this choice, and told her there was no other—and that put a stop to her repeated orders.

As long as your Kid Tyrant feels he has a choice, he can exercise his need for control in an acceptable way. You draw the line if he wants choices other than those that are acceptable to you. But getting into a power play by saying, for instance, "You'll have only one juice because *I say so*," with no options, only stokes his need to take over.

There are times, however, when you shouldn't give your Kid Tyrant options. One 3-year-old Kid Tyrant we know hated eating in his high chair. Says his mother:

It was a major battle I lost. We got him a little table and chair, and that only led to new battles. He was too young to sit still at a table, and I had to work twice as hard to get him to stay there—he'd get up and wander all over the room with his food, which, naturally, left a terrible mess.

Once his mother let him have his way with the seating arrangements, there was no way she was going to get him to stand by her side, eating, let alone to remain quietly at the small table. Since no logical consequences were applied, he did not learn to establish inner controls on his behavior.

Parents have trouble with Kid Tyrants when they don't take into consideration the child's sense of time and timing. Kid Tyrants not only like to be in charge, but they also hate surprises. They require priming before a task or request, such as your saying, "In a little while, we'll have dinner, so finish what you're doing." Says the father of a 4½-year-old Kid Tyrant:

Problems start when I don't give him enough time to do something—then he'll whine, nag, say "No" to whatever I ask. He doesn't know how to wait. He prefers making up his own rules, when to eat, what to eat, what size bites to take.

A contest with a Kid Tyrant can be turned into a collaboration if you give your child options that utilize his assets. By meeting him halfway, you both achieve your goals, and mealtime is made infinitely more pleasant. But this negotiation will work only if you are consistent, and if you don't allow your exhaustion at the end of the day to corrupt your resolve. At first, it will take all your energy to change hostile mealtime patterns to civilized ones—but if you don't make that effort, the behavior will escalate for an infinitely longer period of time.

Saints and *Underdogs* are another mealtime matter altogether. So eager are they to please you that they may overeat. In time they may use food as a palliative when they are upset, a tendency that could lead to excessive weight gain. Using food for reward or punishment is a mistake with any style, but in particular with the Saint or Underdog.

BOTTOM LINE

Loners are often indifferent to food. Frequently they'll say "I'm not hungry," because they are engrossed in a game or a television program. Tell your Loner he must join you at the table, even if he doesn't want to eat, so that you can have time together. So much tension is created by this style's remoteness that you may secretly wish he'd stay in his room; but if you hang in, he may begin to value family participation, and might even grow to like it. Involve him in the mechanics of meals: clearing the table, putting away groceries, and the like do not require chatter, but they do require attendance.

If he does decide to eat, he may not want much. Don't establish a mealtime hassle by insisting that he finish his meals; just remove the plate once he starts picking at or playing with his food. If he's hungry, he'll eat; if not, don't make a big deal of it. Food is not a huge issue for him— don't make it one by your anxiety.

MANNERS

Nearly every etiquette book stresses that good manners are nothing more than concern for other people's feelings and sensibilities. Successful negotiations involve good manners; without respect for others, any negotiation becomes a losing proposition.

Respect and disrespect are first learned at home; your child is never too young to learn to expect respect, and to respect others. There is no excuse for a child, or adult, not saying "Please," or "Thank you." When these amenities are required of your child, and of you, they make family life much more pleasurable.

Good manners seem to be a relic of the past. You walk down a city street and there is a crowd of kids blocking your way; more often than not, they will not move to allow you to pass, so you must walk in the gutter. It is this kind of behavior that increases the stress of daily life. You can teach your child to behave in another way, gearing your values in this department to your child's style.

Manners can be reinforced by your setting an example; they can also be underscored by reminders, but try not to nag. Children who are constantly interrupted with such rubrics as "Say thank you," or "Say please," begin to feel like marionettes.

You can prepare your child's place in the social world in a pleasant way, early, by taking him out for lunch dates, during which he can pretend to be a grownup—mimicking and acquiring good manners. In the same way, when you and your partner treat each other with courtesy, you set an example for your child.

Another way to bring out the civility in your children is to give them an acceptable way to vent their anger and frustrations: this makes it clear that you are not disallowing their feelings but teaching them how to express them. You can place in their bedroom a graffiti wall on which they can draw anything they like, including a picture of you that indicates the degree to which they hate your guts at the moment. Or you can get a large, soft toy they can beat up.

Only the Saint and the Underdog are inherently apt to be sensitive to people's feelings—they seem to be constitutionally suited to altruism—but the other styles can learn polite behavior.

Baby Bullies have dreadful manners if allowed to get away with rudeness. Your Baby Bully grabs the salt at dinner rather than saying, "Please pass the salt." He pushes you aside as he dives under the Christmas tree to be the first with a present.

Such social aggressiveness begins when Baby Bullies are very young and may first express itself with biting. It is tempting to bite a Baby Bully back, just to let him know how it feels. But such retaliation backfires, because it reinforces the habit. If your Baby Bully bites you, hold his arms firmly and say, "That hurts. You are never to do that again." Do not threaten him, because threats are invitations to continue the misbehavior. Do apply logical consequences. If your child bites you again, take him into his room and say, "I see that you don't like me right now. Tell me how you feel with words. You cannot bite." As you leave his room, say, "When you're ready to talk, you can come back to where I am sitting."

ZEROING IN

Physical aggressiveness is a hallmark of Baby Bullies and must be curbed quickly. But even here, there is room for negotiation.

One woman we interviewed bought her 22-month-old Baby Bully a cobbler's bench with a plastic hammer to help him vent his frustrations. The first day he hammered not only on the bench, but also on the chairs, tables, walls, lamps, dog, his mother, and every other available surface. Says his mother:

ZEROING IN

I explained that hitting hurts people and makes bumps on things. He continued to hit. So I said, "If you continue that I am going to take the hammer away from you," and I turned and walked away so he wouldn't think I was challenging him to start up again.

SHIFTING GEARS

He resumed banging away on the coffee table, so I took the hammer away and said, "Let's try again tomorrow. You aren't ready to stop hitting things yet." He cried for a while, but I didn't give in.

OPTIONS

The next day I gave him the toy again, and he started hitting on things. I said, "There are four things, and *only* four, that you can hit: your high chair, the bench, the stool, and the wastebasket.'' Giving him a choice did the trick—he only hits those things. Now when he wants to bang on something, he says, "I can hit the chair, the bench, the stool, the wastebasket," as though it were a great gift.

Sometimes the Baby Bully will try to get around your limit setting regarding his manners by picking a public place to act out his unresolved temper; he'll pull a tantrum in the middle of a restaurant or while you are standing in the checkout line. Do not allow the milieu to alter your limit setting.

You need to prepare your Baby Bully for your expectations of his behavior in a public setting. Prime him by explaining the proper way to act in public, including in a restaurant.

PRIMING   With so many couples working, dinner with the children at a fast-food restaurant, and sometimes at a particularly nice one, is often the easiest way to have some time together with a minimum of labor on your part. Tell your child in advance of an outing that you expect him to stay in his chair, to not throw food, to say "please" and "thank you" to the waiter.

If after all your priming your Baby Bully still decides to have a tantrum, or to toss his food across the table, there are three possible stages for your negotiation:

1. Take the child to the bathroom, or outside, or to your car, and say, "This is not okay. We talked about restaurant manners this morning. I'll give you a few minutes to calm down, and then we'll go back to the table and you can try again. If you still can't behave, we'll go straight home."

BACKUP   2. If the child continues to ruin your meal, follow through: take him home, even if it means the whole family has to go as well.

BACKUP   3. The next time you want to eat out, hire a sitter and say to your Baby Bully, "You cannot come with us this time because you don't know how to behave yet in public. Maybe next time you'll be ready to behave in a restaurant." He'll get the message from this logical consequence, because he doesn't want to be excluded.

Kid Tyrants are generally polite when they are older, but when they are very young need some training in good manners. They will exhibit bad manners through unfettered candor, as in "Grandma, you smell funny."

ZEROING IN

These kids love language, so use it. Say, "That makes Grandma feel bad. I don't like it when you use hurtful words. If you don't like Grandma, tell me how you feel about her. But don't use words that will hurt her."

Sharing, another component of good manners, can be a problem for Kid Tyrants because they are so territorial; they want to control everything, especially all their belongings. You can address your Kid Tyrant's feelings, and at the same time negotiate with him about sharing, without giving him a lecture about selfishness. Here's how one woman we interviewed accomplished this feat with her 2-year-old Kid Tyrant:

TRADE-OFF

Just the word "sharing" used to make her cry. We got her a tricycle, and when a friend was coming to play with her she'd say, over and over, "This is my tricycle, it's no one else's tricycle." So I said, "Yes, it is. Let's put it in the garage for the afternoon. You can find three other things you are willing to share."

This parent drew the distinction between what's important to the child and the need for her to learn how to get along with other people. You don't ask your Kid Tyrant to give up

ZEROING IN

the belonging he treasures most, because you know its emotional importance. But if he refuses to share any of his toys, he's probably not ready for playmates, and you need to establish with him the concept of sharing within the family first. These are logical consequences, not punishments, for an inability to share.

Saints and *Underdogs* will generally be unfailingly polite, so much so that they may try to ingratiate themselves when it is inappropriate—say, with a friend who takes terrible advantage of them. These styles may, for instance, give their toys away to more aggressive children.

ERROR ANALYSIS

Tell your Saint or Underdog that you appreciate his good manners, but that not everyone deserves such generosity. He needs to know that he has value, and that he must not allow himself to be mistreated by others. He doesn't need to be rude, but he does need to set boundaries for his unflagging and indiscriminate largess and goodwill. Point out to him when he is being kind, or overly generous, at his own expense; you intervene on his behalf until he can do so on his own.

Loners often are rude by their silences; they get so lost in their own thoughts that they do not listen to other people during a conversation, and will talk about that which is of interest only to them. This comes out as a total non sequitur; you are discussing something you did at work, he interrupts by telling you that he likes chocolate pudding. He isn't tracking your conversation; he's tracking his own, the one he's having in his head.

ZEROING IN　Make connections for your Loner. Tell him, "I see that you aren't listening to what we are saying. People think you don't like them if you act as though what they say isn't important, just the way you feel if they don't listen to you."

PRIMING　Loners, like Baby Bullies and Kid Tyrants, have trouble sharing. You will have to prepare your Loner so that he can learn to do so when, for instance, a friend comes over to play. Say to the child, "Before Susie comes over, why

OPTIONS　don't you pick out a game you can play together?"
This style needs to get in touch with his own feelings and those of other people, and probably won't if you don't show him how.

CLEANUP

Most kids don't mind clutter, and need to know that for the sake of the group (the family), a degree of tidiness is necessary. You can make cleanup less irksome for your child if you negotiate.

The *Baby Bully* would rather throw things than put them away. You can say to him, "Let's do it together. I'll put away the toys on this side of the room, you put away the

TRADE-OFF   toys on the other side of the room." Be certain that you both participate. The logical consequence for making no effort to clean up is to deny him your help, or to remove his toys for a day; this tactic will not need to be repeated if you enforce it, and if you live through your Baby Bully's volcanic response.

Kid Tyrants tend to be fairly well organized and will not mind your telling them that when they are finished using one toy, it must be put away before they start with another; but they want *you* to put it away. The most important thing is that they cooperate in cleanup so that they don't get the idea that you can be ordered around. Kid Tyrants will look for any opening to be in charge, and know exactly what they are doing. Says the mother of Sharon, a 3-year-old:

> One night we were putting her toys away, and I did ninety-nine percent of the work, while she did one percent. When her father came home I said to him, "Look what Sharon did! Isn't that terrific?" whereupon Sharon said, "I didn't help much."

This kid may be a tyrant, but she isn't stupid. Don't confuse encouragement with hyperbole—most children know the difference, and it is fuel for their manipulation of you (because you lack credibility), as well as of their inability to count on your telling them the truth.

OPTIONS   If your Kid Tyrant balks at cleaning up, you can give him
BRAIN-   a choice, as well as draw on his love of order: "You can do it
STORMING   now, or after two cartoons. How do you think your toys should be arranged?"

Saints can be distracted from cleanup by almost anything, and will cry, or whine, or ask to cuddle, to get out of it. You want your Saint to develop some independence, so you can give him this choice: "I'll help you put some of the toys away, and then you can do the rest." If the Saint makes little or no effort, you can say, "Now you have to do them by yourself. I won't help if you don't do anything." The logical consequence of not taking you up on your offer is losing your "help"—and company.

FINDING COMMON-ALITIES

Underdogs will seldom squawk about cleanups; they are so eager to please that they will almost always be willing to do what you ask. Use cleanup as an opportunity to encourage—say to your Underdog, "I like the way you put the pots and pans away. Now it will be easier for us to find them." You have complimented the child's deed, rather than praised him. Such compliments will help build his self-esteem.

BRAIN-STORMING

Loners don't usually make much mess because they can become absorbed by one activity for hours. But you want your Loner to become a little more sociable, so you might engage his help in, say, picking up the newspapers and magazines and asking him where they should be put. Don't make these sessions long—perhaps 10 minutes at first. But use tidying up as a way to be together in a joint task.

TOILET TRAINING

With so many women in the work force, the issue of toilet training has become urgent; if your child isn't out of diapers, he or she may not be allowed to attend nursery school or even some day-care centers.

Your child senses how important it is to you for him to have bowel control, whether or not you work outside the home. But if you don't approach this delicate issue with respect for your child's style, he'll have control over everything *except* his bowels. One 3-year-old boy we met has learned to use his excretions to pit one parent against the other: he says to his father, "Daddy, change my diaper." When Daddy lifts him up on the changing table to do so, the kid says, "No, Daddy, I want Mommy to do it."

Our aim in discussing toilet training is not to give you the last word on the physiological and technical ramifications of bladder and bowel control—your pediatrician, as well as other sources of expertise, can provide useful information on the subject. Rather, we believe that if you integrate and implement that information with attention to your toddler's style, the process of toilet training will be much simpler and far less traumatic.

Among the things for you to think about is your child's readiness, which is critical to toilet training. There is no hard-and-fast rule as to the moment when the child is ready to take control over his body in this important way. Do not rush your child. Any hurry on your part will backfire, either in the form of "accidents," or in the form of extreme constipation. When your child's diapers are dry for long stretches of time, he is probably physically ready to begin toilet training. His emotional readiness, however, has something to do with both his style and yours.

A Kid Tyrant we know at 2½ walked into his mother's bedroom one afternoon, his sodden diaper draped around his knees. In his hand he held a fresh diaper. "Here," he announced, handing the diaper to his mother, "change me." This child is ready to learn how to sit on a toilet and to keep his knees dry.

Remember, however, that just as you cannot force a child to eat or to sleep, you cannot force a child to use the toilet. But you can make the process easier through negotiation.

GOAL SETTING	*Baby Bullies* and *Kid Tyrants* are eager to be all grown up. If you take either style regularly to the potty after meals and give him a pleasant few minutes on it—whether or not he uses it—he will get the idea and fairly easily want to use the potty on his own. Lack of bowel control is a barrier to moving on to other things—going to nursery school or swimming without a diaper, like the bigger kids—which these children are eager to do.
TRADE-OFF	*Saints* tend to be forgetful because they so enjoy your company, or that of playmates—they are very social at quite a young age—and so may easily forget to use the potty. You can sweeten the toilet training deal by offering a new pair of underpants, perhaps a pair the child picks out, to provide an incentive for your Saint to be less forgetful.

Underdogs and *Loners* cannot be pressured about toilet training; they have other things on their minds (fear of separation for Underdogs, concentration on their inner lives for Loners) or may be immature or developmentally unready, so the big maturational leap of toilet training holds little appeal. Rushing these children can lead to constipation. They are temperamentally programmed to withhold inner feelings, and the same may apply to their bowels. Make toilet training a matter-of-fact, low-key interlude, encouraging their efforts and saying nothing if they do not produce results. Never punish these (or any) styles for "failures."

SHIFTING
GEARS   If either style is not toilet trained by the age of 3½ or 4, it is possible that his immaturity is cross the board and he is not ready for day care or prenursery school or structured play groups. Moreover, the child may have emotional or medical problems. His body is sending you a message—pay attention to it. In most cases, the time lag will quickly vanish if you respect his timetable; and if you do not, other signs of immaturity will persist as the child gets older. It is better to allow him the latitude of time now, rather than pay over the long haul for pressuring him to hurry up.

Although the years from birth to 5 seem brief to you, remember that children accomplish a huge percentage of their developmental tasks during this time, and each triumph—walking, talking, learning generosity and self-control—are giant steps for them.

These are the years when you are shaping your children in a profound way, one that is incalculable in its impact on their future self-esteem and in their relationships not only with you, but with other people as well.

Negotiating skills, such as options and trade-offs, brainstorming and finding commonalities, give children survival and coping skills in the outside world. You are not doing your child a favor, nor are you respecting his knowledge and capacity to learn, if you "make it easy" for him by not beginning to teach him how to negotiate his own needs and wants.

Your strategy for your child includes taking the long view in these brief, but extremely important, years. The negotiating groundwork you lay now will be of immeasurable importance to him as he moves into the school years—and your life, marriage, and parent–child relationship all benefit by the process. You are storing up treasures.

Here's how the mother of a 2-year-old put it:

> I try to keep in mind my long-term goals for him. What we want most is for him to be an independent decision maker. Kids do not wake up one day knowing that they have to learn how to be that. So we continually have him make choices and we support those choices so that he won't be afraid to make them. The fact that he screams or has occasional tantrums doesn't upset me or that plan. I just have to stick to my goals, and keep going forward.

Enjoy these early years and remember the value to you, and your child, of teaching him to become a collaborator in his own destiny, by encouraging his assets and curbing his liabilities. By the time he's of school age, you will have made this "passage" a welcome event because you have prepared him so well for it.

CHAPTER 12

NEGOTIATING WITH GRADE SCHOOLERS

"**E**veryone says that you shape your kids in the ways you treat them," says the mother of three children, "but in a lot of ways you don't have anything to do with how they turn out."

Once your children begin to go to school, this awareness hits you like a gust of wind. Up to now, most of the variables of their lives have been fairly predictable. But now you are sending them out into a wider world—school—where for many hours of the day you have little control over their experiences. You are no longer the only influence on their lives, and in some ways you may not even be the primary one.

The meteoric changes between birth and 5 have mostly to do with children's mastery of the physical world and their bodies. Now, however, they are finding their place in the academic and social schemes of things; this process produces in children personality changes that give you joy and anguish.

As children move toward puberty, parenting becomes more complex. This is a time of children's emerging social, intellectual, and sexual selves, with all the attendant complications. These are the years, if you remember your own childhood, when you were or were not invited to parties or to join a team, when friends were nice to you at home but snubbed you on the school bus, when teasing was rampant, when pressures for good grades began to mount.

In elementary school, children settle into their styles, and compare themselves, and are compared to, the styles of other kids their age. Their styles take on sharper, more recognizable contours. For example, whereas in their earliest years Baby Bullies and Kid Tyrants seemed very much alike, their styles begin to diverge and come into separate focus during the elementary school years. So it is with the other styles.

Secretive children (Loners) become downright clandestine; vigorous kids (Baby Bullies) shake the house. Angelic children (Saints) begin to extract favors from you for each good deed they do, and domineering kids (Kid Tyrants) start giving you five rational arguments for why they should not turn off the lights. Hypersensitive children (Underdogs) become increasingly helpless.

Your children's styles are being modified not only by the family, but also by forces outside it. Your house may suddenly have invisible guests, the echoes of friends and teachers and tutors and coaches and lesson givers. Now your children are saying and doing things that they did not learn at home, and are responding to social consensus.

Modifying the liabilities of a child's style now is critical, because it sets the stage for adolescence when your influence (if not your leverage) dwindles in direct proportion to the child's age.

But that's a while off. Right now you are trying to create a balance— for yourself and for your children—between outside pressures and family life, between freedom and structure. It is a delicate balance indeed. If there is tyranny in too much freedom, there is also tyranny in too little, and it is in these years that children's needs for privacy, for carving out an identity for themselves, and for learning how to make good decisions add to the complexity of finding the right balance.

Some parents have difficulty with the beginnings of their children's independence; parents who are themselves dependent may have trouble letting go, even minimally. One woman we know of, when her child began attending kindergarten, pasted her own picture inside the lid of her daughter's lunch box in the name of her daughter's "homesickness." The child may have been ready for the separation kindergarten brings; her mother certainly was not.

You need to find the middle ground between letting your children fail—within certain boundaries—and letting them succeed. The key to this balance is collaboration within the structure of your family.

Collaboration means working together for the common good and for mutual benefit, and helps your children feel needed. For instance, you want your child to take out the garbage, not because he'll get his allowance if he does, but because this and other chores are part of the teamwork involved in making family life run smoothly; each chore helps everyone.

Collaboration is a notion to which children come only gradually— and in some cases, unwillingly. In their youngest years, they are the centers of their own universes; now you are asking them to share their universe, and to share you.

Cooperation is the first step in learning how to collaborate. Here's how each childhood style, in the elementary school years, begins to approach this new task of cooperation:

Baby Bullies will cooperate only when they see an advantage to them, and only if they can engage in preliminary repartee. Sarcasm is the tone of choice for this style, because behind their replies to your requests is the thought, "What's in it for me?" These kids may try to get you to jump through verbal hoops, but eventually they'll cooperate.

Kid Tyrants will cooperate only if they see guarantees for their efforts; they do not want to extend themselves unless they can control outcomes. Even at this young age, Kid Tyrants want to see a return on their investments, and so they will ask, for instance, "If I clean up my room, will you take me to the video store?"

Loners will pitch in only if it extends their orderly view of their environment, not because they are anxious to gain your approval. And so they will cooperate in an enterprise that calls on their skills—say, repairing a broken object—more willingly than they will to help someone in a joint or team effort.

Saints will promise to walk on metaphorical water for you, but will expect favors in return, and on their own terms. For example, an eager and immediate, "Sure, I'll vacuum the house," is followed an hour later by, "On your way to the store, will you pick up a pizza, and swing by to get Susie, Mary, and Jane? I've invited them over." The team effort of this style has a big price tag.

Underdogs will give lip service to cooperation because they don't know how to say no. Not with words, anyhow. Instead, they get sick, forget to put away the milk, don't call you when they're supposed to. They *want* to cooperate with you, but they're doing so for so many people that they don't have time for family obligations, which are at the bottom of their list of priorities.

Just as you cannot force someone to love you in only one way—yours—so you cannot force your children to cooperate with you in their own character building if it does not suit their styles. The goal—collaboration—can be the same for all children; achieving it depends on sensitivity toward their styles.

We mention this for two reasons. First, you want your family to be an enriching haven for everyone, which requires everyone's positive participation. The other reason is that these five styles of cooperation are blueprints for how your children will address issues that are of paramount importance to them, and to you, in these years.

According to many of the parents and children we interviewed, these issues are:

homework
friends
siblings
messy· room
allowance (money)

As we discuss these issues, remember that certain of them will be of greater concern with some styles than others; homework, for instance, is seldom a source of struggle with Kid Tyrants. And keep in mind that certain negotiating sensibilities and tools will be recurring themes in your strategies for your child: shifting gears, recruiting outside help, your child's readiness (timing), and awareness of your child's feelings.

SHIFTING GEARS. Remember to alter your negotiations as your child moves through these years. If, for example, you want to trade off something for his doing extra work around the house, and he's in the fifth grade, it wouldn't be reading him an extra bedtime story, a nighttime ritual he's outgrown. Tailor your trade-off according to his maturity and changing interests. You need to keep track of what's important to him, and what isn't, at each age.

RECRUITING OUTSIDE HELP. When we talk about outside help, we do not mean simply doing research about child development or attending PTA meetings. We mean the significant people in your child's life who can help you help your child—teachers, therapists, coaches, music teachers, relatives, friends.

If you are married, you have all these people *and* a spouse, who may be able to give you a fresh perspective, if not as fresh as a nonrelative's. And if you're divorced, don't forget that your ex-in-laws, as well as your parents, may be willing to be called upon.

It's very important for you not only not to feel alone, but also to know that sometimes outside support, rather than your own, is exactly what your children need most at the moment; they may feel more at ease discussing certain issues with people other than you. Moreover, you may not know your children as well as you think, because their public face—in all likelihood, like yours—is very different from the one they reveal in private.

READINESS. Readiness refers to your child's ability to handle certain responsibilities and choices; it also means his ability, whatever his age, to cooperate with you in the administrivia of running the household. Children in the elementary school years are able to do a range of chores, from setting the table to running the vacuum cleaner; some kids are ready to take on more adult chores, such as preparing dinner.

But if you have not involved your child in these activities before now—if he hasn't, as one parent put it, been "programmed" to help—it may be more difficult to get him started now. Nevertheless, it's possible to get him into the habit of cooperating, with a minimum of nagging, if you begin negotiating now.

ADDRESSING YOUR CHILD'S FEELINGS. We have discussed the importance of being sensitive to your child's emotional makeup when negotiating with him. The difference now is that he is more vocal, or more passive, or more sensitive, than he was in the preschool years.

Try to respect his emotional circuitry and allow him to express his feelings before you embark on a negotiation. You may be able to forestall the need for a negotiation as, for example, when you say to your cranky child, "You don't sound happy today," and he or she bursts into tears and tells you what's *really* going on inside.

Remember that while cooperation can be between two people or among the entire family, negotiations with your child are nearly always set into motion when you are alone with him, or with only your partner, if you have one, present. When you have more than one child, sibling rivalry only exacerbates whatever conflicts your child is going through. Do not embarrass him in front of anyone in or outside the family.

Privacy for negotiation needs to be scheduled into your day if you work outside the home. Says the mother of a 7-year-old boy:

> One or two evenings a week I sit down with him, not to interrogate him, but to get him to tell me what's been going on in his life. I try to make it a special time and I find out all kinds of things—what he's doing in school, things he's having trouble with.

We interviewed the father of a 10-year-old girl and he admitted that his relationship with his daughter—hence, his awareness of her feelings—

has never been as open as he would like because he doesn't schedule time for her. He says:

> I sometimes feel rejected by her, and I guess I'm jealous of the closeness she and her mother have. I think my daughter would like to communicate with me more, but we've never done it much. One day not long ago I tried; we were talking about sports, and I asked her if she had ever been benched in soccer. I said, "Come on, tell me the truth," and I kept probing. Finally she leaned forward in her seat, looked me straight in the eye, and said, "Look, Dad, you live your life and I'll live mine."
>
> I know I am lacking in her life. She doesn't respond to me. But I don't know what to do about those years when she was growing up.

When you can address your children's feelings, even if you are new at it, they begin to see that you are more interested in what they think than in their successes or failures in school; in short, you become an ally. For children to trust the negotiating process, they need first to trust their emotions, and your ability to listen to them uncritically.

Moreover, by knowing your child's emotional makeup thoroughly, you will be alerted to attempts at manipulation through tragedy—as in the difference between when your child says she didn't do her homework because "I'm so *depressed!*" and when she is really on the emotional ropes.

All this is quite a lot to think about. As we have said, be patient with yourself as you begin to negotiate the following issues. Learning to see them through the prism of negotiation takes time and practice; you'll have setbacks, even failures. But in time the process will become automatic, and the list of issues shorter, because the child will learn how to negotiate many of them on his own.

Here's how you can negotiate the primary issues of this age, by style:

HOMEWORK

This is a thorny subject for many American parents, because making the grade early in order to get into a college later—even *much later*—is of paramount importance to them.

Doing well in school concerns some children more than others, but it is *their* problem, not yours. If you push for scholastic achievement, you effectively take it away from your child, even if he gets straight A's. He may be ranking well, but he may not necessarily be learning, let alone enjoying, his school work.

Just as your child has his own personal style, he also has a *learning* style. As John Grinder and Richard Bandler discovered in their development of neurolinguistic programming techniques, the visual student learns best by illustration; the auditory student learns best by hearing; the kinesthetic student learns best by writing things down, or, when possible, becoming physically involved with the material (scientific experiments, for example). The imaginative and perceptive teacher will adjust to his or her students' different styles of learning.

Part of your strategy is to get a handle on your child's learning style so that you can intervene on his behalf with his teacher. You or your child may want to negotiate with the teacher for extra time, before or after school, to reinforce material that cannot be tailored for the child's learning style in class. Or your child may need to be tested to rule out or identify a visual or learning disability.

Regardless of your child's style, he must believe that the *choice* to work on his studies is his, and so are the consequences for his not working. You can guide, you can encourage, you can even, to a degree, help—as in taking your child to the library, or watching educational television programs with him, or not interrupting him when he is doing his homework. But you cannot do the work for him.

The purpose of the following negotiations is to remove yourself from any arguments about homework:

> *Baby Bullies* will put up a terrific fuss about homework. To begin with, there is the physical factor of their extraordinary energy, which makes it hard for them to sit down in one place and to concentrate. They'd rather be outside playing, or running around the house; their creativity kicks in with their charming ability to give you a list of reasons why they shouldn't do their homework until later, if at all.
>
> Sandra Cooper describes her first-grade Baby Bully's attitude about homework this way:

> > In the beginning of the year, he'd come home from school, sit down to do his studies, and look out the window, break pencils, doodle, get up and walk around. He simply couldn't sit there and do the work. So I

TRADE-OFF   would say "Go outside and play for fifteen minutes—then come back and do your work." The physical activity would pep him up—he couldn't work without doing that first.

TRADE-OFF   We don't have a TV, so when he finishes his homework we tell him he can go to a friend's house to watch television, but not until. We also try to have him do his work when we're around—say, right before dinner when I get home from work. That way I'm on deck if he needs help going over directions, or needs something for a project.

The most important thing I've done about homework is programming him so he doesn't have to spend a lot of time on it. When he began school this year, I told him, "If you listen closely in class, the teacher will tell you almost everything you need to know. Homework is just to make sure you know the material."

AGENDA   The combination of physical activity and intense listening in school has reduced the hassles about his homework.

Do not ask your Baby Bully to chain himself to his desk, or the kitchen table, to do his homework the minute he comes home. Give him a half hour or an hour to play first so he can dissipate some of the kinetic energy that gets stored up after several hours in school. In his case, pleasure—for a set amount of time—comes before work. You can set a timer so that he knows when playtime is over.

If after an hour of studying your child still hasn't completed his assignments—presuming he has not needed your interpretation, say, of a homework question—do not get into an argument with him about his "irresponsibility."

FISHING   Instead, gather information from him to find out if he's having trouble with the material or if he's simply bored—he may be over his head, or he may know the work thoroughly.

TAKING   If neither is the case, ask him, "What does your teacher
STOCK   do when homework isn't completed?" He may hedge by

ERROR   saying, "It's no big deal, I'll do it in the morning." Your
ANALYSIS   response could be, "I know homework is an important part

of your grade. You'll be disappointed if you get an F. How do you think you can keep that from happening?'' Such statements take you out of the middle, and get him to take responsibility for his decision not to complete his work.

BOTTOM LINE   He may decide at 9:00 P.M. to knuckle down, but that's his bedtime. So you say, ''It's time for bed; it's too bad you weren't able to do this earlier. Perhaps you will tomorrow.'' End of discussion. He may holler and give you a hard time. You merely need to calmly enforce the bedtime rule and let him face his teacher in the morning. Apply the same logical consequence if you have to take him for a doctor's appointment, or any other scheduled task, and he claims he can't go because he didn't do his homework.

In no case should you write a note to the teacher excusing him from doing the work, unless there is a legitimate reason—such as illness or a death in the family—to do so.

Kid Tyrants will almost never fail to do their homework. They are eager to achieve and to lead, and know that one way to do that is to do well in school. Their controlling nature extends to their homework, about which they are usually dependable, sometimes to the point of obsession.

Says the mother of a 10-year-old Kid Tyrant:

> I get impatient with her because she's so exacting. She sees the world in black and white, and she tends to be unable to expand. She'll read a sentence and say, ''What does this word mean?'' It's much more difficult for her to read that sentence and get meaning from it, because she needs to know what each of those words means *exactly*. But the payoff for her is that she gets straight A's—it's very important to her, much more so than to her father and me. She's extremely competitive. We try to kid her out of her concern about grades, which she doesn't find terribly amusing.

Saints give their parents grief because of their procrastination. Along with Baby Bullies, they are the style most likely to put off doing their homework. Saints tend to be extremely disorganized and panic because they cannot find their books or their homework assignments. You want to say to them, "No wonder you can't find them—you're a slob!" An argument erupts over messiness and the homework gets ignored.

Here's how a father describes his 8-year-old Saint's approach to homework:

> Liz's school has a gifted track for the better students, and she has a very high IQ. She's capable, but she isn't competent, because she gets scatterbrained. It's hard to teach kids competence and it takes time—you have to let them bungle, to make mistakes.
>
> She wanted to get into the gifted program, because her closest friends are in it, so we told her that she had to structure her day so that her work would get done. She was supposed to do a special science project, and didn't complete it in time, so she was left out of the gifted program. She was heartbroken. I think her disappointment taught her more about becoming competent than I ever could teach her.

But sometimes the issue is deeper. Says the mother of Linda, a 6-year-old Saint who has an identical twin:

> When it came time to start kindergarten, Linda was terrified; all I had to say was the word *school* and she'd start to cry. We sat down to talk about it one day, and she said, "I can't read." Her sister already knew how to read, and Linda just didn't have her sister's skills.

FINDING COMMON- ALITIES

> So I said, "It is very unusual that your sister has a talent that very few students have. You're going to be just like most of the other kids in school." I think that helped her a lot—that, and the fact that she had a very understanding teacher who reassured her the first day of school and gave her a hug.

Loners are sometimes thought by their parents and teachers to be not terribly bright when in fact they may be quite intelligent. The problem is threefold: they don't easily reach out for help; they are perfectionists; and they work slowly. If they don't "get" something the first time, they may give up. If their homework has an erasure on it, they'll tear it up.

Nine-year-old Robert confounds Lydia, his mother. After a recent conference she had with his teacher, she said:

> She told me Robert doesn't talk in class, which amazed me, because he does talk at home. Her main criticism is that he works slowly and carefully—he's a perfectionist. I try to motivate him to work faster by giving him gold stars, or stickers, or an increase in his allowance. Money seems to motivate him—he'll work harder for outside reward, but he has no inner motivations. The work that does get done is fine—it's what doesn't get done that worries us. His report cards aren't that good. So I don't show them to him.

ERROR ANALYSIS

Lydia's negotiating error is not telling Robert the truth about his grades—she is overprotecting him. He won't learn logical consequences unless she is honest with him—and so she should show him his report cards and discuss them. Moreover, she should remove the reward system so that he can begin to learn about the inner rewards of completing a task. The issue here is not prizes—it's Robert's self-esteem.

ZEROING IN

Here's how Lydia can negotiate with Robert about his homework. First, zero in: "I got a call from your teacher today about your work. She says you understand the material, but that you aren't doing the work." By beginning her negotiation with a positive comment, she'll get his attention for what follows.

FISHING

The next item to be discussed is what Robert plans to do about his school work. She can ask him, "What do you think the problem is?" If he replies, "What problem?" she can say, "What concerns me is that the work isn't getting done, and you're being penalized for it by getting poor grades. What can we do about it?" Lydia should then give

BRAIN- STORMING

Robert the opportunity to come up with some options—he might say, "You could write me a note," which is not an acceptable option. Neither is being paid to do his work, nor not doing it at all.

OPTIONS   Lydia may need to guide him, at first, in finding appropriate options: "There are several things you can do. We can set a timer while you are doing your homework, and each day reduce the time by a couple of minutes—maybe you can learn to work a little faster."

BACKUP   If that doesn't work, one backup plan is to teach Robert to negotiate with the teacher. He can say to her, "I know the material, but I get nervous doing my homework. Could I tell you what I know to show you that I know it, and maybe **TRADE-OFF** you could give me fewer problems to do? I'll try to work faster on the homework you do give me." His mother can follow up his negotiating efforts by saying, "I'll call the teacher after you discuss this with her."

Lydia needs to recruit Robert's teacher's help in her strategy to help her son become more patient with himself, and to see to it that he isn't setting himself up for failure. Kids who are perfectionists often have low self-esteem; it won't help if his teacher is also a perfectionist. Often a **BRAIN-** conference with the teacher will help reinforce your plan **STORMING** regarding your child's school work, or even produce other solutions and suggestions to help him.

Let us say, however, that this plan is acceptable to neither Robert nor his teacher. Lydia still has an option: She can **BACKUP** say to Robert, "Which after-school activity are you willing to give up so you'll have more time for homework?"

BRAIN-   She can also ask him to design a work schedule with **STORMING** which he feels comfortable. If he doesn't have any ideas, she can say, "Why don't you work for an hour. You can take a short break every twenty minutes."

BACKUP   Lydia has one more option: allowing Robert to repeat the third grade. If none of the other strategies works, it may **BOTTOM** be that he is simply overplaced, and perhaps should have **LINE** the option of repeating a lower grade. Many parents resist this option because they feel as though they have failed; some kids may resist it as well because they are worried about social approbation.

Giving your child the gift of time in this way is extremely important—he can go from feeling as though he's the worst student in the class to discovering what it feels like to be one of the best. The Loner in particular may not balk at the idea because he isn't terribly concerned about what other people think about him. What matters is what he thinks about himself, and without his parents' intervention, his self-esteem may not improve. We've discovered in several interviews with the parents of underachieving Loners that often one of the parents is a Jungle Fighter or a Dictator. Neither style is terribly interested in intangibles such as "self-esteem"—they are more result oriented.

SHIFTING GEARS

BOTTOM LINE

In Robert's case, his mother and father have been aware since the first grade that he has trouble with his school work, but because of their denial have done nothing about it. They need to do some further exploring—say, having him tested, or seeing a psychologist, to find out if he has cognitive or emotional barriers to learning.

Underdogs tend to be either overachievers or underachievers in school because their academic performances are frequently efforts to please the teachers or their parents, who may be giving them less individual attention than this style requires. Because good grades are so important to so many parents, many Underdogs will use homework as leverage to get Mom and/or Dad to sit down with them to explain the work, to help them with it and, in some cases, to do most of it.

The Underdog's need for approval may be so great that he doesn't listen carefully in class—he's afraid of being called on and looking foolish in his response. He may be very bright, but his nervousness skews the learning process. And so he may approach homework with a sense of dread, defeated before he begins. Some Underdogs are perceived as being unintelligent because of their fearfulness, and because they tend to daydream.

The main problem for you is that you want your Underdog to tell you about his feelings—his anxiety, his fear of failure. If he can learn to state his feelings, you can begin to help him beef up his self-esteem about his schoolwork. Underdogs can't be pushed—they can only be encouraged.

You need to figure out what your Underdog needs at a given moment in order to help him learn how to study. Is he simply in need of attention? Is he on stress overload? Does he not understand the material?

TRADE-OFF

The easy part is attention getting: if your Underdog needs more time with you, you simply arrange to do more things together on a regular basis. Having done so, you can, when the demands on you become too great, say to him, "We spent a lot of time together on Saturday. Right now I have to do something else, and you have your studies; after dinner, let's play a game together."

BACKUP

If his problem is stress, it may be that his teacher doesn't understand his learning style, and you will have to enlighten him or her. That's what parent–teacher conferences are for. You can also enlist the teacher's help in encouraging your child to get involved with school plays or the presentation of skits in class to help him get used to speaking before a group, if that's his problem.

Let us say that you've sorted out his feelings, and his stress. Now the issue is doing his homework. Here's how to negotiate that task with your Underdog:

AGENDA

When he sits down to do his work, tell him he must read the assignment and materials for 10 minutes, and begin to work by himself. If after that time he is unable to do the work, tell him he can discuss it with you, but that he cannot simply say, "I don't understand." You want him to learn to formulate questions, which means he has to think about the work and digest as much of it as he can before coming to you for help.

For example, if he's working on his math, he may say to you, "I don't understand the difference between fractions and decimals." If he is being specific in this way, it means he really is doing his homework, at least partially. You are helping him become autonomous.

Sometimes your child's friends will come to his aid. One Underdog fourth-grader we know, who hates math, is extremely lucky in having a creative and kind Loner friend. One day the two children were doing math homework together, and the friend suggested that they put the times tables on a large piece of oaktag, color-coordinating the numbers in different hues. Together they finished the colorful project—which hung in their classroom for weeks—and the Underdog got an A in math that semester.

FRIENDS

The elementary school years are those in which you'll have the most influence over the kinds of friends your children choose. The issue is not so much whether or not you like those friends—the issue is why your children choose the friends they do. Once they reach junior high, which is the apogee of peer pressure, the nature of their friendships will be telling in terms of how much of that pressure they have learned to deflect.

You can't force your children to like or dislike certain kids, but you can teach them to evaluate how they treat their friends and how their friends treat them. You can raise these questions:

"How do you feel when your friend doesn't give you a turn with a toy?"

"What do you like about your friend?"

"What don't you like about your friend?"

As you help your children analyze their friendships, you are preparing them for negotiating with them and learning how to define problems. In childhood (as well as adult) friendships, there is a vast difference between kindness and control, between leadership and dictatorship, between a request for help and exploitation. You may need to point out the differences as your children discuss with you their experiences with other children.

There may be times when you need to intervene on your child's behalf, as, for instance, when he is punched at the school yard; you'll want to discuss such behavior with the school authorities and, perhaps, with the offending child's parents. But generally you want your child to solve friendship troubles himself, and to make him aware of the ways in which he may encourage abuse. You want him to recognize the patterns of his relationships, so that he can correct them. Here's how each style approaches friendship:

> *Baby Bullies* are seldom at a loss for companions, but are often short on real friends because they tend to coerce other kids into doing their bidding. One woman we interviewed describes her 8-year-old Baby Bully daughter, Edith, this way:

Of my four children, Edith is the most outgoing socially, but she's also the most outspoken and the toughest. She can't stand not being the center of attention. If I tell her she can't see a friend, she'll kick the door, scream, and even run away from home. And when friends do come over, they almost always play the games Edith wants—and heaven help them if they beat her, because she goes bananas. She'll cheat at Monopoly, for instance, in order to win.

Edith's mother has not been able to modify her child's liabilities—withholding her allowance, spanking her, talking to her about her behavior produce no change in her uncontrolled temper.

The negotiating strategy that works with many Baby Bullies is to remove that which they most need for a sense of self: an audience. If your child is treating a friend cruelly, you can go directly to your bottom line, and take the friend home. One woman we know did just that:

BOTTOM LINE

I explained to the child that my son was not in the mood that day to have friends over, and that perhaps another day he would be.

When I got home, I said to my son, "It seems that you don't want to play fairly with your friend. We'll try another time."

You can use the loss of companionship as the logical consequence for other negative behavior. For example, 9-year-old Tommy was constantly getting into trouble in school because he talked back to teachers in front of the class and mimicked other kids when they were at the blackboard. The teacher called his parents to register his disapproval of the boy's behavior and asked them to work on it at home.

Tommy's parents called a huddle with him, and his mother said:

ZEROING IN

You do not know how to behave in class. It is rude to speak that way to your teacher, and it is cruel of you to make fun of other children. You wouldn't like it if they

BOTTOM
LINE
treated you that way. For one week, you may not have any play dates. If you give us an argument about it, or if this behavior in school continues, you will not have friends over for another week. Only after you have shown us that you can behave politely and with kindness can you see your friends after school.

Going directly to your bottom line with your Baby Bully is imperative, for three reasons: first, this kind of behavior is unacceptable in any situation, home, school, or at a friend's house, and is nonnegotiable. Second, there are times when children should not be given options, and with this style, this is one of them. Third, your child needs to know, early in his life, that you mean what you say. If he does not, his behavior could become uncontrollable by the teenage years.

PRIMING

OPTIONS

FINDING
COMMON-
ALITIES

Once you have jolted your Baby Bully and made him examine his behavior, you can follow up by forming a strategy for his playtime with his friends. Prepare your child for the appropriate way to treat friends, and engage him in decision making. Suggest to him that they play outdoors so that he can siphon off some of his energies. Let him select the possible outdoor activities—baseball, tag, footraces. But tell him that he must allow his friends to narrow down the final selection to one or two things that they would all enjoy. After that they can come indoors and play games or watch television, again deciding together what they want to play or watch.

Your Baby Bully may discover, on his own, that his behavior is reducing the number of playmates at his disposal. While other kids may "yes" him on the playground, they will often have told their parents about him, who will refuse to let him visit their homes. If this occurs, point out to your child that this is a logical consequence of his behavior.

ERROR
ANALYSIS

You'll have to do some fishing to find out whether or not he understands what is going on. Baby Bullies usually pick on Underdogs. So you can say to him, "I know you play with Johnny on the playground. Have you ever been asked to his house?" If the answer is no, ask "What do you think is the reason?'' The child may say ''I don't know.'' Then you can say, ''Maybe he feels bad. How do you think your friends feel when you pick on them?''

Your child may deny his behavior by saying that his friends are fat, or stupid, or slow. Address your child's feelings by saying, ''I know it makes you angry or hurt when your friends don't like you. What do you think you are doing to make that happen?'' Whatever his response, you have asked him to assess his behavior.

By addressing his feelings, he knows that you love him, even if you don't approve of some of the things he does. You can point out to him the things about him that you do like—his humor, his creativity, his spontaneity—adding that

**GOAL
SETTING**

these qualities will get him real friends, not just kids who, because they are afraid of him, he cannot trust. You also set into motion the thinking process that will help him learn to apply some inner controls to his bullying.

Kid Tyrants often have a lot of friends because they are born leaders. But they may have a problem with bossiness— telling their friends where to sit, what to do, and when to do it. When they have guests, you need to create experiences with their friends in which they are not in charge.

PRIMING

Prepare your Kid Tyrant for sharing authority before a friend comes over to play by saying, ''Last time Jenny visited, you told her what game to play instead of asking her. It might be a good idea if you give her a choice this time.''

**ERROR
ANALYSIS**

Follow up in a huddle similar to that with Baby Bullies to make sure your Kid Tyrant pays attention to the feelings of others.

Saints, more than any other style, are interested in being popular, a need so urgent that they tend to be indiscriminate about their choice of friends. So much are they defined by the people who like them that it is hard for them to know what they want, or to feel secure.

Saints like to make their friends dependent on them, and to that end will provide all kinds of solace and do a variety of favors, whether or not the friends want to be helped.

They tend to manipulate their friends, making them feel guilty when they do not call, or if they display what Saints construe as disloyalty, or do not express gratitude.

Many kids long to be popular, but for the Saint, not being included feels life threatening: the Saint pays a high price indeed for his or her social needs. Says the mother of 10-year-old Dorothy:

She's been loyal to friends and it's hurt her. She takes her friends very seriously; recently two of her friends were being mean to each other and they want her to take sides. She's been losing sleep over it.

ZEROING IN

I said to her, "You have to learn not to allow yourself to be taken advantage of. Half the responsibility is yours by not saying you won't take sides. You can get yourself out of this, instead of wallowing in it. I've done that all my life—please don't do it to yourself."

FINDING COMMON-ALITIES

ZEROING IN

Saints may need to be reminded that they may never be thanked for all the help they give, willy-nilly, to so many people—that, in fact, they lose others' respect by their lack of discrimination.

TAKING STOCK

Teach your children to assess their friendships by writing down the names of all their friends and listing next to each name the things they like and dislike about each friend. They may discover, from this exercise, who their real friends are. One way to encourage this endeavor is to point out that by narrowing their choice of friends, they will have more time to devote to the remaining friends, as well as to themselves.

ERROR ANALYSIS

At the same time, ask your Saint to list the things her friends dislike about her, including criticisms they've given her, if any. While at first the Saint may grow faint from admitting the lack of praise, you can help her understand that everyone has an unattractive side, and that maybe these criticisms are really demonstrations of friendship, assuming they were honestly stated.

One liability of Saints is their possessiveness. Tell your Saint that one way to be a good friend is to give one's friends the latitude to leave—if only to play for the afternoon with someone else—and to come back out of choice, rather than guilt.

The *Loner* may have as much trouble dealing with your anguish over his lack of a social life as he has with making friends in the first place. It is important not to make this style feel like a freak if he hasn't got a lot of playmates.

ZEROING IN

He needs to be made aware of the ways he may unwittingly hurt the feelings of the friends he does have. Unlike the Saint, who can sense a mood shift that indicates hurt or anger, the Loner just doesn't notice; you'll have to teach him how to do so.

This is most efficaciously done when your Loner is in the lower grades and his feelings are less hooded. If your first- or second-grader seems to be spending most of his time alone after school, rarely playing with friends, you might have a huddle with him to find out how he feels about his habitual solitude.

FISHING

It may be that he doesn't know how to begin to make friends—asking someone to sit with him on the school bus, say, or inviting someone over after school. Ask your Loner to tell you the names of three kids he'd like to be friends with, and, with his permission, ask his teacher to give you their parents' names and phone numbers. When their children are in elementary school, many parents make such arrangements on their children's behalf and work out transportation plans.

BRAIN-STORMING

FINDING COMMON-ALITIES

Then, in preparation for the play date, you can ask your child to offer suggestions about how he and his guest can use their time together. Be sure that the agenda includes activities that appeal to his style—working or playing with a computer, or building a sailboat from a kit. These activities require more activity than talk, but are a far cry from total isolation.

TAKING STOCK

Try to keep the initial visits relatively brief—say an hour or two. After the playmate goes home, ask your child if he had fun and what he liked, or disliked, about the friend. It may be that the two kids had little in common. You don't want your Loner to become discouraged from the friend-making process, so you can call on the other two names to arrange another date a few days or a week later.

The Loner's most important asset is his extraordinary loyalty—given the opportunity to make like-minded friends, he will very likely keep those friends. As your Loner displays this valuable trait, be sure to encourage it by pointing it out to him.

In no case do you force your Loner to form friendships. But you can make socialization easier by giving him an opportunity to talk and to listen at the dinner table, to accompany you on errands, so that the idea of being with people becomes easier for him. Watch his reaction to other people as you make your rounds, and encourage him to discuss it.

Nor should you pressure your child to join teams, clubs, and other group activities. This does not mean you remove him from any opportunity to join up. If you and your family regularly go skiing or ice skating, for instance, your child may at first be reluctant to participate—but if you don't push, he will be more likely to try it when he is ready.

Underdogs, like Saints, tend to have low self-esteem because they are so concerned about the reactions of others. But unlike the Saint, the Underdog tends to be victimized a great deal and has fewer defenses.

Here's how an 11-year-old Underdog describes her attitude toward friends:

> If any of my friends said anything bad about me, I'd die. My best friend is the stronger one in our relationship—I always say, "You decide what we're going to do." Sometimes, walking down the hall in school, she'll leave me behind, and I'll say, "Wait for me." She's always leaving me behind, or leaving me out.
>
> I don't feel I can do anything by myself. Right before school starts in the fall is the worst time for me—my stomach gets upset and I don't want to go to school without knowing someone in my class. I have to know at least one person or I'll totally die.
>
> So I'm nice to people, even though they aren't al-

ways the greatest, and I smile at everyone, because I don't like to give the impression that I'm unfriendly.

Underdogs are so concerned about the opinions of others that their perceptions and judgment can become terribly distorted. Diane, a 10-year-old Underdog we know, came home from school one day and told her mother that a friend of hers had said, "You're so lucky, you've got friends and you get invited places."

Says Diane's mother:

TAKING STOCK

Diane felt so guilty. I said to her, "This is your life, and you have to enjoy it. What other people's lives are like is not your responsibility, unless you've made their lives worse. You must not think less of yourself because someone else is envious."

You need to help your Underdog see himself through his own eyes, rather than through others', because of his tendency to devalue even his assets in this self-destructive way.

ERROR ANALYSIS

Help your Underdog to understand the ways in which he allows himself to be manipulated. Ask such questions as, "Does this friend really like you, or do you think she just wants help with homework?" and "How do you feel when your friend promises to call and then forgets?"

Teach your Underdog to learn how to say no. This can be done by the child's saying any of the following:

"I'm sorry, but I have too much to do this week."

"I can't right now, but I'd be glad to next week."

"I can help you with your homework for a half hour on Thursday."

The child can sweeten his refusal by adding, "But why don't we go to the movies on Saturday?" This last will help the child learn which friends really like him—those who accept the invitation, or who make another plan to get together.

SIBLINGS

Many parents find that the rivalry between their children is one of the biggest sources of turmoil within the household. Helping your kids learn to get along is not unlike teaching them about friendship, and the above negotiating strategies often work with siblings.

But there is this difference: kids can choose their friends, based on shared interests and values, but cannot choose their brothers and sisters. Moreover, because they live together, there are more opportunities for disagreement and more fuel for hurt—secrets and fantasies, known only to the family, are vulnerable to exposure and ridicule.

Siblings are not required to love one another, but they must learn to sort out their differences if your home life is not to be one running battle. You will need to encourage your more assertive children—Baby Bullies and Kid Tyrants—to pull back on their dominating traits, and your more passive kids—Saints and Underdogs—to become more assertive.

It is far better for them to fight their own battles than for you constantly to step in to protect them; but you can mediate where necessary, and help them learn to negotiate for themselves. Put a time limit on your kids' squabbles by saying, "If this isn't resolved in ten minutes, I'll resolve it for you." They may prefer a grudging truce to your logical consequences—say, being sent to their room, or forfeiting altogether the item over which they may be railing.

Sometimes you can use negotiation to forestall disagreements, as, for example, over who gets to use the new bicycle first. You can suggest this agenda: "I want you to work out a time schedule for riding the bike and to figure out what should happen if the other person takes more than his time." As numerous colleges have learned, sometimes a court of peers, as in the honor system, can mete out harsher penalties than any administrator could.

Another tactic is to call a huddle and say to your children, "What is each of you willing to give up for the extended use of the bike?" Kids can trade off chores, for instance, or find other options. Your goal is to teach them the benefits of cooperation and to use negotiation to reduce sibling rivalry.

Having set into motion negotiating strategies for and between your children, you may need to follow up with private, and occasionally, family meetings with your children to help them learn how to field the liabilities of their siblings' styles or to curb their own liabilities. What follows is the language you can use with each style:

Baby Bullies can be the cruelest of all, so hell-bent are they on winning any contest. They'll tease mercilessly, or dream up practical jokes, or punch a brother or sister. Baby Bullies, it seems, are always getting into trouble.

For example, the Schwartz family drove to the beach for an outing, and in the back seat of the car Daniel, a 7-year-old Baby Bully, became annoyed with Ann, his 5-year-old Saint sister, for pestering him. He lost his temper and grabbed Ann by the neck, whereupon Ann promptly threw up on him.

BOTTOM LINE

ZEROING IN

Lest he fail to see the logical consequence of his violence, his mother said, "You cannot do that. When you grab too tight you can hurt her, and she gets sick." She added in our interview with her, "Daniel saw the results of his behavior and he learned. I love it when bizarre things happen like that because the situation corrects itself."

OPTIONS

But situations do not always correct themselves. You may have to discuss privately with your Baby Bully the unacceptability of his violent behavior by saying, "I never want to see that happen again. If you're really angry, write on your graffiti wall or write a note to your sister or to me. But you may not physically hurt anyone."

At the same time, know that your Baby Bully can be provoked by a Saint to consider strangulation. Kids pick up on each other's liabilities, and the Saint is a master of sneakiness and of conveying the appearance of being angelic.

FISHING

ERROR ANALYSIS

BRAIN-STORMING

By pestering him, Ann set her brother up for parental reprisal. His mother should have followed up her talk with him by saying to Ann, "When you keep bothering your brother, what usually happens?" Ann could easily figure it out: "He hits me." His mother can add, "Today you almost got seriously hurt because you kept egging your brother on. What he did was wrong, but you asked for it. When you're in the car, what can you bring along to play with so you won't have to pick on your brother?"

Baby Bullies are often targets for blame, but they aren't always the instigators of trouble.

Kid Tyrants will try to boss their siblings around, telling them what to do. But they are also adept at dividing and conquering. Here's how one woman describes her 10-year-old Kid Tyrant daughter:

> She's the second oldest of my four kids, and the one most likely to say, "Let's gang up on Jimmy." Even if the other kids get mad at her and decide not to go along with the plan, she doesn't care. She's fiercely independent, even with her siblings. She likes to mix it up, even if she's left empty-handed.

This woman discovered that the way to curb her daughter's attempts to dominate her siblings was to remove her from the situation by sending her to her room, a logical consequence for her inability to get along with people. Says the mother, "It drives her crazy to be apart from people. Lately she'll do almost anything to avoid it. So she's learning to get along with her brothers and sisters."

Loners drive their siblings into frenzies because they are singularly recalcitrant about group efforts, and because they seem to be immune to criticism.

For example, Sunday for the Hopkins family is the day when relatives usually drop by for an early dinner, and so the three kids—Mary, 17, Stacy, 14, and Mike, 9—are supposed to help get the house ready and to set the table. The problem is that Mike, a Loner, sits slumped in front of the TV set while his siblings race around doing their work *and* his.

At first, their mother tried letting his sisters deal with his unfairness directly: they told him they resented his attitude and that they weren't going to play with him or talk to him—which suited his entrenched Lonership just fine.

When she realized that without her help, the problem would not be resolved, their mother called a huddle with the children. She said to Mike, "This is not all right—your sisters are pulling their weight and yours, too. What are you willing to do to make it different?" In true Loner fashion, Mike grunted, "Nothing."

ZEROING
IN
OPTIONS

**SHIFTING
GEARS**

His mother outlined this strategy. She asked the other two children to write down the things they often do for him: Mary drives him to and from his best friend's house, and Stacy types his book reports. The mother added her own list: buying his school supplies, taking him shopping, chauffeuring him to the local Y for swimming.

BACKUP

**BOTTOM
LINE**

**TAKING
STOCK**

The children and their mother presented their lists to Mike. His mother said, "These are the things we are no longer going to do for you as long as you don't help around the house." When he realized how much he had to lose by his stubborn refusal to assist in cleanup efforts, he burst into tears. From then on, he did his share of chores.

Underdogs are generally the most obvious victims of sibling rivalry because they practically volunteer for it. Indeed, through sibling rivalry, they learn to rely on their victimization for parental attention, rather than learning how to become stronger. You need to use the sibling struggle to help your Underdog defend himself, rather than relying on you to do it for him.

Here's how a mother taught her 8-year-old Underdog, Ruth, to cope with the teasing by her older siblings:

**ZEROING
IN**

I could see Ruth patterning herself after me, and I have always had trouble asserting myself. When my three older children would pick on her, she would cry, and the more she cried, the more they teased her.

FISHING

**ERROR
ANALYSIS**

One afternoon when this was happening, I took Ruth into another room and asked her why she was crying. She replied, "Because they keep teasing me." I said, "If you cry, they don't respect you, and you don't respect yourself."

**BOTTOM
LINE**

Then we rehearsed what she should say to them. She walked back into the den and at the top of her lungs yelled "I'M ANGRY AT ALL OF YOU FOR TEASING ME AND I WANT YOU TO STOP IT!" and turned on her heel and stomped out of the room. Their jaws dropped. I kept reinforcing this strategy with her so that she could learn to negotiate for herself without tears.

If siblings can hurt one another, they can also help in a profound way. In one family we know in which the kids are 3, 8, and 9, the 3-year-old had not yet begun talking, not because he was incapable of it, but because the two older kids—a Baby Bully and a Kid Tyrant—did all his talking for him.

The kids' father called a huddle with the other children and presented this strategy: "When your brother points to something he wants, I want you to say to him, 'Tell me what you want. I won't give it to you unless you do.' " The idea was to have everyone in the family help the little one put his needs into words. Because the family was united in carrying out the strategy, the 3-year-old soon began talking.

MESSY ROOM

Next to sibling squabbles, this issue is the one most likely to turn your hair gray. It isn't simply that you cannot fathom how anyone can *live* that way, with eight consecutive days' worth of clothing on the bed, under it, and scattered around the room; it is also that you find yourself nagging and talking about it almost more than any other issue.

Messy rooms can be a smoke screen for other issues. Extremely controlling parents often find that one or more of their kids is a pack rat in his or her room; it may be that that is the only place where the child can exercise *any* control or self-expression—as, for instance, in the hanging of posters or collecting of necklaces that dangle from a nail on the wall.

Perhaps the greatest undercurrent to this issue is the question of privacy. As children go through the elementary school years, they are making the gradual transition from babyhood to puberty; tandem with that development is an increasing inward turning. Diaries become important, as do whispered phone conversations. Souvenirs and objects of unknown nostalgia crowd dresser and desk drawers.

While the house is yours to maintain and pay for, there needs to be someplace within it where your children have a haven from prying eyes and questions; that place is their room.

And so we recommend this policy: just as homework is children's responsibility, so are their rooms. If they want their rooms to look like a dump, that's their department (short of collecting food that draws insects and other critters). If the room bothers you, *close the door.*

But where there is latitude, there are also logical consequences: if your child finds he has nothing to wear, that too is his problem. You can teach your child, except when he is very small, to run the washing machine and dryer, with your supervision. The logical consequence for not putting away his clothes is for your child to have to repeatedly wear an ensemble until his wardrobe is laundered, which for some styles (the Saint and Baby Bully) will rank with capital punishment. He'll either put his clothes away or head for the laundry room.

As for messiness in other parts of the house, you go right to your bottom line: put the errant belongings into a large garbage bag, place it in the garage or trunk of your car, and make this announcement: "If you have not dispatched this stuff within twenty-four hours, I'll assume you want it thrown out." If you follow through on this policy a couple of times, the kid will see the logical consequence for his indifference to tidiness.

With this preamble in mind, here are the ways the various styles approach their rooms, and what you can do about it if you are unable to tolerate messiness:

> *Baby Bullies* and *Saints* are the sloppiest of all styles. Saints in particular cannot bear to part with any item, from broken rubber bands to a gum wrapper given to them by a favorite friend. Birthday cards, spent balloons, a lock of hair cut off 4 years ago, vie with their beds for floor space.

Here's how a 10-year-old Saint feels about her room:

> My parents and I fight about it all the time. But I know where everything is. They think it's unorganized—nothing's folded in my drawers, and there's stuff all over the place. But I can't see a reason to clean up, because I can find anything I need.

There are times when the mess becomes unbearable to her mother. Here's how she negotiates the cleaning of her daughter's room:

> I've learned by trial and error. Every so often I stick my head into her room, instead of letting the mess and my anger pile up. When I explode, I go out of my mind and her room has to be cleaned that minute, despite her pleas.

PRIMING   Now I act sooner. I say, "By suppertime tomorrow, I want your things picked up from the rug and the books back on the desk." Barring extenuating circumstances, such as a sleepover, she'll do it.

Kid Tyrants and *Loners* are generally fairly tidy—they put great stock in being organized—and so will present few problems about their rooms.

Underdogs, like Saints, often have unkempt rooms, but in this case it's because they are so often let off the hook regarding household responsibilities. Moreover, their messy rooms may be a metaphor for their lack of self-esteem.

One way to help your Underdog feel good about himself is to make his room feel like a special place, just for him. You might want to make a project of fixing it up to his liking—perhaps you could paint the room with him in a color of his choosing, or help him buy something special for it—an inexpensive stereo. Or you might ask him to pick out some posters that reflect his interests—such an offer might help him form some interests.

The Underdog's room can be a place where friends can play, and if the room is inviting, your child might have an incentive to keep it neater. But the issue is not neatness—the issue is how your Underdog feels about himself, of which his room is a reflection.

Don't clean his room for him, because you will be encouraging his tendency to let others take over his life and decisions. By making him responsible for his room and belongings, you help him have higher expectations of himself.

ALLOWANCE (MONEY)

One of the ill-advised trade-offs of many working parents is giving their children more spending money than is appropriate out of guilt at being away from the house a great percentage of the day.

Part of the problem is the confusing of family responsibilities with "jobs." One woman we interviewed gets her child to clean her room in exchange for her allowance; another pays her son to shovel the sidewalk in winter. These two items are responsibilities connected with being part of a family, not labor for which one should be rewarded.

Money is often used as a substitute for love; for instance, you buy your daughter a $100 sweater because you couldn't attend her school play. Indeed, arguments over money often stem from a paucity of parental attention, and so how much money children receive becomes a barometer for how much they are "loved." You may need to do some error analysis to find out if that is the case; rearranging your priorities and work schedule may be in order.

Kids' attitudes about money begin in their earliest years, and often they compare how much they have to how much their friends get. In some families, for instance, the "tooth fairy" leaves a dime under the pillow for a lost baby tooth. The child runs to school to proudly display the dime, only to have another kid say, "Big deal, I get a dollar." Upon returning home, the child demands a raise from the tooth fairy.

Rather than scream at your child, "You never have enough—you always want *more!*" it may be necessary to have a huddle. The issue of insatiability may have more to do with a lack of affection and attention than with financial want.

Our view of allowances is this: when people live together, they are all equally responsible for the running of the household, and so collaborating in that endeavor is part of being a partner in the family. One does household tasks because it is part of the trade-off for being housed, helped in achieving one's goals, and enjoying the benefits of family life. Children are part of a team, not a payroll. You don't pay children for pulling their weight within the family, just as you are not paid.

At the same time, children need a certain amount of spending money for food, emergencies, a reasonable amount of entertainment, such as going to the movies; you can negotiate how much and the purpose of such monies.

You need to help your child have a healthy and responsible attitude about money early on, and to understand that while he may have less money than his friends, it is because you respect him too much to let him think that money should not be earned. If he needs extra money— say, for ice skating—that is a negotiable item. But if he asks for $25 a week so he can go shopping after school with his friends, that is another story. He needs to earn it, rather than have you dole it out, and you may be able to help him find an after-school, part-time job, such as mowing lawns or washing cars.

The issue here is not so much allowances as how your children handle money and what their attitudes about it say about their style. Says the mother of three kids, age 14, 11, and 8:

My oldest [Kid Tyrant] stopped asking for his allowance once he started working after school, which the other two thought was crazy. My middle one [Saint] forgets to ask for hers, and my youngest [Underdog], when he went to camp, said, "Will I still get my allowance?"

Here's how each style approaches the issue of money:

Baby Bullies are extremely enterprising and often target their creativity to entrepreneurial endeavors. Indeed, numerous studies have shown that it is the risk-taking maverick who tends to become a great financial success, rather than the more plodding, careful types.

Your Baby Bully is first on the block with a lemonade stand in summer; first to start a snow-shoveling business in winter; first—yes—to dabble in the stock market with his earnings.

When he is older, he may also be the first to sell the answers to tests—be sure you monitor the morality of his financial wheeling and dealing. Some Baby Bullies start a small business, such as forming work teams for spring cleanups; make sure your child is not underpaying his colleagues in his eagerness to make a lot of money. But do not discourage his creativity in earning it.

Kid Tyrants will not work for money unless they are sure of how much they will get, and will, even at an early age, try to negotiate the sum higher than the first offer they receive. We're reminded of an 8-year-old Kid Tyrant who wanted to earn some money for a pair of red Reeboks. Her mother said, "Why don't you clean out the kitchen cabinets?"

"How much will you pay me?" said the child.

"Fifty cents an hour."

"Are you kidding? That's not even minimum wage!" replied the child, aghast. Mother and daughter went back and forth and settled finally on $1 per hour.

Kid Tyrants are also entrepreneurial, but they take calculated risks rather than impulsive ones. One second-grader we know noticed that a lot of his friends had money for gumball machines. So the child asked his mother to take him to a gumball wholesaler, borrowed from her the money to buy 500 gumballs, and made $30 a week selling them. He did not squander the money—he set up a savings account.

Kid Tyrants are tough negotiators because they would rather have no money than less than they feel they deserve for their efforts. You need to help your child understand that life requires a certain amount of dues paying, and that today's work for low pay provides the intangible, and ultimately financially rewarding, payoff of experience.

Saints and *Underdogs* will take the first sum they are offered for a job—either in the house or out of it—and you must help them learn not to sell themselves short. They are loath to set the wage, for example, for baby-sitting—which many kids do beginning at the age of 11 or 12. You can rehearse financial negotiation with them, involving them in tasks around the house, other than their routine responsibilities, for which you will pay them.

Help your Saint and/or Underdog to understand that the older he gets, the more mature and valuable he becomes in a job market—and if he feels you are underpaying him, he should negotiate with you. You do not want these styles to undervalue themselves, emotionally or financially, nor to be exploited as a result of their eagerness to please and to be loved. It is a lesson that cannot be taught too soon, as many underpaid adult workers in the job market have found to their detriment.

Be aware also that these styles tend to give their money away to friends, lend it with no hope of repayment, and buy expensive gifts for chums.

Their generosity extends to things you have bought for the house. Says the mother of an Underdog fifth-grader, "I've always taught him to be kind to people. So he gave away our humidifier. I told him to get it back—it's been six months!"

Saints and Underdogs will also squander their money on impulsive purchases, and seldom save it. You can help both styles become aware of the future and learn to set agendas by encouraging them to save a portion of what they earn. Allowances are not entirely without strings; they are a privilege, and so while you give your child some latitude about what he does with his money, you still have a legitimate right to teach him how to handle it responsibly. He cannot, for instance, use it to pay for a friend's snacks every day in school because the friend always forgets to bring his own money.

Loners treat their money the way they do their feelings—saving a lot, giving little. They need to be taught generosity, not necessarily in terms of donating their sums to charity, but in terms of being able to spend it on others and on themselves. Today's tightfisted Loner will be tomorrow's Silhouette Scrooge.

All these negotiations, which can be applied to a myriad of situations, will stand your children in good stead by the time they hit the teenage years. By formulating strategies to bring out the assets of your children's styles, you are preparing them—and yourself—for the enormous change that lies ahead: adolescence.

PART V

NEGOTIATING WITH TEENAGERS (JUNIOR AND SENIOR HIGH SCHOOL)

CHAPTER 13

ADOLESCENCE: THE HOMESTRETCH

Your child's teenage years are in many ways the best of times, and the most rewarding of your parental experience so far. All your efforts—teaching and guiding, exposing him to new ideas and people and places—begin to coalesce into your child's mature identity. Where once you had to tutor him in basic negotiating skills, now he employs many of them automatically. It seems as though only yesterday he was taking his first step, and now he is striding into his adult apprenticeship, while you observe with pride his dwindling dependence on you.

His adolescence is an exhilarating time for you both. These are the years when he becomes the results of all your good work and provides glimpses of the adult he will soon become. Closer to maturity than childhood, he is bringing something new to your life in the form of his projects, perceptions, achievements, insights, and excitements: he is coming into his own emotional and intellectual inheritance.

At the same time, adolescence can be the worst of times. Of all the levels of childhood, none is so stressful as your child's teenage years, for him and for you—and little about his previous behavior quite prepares you for it. Where once your negotiating skills produced collaborative growth, now they are often inoperative, as though the keys to his style no longer fit because the locks have been changed. Your child is exiting from his childhood, and your former strategies are obsolete.

It is no comfort to know that there are 25 million other American teens who are also confounding their parents. These are the kinds of statistics that keep parents up nights:

- 17 million teenagers have driver's licenses.
- 65 percent of 13-year-olds have had alcoholic drinks in the last year, 35 percent at least once a month.
- By the age of 19, 70 percent of girls have lost their virginity.
- 5,000 teenagers kill themselves each year.

When your teenager is in the house, there may be times when you ponder how to get him to stop being fresh or to start talking to you like a person; when he is out of the house, you wonder if he will survive the day unscathed.

Now you are living with a kid who, compared to his elementary school years, may seem unrecognizable to you: he drives a car or gets into his friends' cars; he goes to parties where drinks and drugs are available; his hormones are on overdrive; he tells you partial truths or flat-out lies.

He may have no trouble either telling you to go to hell or suddenly speaking in grunts. His conversations with you, as the old joke puts it, often go something like this:

"Where'd you go?"
"Out."
"What'd you do?"
"Nothing."

But it may be that these years with your teenager are an agonizing limbo; your child may be neither a paragon of virtues nor a hell-on-wheels but, instead, show few signs of maturity, of appropriately breaking away. Perhaps you worry that he hasn't begun dating, or that he keeps putting off getting his driver's license, that he has no friends, that he's too timid to get an after-school job, that he hangs around you all the time.

He may be reluctant to go away to college—you can't get him going on his applications, or to consider an out-of-state school—or to prepare, if he decides not to continue his academic education, for the world of full-time work. And so you are beginning to wonder if he will *ever* leave home.

Whichever mold your teenager seems to fit into, there is this timeless given about parent–teen relationships: the biggest task for teenagers is to learn to separate from their parents with a sense of mutual love, emotional support, and approval; the task of being the parent of a teenager is to help make that possible. The latter is what negotiating with him now is all about.

CONTROL

The issue for both of you may be control. Once your child begins junior high school, you may find yourself feeling the beginnings of 5 or 6 years of mounting helplessness. He's going through dramatic mood swings and rapid changes. Suddenly, or so it sometimes appears, you carry no weight with him. Where he used to respond to disapproval or affection, now you occasionally feel as though you are speaking into a vacuum, because he'll often do anything to avoid interaction. Everything that you did before no longer seems to work.

Now, more than ever, it is important to learn how to negotiate, or to alter your negotiating strategies, with him.

Navigating through your child's teenage years turns on this premise: you have to take the long view, by thinking in terms of these goals for your adolescent:

- To have your youngster be open to discussion, even though engineering a candid conversation with a teenager is often like maneuvering through a mine field
- To have your child be able to reach out for help and understanding with questions about drugs, alcohol, sex, and peer pressure without thinking that his or her integrity and identity depend on resisting your guidance
- To have your child acquire healthy, circumspect independence
- To have your child look forward to, rather than dread, the future
- To have your child love you, and you him or her, even as your relationship is changing

But life in your house, whatever your adolescent's style, may feel at times like a Mexican standoff because you often feel that all you do is pay the bills and take a lot of guff.

Take heart: you may sometimes feel you have lost control, but you have not lost authority. These years will be made easier for you if you understand that your child must begin to separate from you now if he is to be able to stand on his own as an adult. Do not believe that he isn't listening—he is, as you will discover; remember the Loop, wherein you say something sage to him, he pretends he doesn't hear it, and a month later, having internalized your beliefs or values, says exactly the same thing to a friend.

Do not be afraid of negotiating with him. Many parents over- or underreact to their disaster fantasies: they think that if they supply limits, the kid will run away, or attempt suicide, or openly defy or simply ignore them.

Remember also that the teenage years are the greatest bottleneck of pressures—hormonal, cognitive, physical, emotional, developmental, educational, and social—of all the years in the life span, and try to retain your sense of humor.

One woman we know, who was heavily steeped in psychology, dreaded her 11-year-old's impending adolescence, and thought she could dampen its force by discussing it with her child in advance. She said to her daughter, "The teen years are the toughest of all; your body and moods go through a lot of changes, just as women do when they go through change of life. We'll probably have lots of fights, but I hope we'll still be able to talk about things."

Her daughter replied, "My luck: I'll be going through puberty at the same time you're going through menopause."

Another woman, in explaining her feelings of powerlessness with her teenage son, joked, "I can always swallow the car keys."

Your child's cataclysmic changes are *temporary*. Most teenagers emerge on the other side of this tumultuous period intact, and many of them later say to their parents, "How could you stand me? I was horrible." And most parents find new richness and delights in their relationships to their teenagers now that they are no longer children.

RENEGOTIATING THE RELATIONSHIP

Critical to your mutual survival of these years is understanding that *the relationship is being renegotiated*. Previous strategies no longer apply. Your teenager's needs, desires, and ways of behaving are changing dramatically. Keep in mind that he is midway between his childhood style and its adult equivalent: from Baby Bully to Jungle Fighter, from Kid Tyrant to Dictator, from Loner to Silhouette, from Saint to Big Daddy/ Big Mamma, from Underdog to Soother, from Winner to Win/Winner.

The renegotiation of your relationship should bear this stylistic evolution in mind. The teenage years may be your last opportunity, in terms of time with your child, to prevent the domination of the worst characteristics of those adult styles and to help the best qualities to jell permanently.

Paramount to your renegotiation is the realization that your adolescent has only one thing on his mind: himself. He's not thinking about you or your feelings very much. Instead, he's thinking about college, about future careers, about sexual relationships, about parties where booze and drugs are served, about driving a car.

If you don't prepare him for these activities and for their attendant temptations and decisions—if, in fact, you don't begin preparing him for adulthood—his adolescence may either be prolonged or he may derail in ways that the protected, childhood years precluded. You have to take the long view, because he may not be ready for it: you have to help prepare him for future negotiations.

Now he needs to learn more about problem solving, because the problems are profound and in some cases life threatening. You can no longer shield him from outside forces that can harm him—he needs to learn how to protect himself.

One woman we interviewed learned this the hard way. Although she and her daughter had always had an extraordinarily close relationship, by the child's teens it was becoming suffocating to the child, who began pulling away.

The woman claimed never to apply pressure for grades, but she would ask her child if she had finished her homework each day and be silently rebuking if she had not. She would ask her daughter why she did not have more friends, but would praise her for her ability to spend hours by herself.

Her daughter was drowning in a sea of double messages.

This woman's overidentification with her daughter, who felt she had no room for privacy or decision making or failure, backfired in the form of her daughter's full-scale adolescent rebellion.

Formerly the "perfect child," her grades began to fall; she would brag to her mother that she had spiked her sodas with vodka; she would, if forbidden from attending a party with a crowd known for drinking and using drugs, threaten to sneak out of the house. She and her mother argued constantly about money—whatever her mother bought her, she wanted more.

Finally the daughter swallowed a bottle of aspirin.

"It was at that moment," the mother recalls, "that I realized I did not know my daughter at all."

Understandably, the woman became frantic and forced her daughter to see a therapist. The teenager stonewalled with the therapist, refused to talk, and would not go again. (Note: You can make a child go, once, to a therapist, but you cannot make him or her continue; therapy will not work unless the patient cooperates in the process.)

Finally, feeling like "an abused mother," the woman herself went into therapy. There she learned that she had failed to alter her treatment of her daughter as the girl got older—she was still babying her, still overly concerned about the child's popularity, still imposing fears where none had existed. To call her mother's attention to the fact that she was no longer a child, the daughter chose alcohol and a suicide attempt.

It worked: her mother began to take stock of the ways she had pushed her daughter to this extreme behavior.

And so the woman shifted gears. She stopped asking questions about school, typing her daughter's papers, and buying her clothes that she did not need. She removed her daughter's curfew and refrained from commenting on her daughter's friends. She gave her daughter a $10 per week allowance, and said that the amount was to cover all her expenses—lunch money, entertainment, and clothing.

The woman also apologized to her daughter for having made life so difficult for them both, and promised that behavior was at an end. Moreover, she said, from then on her daughter's decisions were her own, as were the consequences of those decisions.

At first the child was stunned: she no longer had any buttons to push in her mother, although she tried to find some, repeatedly. When her mother was unable to drive her to a friend's house, for example, the teenager would say things like, "You're a lousy parent," or "Bad kids aren't born, they're created." The mother would not respond, except by walking away, and was resolute in her plan to make the girl become more autonomous.

It took a year of the teenager's fighting, arguing, silence, tears, threats, and insults for the girl to accept the necessary renegotiation of their relationship that she herself had set into motion. But now, in her senior year, she is on the honor roll; she has been accepted by a first-rate college; she has an after-school job; she has replaced her former circle of unsavory friends with new ones, people she respects.

In addition, she and her mother have become close once again, but in a different way: the daughter seeks the mother's advice on most subjects, knowing that the final decision is hers. As for the mother, she has since come to terms with her former need to force her daughter into her vision of perfect childhood, and she recognizes that they are different styles.

The mother saved this relationship by:

- shifting gears, and realizing that dramatic changes had to occur in the parent–child relationship before any other issue, such as grades, could be addressed
- setting limits—in this case, teaching her daughter that the price of freedom is responsibility—and making them stick

While this scenario may neither apply nor work for every child, the point is that you can turn your teenager around if you finally recognize that by high school, most of his decisions *must* be his own, as must his successes and failures, and that they have nothing to do with your love for him and his for you. This is the most important reason why, for example, you do not pay your child for good grades, or punish him for bad ones.

None of this means that you do not set limits; it does mean that, having done so, the decision is still his to abide or not abide by those limits, and to live with the logical consequences if he does not. And at no time can your child be permitted to treat you abusively; if he does, there are consequences here as well, in the form of curtailed privileges.

Your most important negotiating skill in the teen years is *shifting gears*. Learning to let go becomes easier if you know that the teenager is intellectually more capable of negotiation than he was in the single-digit years; he can tolerate ambiguity in ways that were not possible before. His thinking processes embrace sophistication and subtlety. Shifting gears becomes smoother because he is more capable of understanding cause and effect.

Your child's most important negotiating skill in these years is *finding healthy options*. He has more of them, due to his maturity, thinking ability, and increased verbal skills, than he did in elementary school. Most of the perils of your child's high school years are almost always the result of one problem: He may not yet *know* what his options are, and often feels trapped by the pressures that are mounting up around him.

IS IT TOO LATE
TO NEGOTIATE?

The balance between freedom and structure that you struck in his earlier years now is put to the test: has your teenager internalized that structure so that he can put limits on his own behavior, and erected barriers against destructive peer pressure? If you have not negotiated before, is he doomed?

The answer is no—with an explanation.

In a 1986 study* of adolescent personality traits and what role they play in drug abuse, the researchers discovered that while most characteristics of temperament persist, how children are treated in the teen years—their environment—can determine the quality of their adolescent rite of passage. Children who have been underachievers, or depressive, or aggressive, can be transformed by certain experiences.

The researchers found that of all the factors contributing to change, achievement was the thing that was most effective in helping troubled and troublesome teens begin to put controls on their own behavior.

The most obvious achievement is getting good grades in school. But another achievement is getting involved in student government. We are reminded of one high school student who was elected president of the student government as a lark by an indifferent, cynical electorate—she had had the reputation of using drugs, having no limits at home, doing poorly in school. Voting her into office was a nose-thumbing gesture aimed at the administration.

The gesture backfired. Once she began her student government leadership, the president-elect underwent a profound change: she stopped using drugs, began getting good grades, abandoned her punk demeanor. Having, in a sense, had greatness thrust upon her, she took it seriously and, with no previous achievements, rose to the task.

The lesson in all this is that even if you have not begun setting limits with your child or applying logical consequences or using negotiating skills, it is not too late to begin to do so now. You can provide for your

---

*"Dynamics of Childhood and Adolescent Personality Traits and Adolescent Drug Use," by Judith S. Brook and Ann Scovell Gordon (both of the Department of Psychiatry, Mount Sinai School of Medicine), Martin Whiteman (School of Social Work, Columbia University), Patricia Cohen (New York Psychiatric Institute, Columbia University), *Developmental Psychology*, 1986, Vol. 22, No. 3, 403–414, copyright 1986 by the American Psychological Association, Inc.

child opportunities for achievement at home, *geared to his style*, that could motivate him to begin to take stock of his negative behavior and to change.

The child who is interested in rock music, for example, can be given guitar lessons, which could lead to his joining a band, which could inspire him to practice, which could lead to payment for performing at parties, which could enormously boost his self-esteem. Rock music may make you gag, but it may be important to him: his achievement with it will make him much more likely to want to collaborate with you and with others. Personality may not change a great deal, but the manifestations of it can.

And so we will show you how to negotiate with your child through his junior and senior high school years. There are, of course, some differences between these two age groups.

JUNIOR HIGH SCHOOL

Junior high is the bullpen for adolescence. It is the period when children begin to menstruate, to shave, to pair off romantically, to flex their stylistic muscles, and to find their niche. For most kids, these are the years when their peers are the cruelest—forming cliques and cutting the "losers," comparing clothes and money, gossiping and fueling rumors, applying labels such as *nerd* and *airhead*.

Junior high is a time of utter public conventionality and private metamorphosis: emotionally at least, many of these kids still have one foot in childhood and the other in preadolescence. They are aware of what's just around the developmental and educational corner—they long to be like the high school kids, and begin imitating them—and you can see shades of difference in their behavior and maturing interests.

The time between elementary school and high school—junior high—is a quantum leap for your child. Negotiating strategies change, because what was important to your child in the sixth grade, the final year in most elementary schools, suddenly becomes moot in the seventh. Many parents cite the middle or junior high school as the "weak link" in their community's school system; as a rule, the only "weakness" is the fluctuating identities of its students.

HIGH SCHOOL

Once they begin high school, young people start to recognize their own ways of reacting and of doing things—their styles—and to seek out friends who are like them, rather than to take on the heartbreaking task of trying to be like someone else. Not all high schoolers are successful at this solidification of identity; some still try to "belong," rather than to look for like-minded peers. But in general, high school is when teenagers break off into subgroups: the jocks, the partyers, the preppies, the artsy crowd, the punkers, the greasers, the grinds.

Dealing with teenagers calls for certain strategems. They are:

1. Know what your and your teenager's styles are.
2. Deal with your adolescent's problems—do not avoid or deny them.
3. Pay attention to timing.
4. Formulate a strategy, or plan of action, geared to your teenager's style.
5. Be clear in stating your concerns to your teenager.
6. Create one or more backup plans—teenagers are often unpredictable.
7. Know what you, and your teenager, are willing to trade off.
8. Keep focused on the problem—do not be distracted by adolescent mood swings and avoidance mechanisms.
9. Recognize that there is a pattern in what works, and what doesn't, in your negotiations with your teenager.
10. Seek outside help from the community and the school.

This last strategem is important for two reasons: First, these are the years when your child is beginning to seek and be part of the world outside his home. Second, because his identity is being influenced by that outside world, you can no longer solve all the problems with your teenager within the context of your family, particularly if the community in which you live has values that are not necessarily yours.

Let's say that your teenager hangs out at the local deli or convenience store with a group of kids who drink and are undirected and, when you object, he says, "There's no place else for me to go." Parents often complain that they don't like what goes on in their towns, but may feel helpless about changing the complexion of their communities.

Many programs in high schools and communities begin with a single parent having the courage to say, "Enough. If I'm not part of the solution, then I'm part of the problem." In one community we know of, when the legal drinking age rose from 18 to 21, a parent put together a group of other concerned parents and got local government and school support to start a disco club for teenagers in an unused elementary school, complete with laser lights, disc jockey, and soft drink bar.

In other communities across the country, PTAs sponsor all-night proms at the high school, where alcohol is not available, parents serve breakfast at the school in the wee hours, and school buses drive the kids to and from a day at the beach.

While some teenagers, and their parents, may not abide by or participate in these community activities, at least such programs apply social pressure on them to find healthy outlets for their considerable energies and drives. You can create a community that takes more seriously the problems of its young by setting up programs with the help of other parents, the local town board, police department, and board of education: such programs include Safe Rides; a drop-in office at the school or in town where kids can go to rap with a sympathetic adult or counselor; Varsity Athletes Against Substance Abuse (VAASA); Mothers Against Drunk Drivers (MADD); Students Against Drunk Driving (SADD).

Such programs can help teenagers whose home life does not give them a sense of indispensability to feel needed in a broad, community sense by providing them with the opportunity to take a leadership position in helping other kids.

The list of negotiating issues regarding teenagers seems endless—the car, curfews, clothes, money, sex, vanity, choice of friends, grades, college applications, jobs, self-centeredness, and rudeness among them. But it isn't the car, or curfew, or any of these issues, per se, that create problems between you and your child. Rather, it's how your teenager deals or doesn't deal with those issues.

If you are able to step back and evaluate your child's behavior in all of these areas, you will discover three primary categories of concern, which will be the heart of your negotiations regarding them:

- *Defiance, or rebellion:* This includes such topics as curfews, clothes, money, and talking back
- *Grades, or gearing up for college or full-time jobs:* This includes your teenager's academic and/or professional future

- *Peer Pressure:* This includes your adolescent's temptations to become involved with drugs, alcohol, and sex

In the next three chapters, we will discuss each of these issues and how to negotiate them with your child according to his or her style.

CHAPTER 14

DEFIANCE (REBELLION)

Hating one's parents, or at least occasionally giving the impression of it, goes with the territory of being a teenager. One 15-year-old told us, "I really love my mom, but I say to my friends, 'She's such a worrywart,' or 'I can't stand her,' because it's expected. They don't believe me when I say I tell her everything—which I do, eventually."

Even if you are a fit with your child, inevitably he will begin to do or say things that differentiate him from you, many of them arbitrary: You say "black," he says "white." The fact that you are a fit will make this period more painful for you, because you will feel rejected. And if you are not a fit, you may sometimes think that the teen years are proof positive that either you are a rotten parent or he is a rotten kid, when neither may be the case.

Remember that while teenagers may behave defiantly, they do not want to have ultimate control over you. As one 18-year-old girl put it, "Some of my friends who get into trouble don't worry about the consequences, because in their families, they say, 'it'll all blow over.' I know that if your parents care, it won't."

One of the primary issues about which teenagers and their parents argue is curfews. We believe that by the time your teenager is in the upper high school grades, he is old enough to be trusted to come home at a reasonable hour. Part of helping him to become autonomous is to encourage his ability to make appropriate decisions, and one of them is the hour at which he comes home at night. In our experience, when you give this decision over to your teenager, he will respect you for it, and be less inclined to abuse your trust.

Within this responsibility, however, resides another; you have a right to know where he is and the approximate hour he will be home, even if you are not up to greet him when he returns. Said one parent, "There's a squeak in the front door that I will never fix."

Your teenager needs to earn the privilege of setting his own curfew. Here's what the mother of a 16-year-old said to her son when he failed to show up one Saturday night: "You knew you were all right. I didn't. I am your parent, and you have an obligation to let me know if you will be late, or if you are spending the night at a friend's house, so I won't worry." The logical consequence for his inconsideration was that he was grounded for a week; he never failed to call after that.

Adolescents are testing their own values, which requires a degree of straying from the family norm. Just as a new pair of shoes is not really comfortable until they have been worn and molded to your feet, so it is with values that your child learns at home. Until your child "wears" them, takes them off and puts them on again, your values are not truly his.

All that is philosophically fine, but the reality is not so neat. There are times when you feel like plunging your fist through a wall, or into your child's once-angelic face, because of his treatment of you—being discourteous, for example, which is completely unacceptable. Here's how one woman describes the foulmouthed behavior of her 14-year-old son, and what she did about it:

> I was infinitely patient with his mood swings, until one day last summer, when I finally cracked. I had asked him to clean up his room, and he said "Fuck you." Suddenly, I lunged out of the chair, and he got this look on his face and edged toward the door. I moved toward him, and he took off down the street.
>
> I ran after him in the middle of the road, screaming, *"That's one 'fuck you' too many!"* and only then did I realize that I was still in my nightgown!

So while you want to give your teenager more latitude, even in terms of testing your and his values, there still are limits to be set—which inevitably can lead to defiance, either passive or explosive.

There is no way you will win a test of wills with your teenager, because he holds this trump card: your guilt. You cannot be hurt by someone to whom you are indifferent. And so if your child runs away from home, or tears off down a street, even if he comes back intact, your fantasies will have put you through nine rounds: he's been hit by a truck, he's pushing drugs, he's breaking into houses, he's a criminal and I am a terrible parent.

Assertive children (Baby Bullies and Kid Tyrants) whose equally assertive parents (Dictators and Jungle Fighters) try to coerce them into obedience may indeed get into trouble with the law, or with drugs. As for Saints and Underdogs, if their parents have not given them any decision-making skills or privacy, those styles may become the pawns of unsavory peers. Loners who are overcontrolled may recede deeper into themselves, and, in extreme cases, could explode violently sometime in the future.

Keep in mind, as you read the following examples of defiance, that the negotiations regarding them can be applied to a variety of rebellious behavior and are blueprints for dealing with it.

Collisions between teenagers and their parents can be avoided if you negotiate. Here's how to navigate your child's defiance, overt or passive, by style:

> *Baby Bullies* worry parents because theirs is the loudest and most dramatic of styles. They are impulsive and hot-headed, and don't see cause and effect.
>
> This style pushes you to your limits almost before you know it's happening. Here's how one man describes his 13-year-old Baby Bully:
>
> > On any given thing, it's a contest of wills—it's an automatic "no." If I say, "Jimmy, let's go to a ball game," he'll say, "I don't want to go out." And he lies. Once he hid a friend's bike and said, "I didn't do it," when I knew he had. He has a streak of trying to get away with things. He's always getting negative attention from adults but positive attention from his peers, because he's a daredevil and a cutup.
>
> Parents of Baby Bullies often feel that they have the least control with this style. Your Baby Bully will listen for the first sign of your weakening, as though it were a tiny rip in your resolve, and keep picking at you, until finally you either cave in or explode.
>
> This is partially why Baby Bullies seldom apply inner

controls: because they have always pushed their parents to make decisions for them, often by force, they have not been held accountable through the calm application of logical consequences.

Now, however, the ways they try to get that response are potentially dangerous—as, for instance, when in a fit of temper they take the car and race away at top speed.

You need to begin negotiating and setting limits with your teenage Baby Bully as soon as possible. Here's how one father handled the defiance of Patty, his 15-year-old Baby Bully:

> One day we had company over, and we'd recently begun allowing Patty to take the car in and out of the garage, just to get her used to driving, but not allowing her out on the road. On this particular day, our car was blocking a guest's car, and we asked Patty to move ours so our guest could get out. I gave her the keys to the car, and the next thing we knew, she was gone. When she returned twenty minutes later, she said, "When I moved the car, I couldn't find a place to turn around." I said, **OPTION** "You had the option of turning it off and leaving it at the end of the driveway." Patty said, "I thought it would be easier just to drive it around the block."

> **BOTTOM LINE** Her punishment was that she couldn't get behind the wheel of a car until she was 16 and eligible for a learner's permit. She blew it. She lost nine months of practicing.

This Baby Bully is having her liabilities curbed in an effective way because her parents are willing to say no appropriately and to stick to their decisions.

But what of the teenager who is beyond such simple solutions? What, for instance, if you have a Baby Bully who is a habitual liar, who repeatedly ignores your rules, who cuts school and skirts the law, who abuses you verbally and even, perhaps, physically?

If you have a child like that, chances are that logical consequences have never been applied, that you have been inconsistent in dealing with him, or you have denied to yourself the evidence of his behavior. Is it too late to change the behavior of such a teenager?

It won't be easy, but it is possible to put the brakes on his apparently incorrigible rebelliousness. Here are the steps in dealing with an "uncontrollable" Baby Bully:

1. Begin your negotiation with information gathering. You may want to find out from the police and the school authorities what your rights and those of your teenager are, and what they can do, in the form of bottom lines and logical consequences, to help you with your child. They may offer assistance that you didn't know was available in curtailing the liabilities of an out-of-control Baby Bully, and in getting him back on a healthy track.

In some communities, for example, if your child wants to go to a party where you know there are other kids you don't approve of, you can ask the police to investigate, even ask them to tell your child that you called, although they cannot remove your child from the party unless he has broken the law. Nevertheless, you make your child publicly aware that you do not condone his behavior, a lesson he will not soon forget.

Moreover, many police departments have youth officers whose job it is to advise parents and teenagers on the best ways to keep children out of trouble, or to get them out of it. We know several such officers who are sympathetic and understanding. Remember—they've seen and heard it all, and know what you may be going through. It is their job to help you and to keep your conversations in confidence; do not be embarrassed to call upon this important source. It is in their interests to come to your aid.

The school may also be able to help. If, for example, you refuse to write notes excusing your child from doing his homework, and if you discover that your Baby Bully has forged your signature and written his own, you must tell the principal. Your child may have to flunk a course to see that there are consequences for his behavior.

BOTTOM LINE   2. Go immediately to your bottom line, without the preamble of priming. Call a huddle with your Baby Bully and inform him of the information you have gathered from both sources. He needs to know what logical consequences the community can mete out in response to his behavior, and he needs to know further that *you will call on them.*

It is here that many parents fall apart. So afraid are they of their Baby Bullies, and so concerned are they about their and their child's reputations in the community, that they will do almost anything to avoid confronting this issue. It is such avoidance that contributes to the Baby Bully's troubles.

There are other measures, which may seem extreme, that you can take to reassert your parental authority with a Baby Bully who shows no regard for your feelings and wishes.

For example, we know one 15-year-old Baby Bully who repeatedly refused to comply with her parents' request to call and say if she would be coming home later than she said she would. Nothing—neither threats nor taking away driving privileges—would cause her to mend her ways. Moreover, she would scream and swear whenever her parents attempted to discuss her behavior.

One Saturday night the clock struck 3:00 A.M. and the teenager still had not come home, although she had said she would by around 1:30. At the end of their ropes, and knowing that she was with a friend at whose house she could spend the night, her parents locked the door and the windows of their suburban home and went to bed. When the girl finally came home at 4:00 and couldn't get in, she went to the friend's house.

The next morning she returned, shocked and furious over what they had done. Her father said in a quiet and even voice, "We cannot leave the house unlocked at night. If **BOTTOM** you cannot be home when you say you will, or if you don't **LINE** call, you can't come home at all." From then on, she let them know if she was going to be late.

This solution may seem excessively harsh. But with an out-of-control Baby Bully, you *begin* your negotiation with your bottom line, because he won't take anything else seriously. Says a guidance counselor we interviewed, "I've seen kids like this destroy their parents. You can't let them ruin your life." Once you have reached your bottom line and acted upon it, you can then employ other negotiating tactics.

3. After you have gotten your Baby Bully's attention in this way, you call a huddle and start sorting out what to do about the child's attempts to disrupt the family.

ERROR ANALYSIS   Begin by using error analysis. Say to your child, "We have not done our parts before. We've let you get away with this treatment of us, and of yourself. All that is over. This is our house, and our life, and you cannot destroy it. You have lost all privileges. Now let's figure out how you can get them back."

FISHING   Next, try to gather more information. Get your child to tell you what he hopes to accomplish by his behavior. If he says "I want to party all the time," for example, tell him what the disadvantages are, and remind him of the logical consequences you have already applied. This is not a threat: He knows you mean it because you've already demonstrated your bottom line.

ZEROING IN   If you are very lucky, the Baby Bully may admit that his behavior is an attempt to get attention. Your job is to help him understand that there's positive and negative attention, and you need to help him learn how to get the former.

He may tell you that he feels he doesn't count with you, or that you neglect him, or that all he ever got from you is criticism. Be prepared to listen to these reactions without **TAKING A BEAT** comment. If you aren't ready to respond to them, say, "I'll have to think about that." But do consider it: he may be right.

On the other hand, he may not want to verbalize his feelings, or he may not have sorted out what they are. Then you may have to give him the ground rules for earning back your trust.

BACKUP   Tell him that until his behavior at home improves, you are no longer going to perform any parental tasks other than housing, feeding, clothing, and providing medical attention for him. These are your only obligations; everything else— money, having his clothes drycleaned and his shoes repaired, use of the car and telephone, presents, going out to dinner, TV, stereo—is gravy. You must be prepared to stick to this plan—if you do not mean it, he will know it.

ERROR ANALYSIS   Having said all that, you need to do some private error analysis on your own. Negative behavior, whether mild or extreme, may be a result of your denial of problems in the parent–child relationship, or of your failure to follow through or to engage your Baby Bully in decisions that are appropriate to him.

But negative behavior may also be a reaction to your hypercriticism, when your child feels he can never do enough to please his parents. It may be that you (or your spouse) are a Jungle Fighter and/or a Dictator, and that you need to examine your own liabilities, which may include your perfectionism, inability to show affection or encouragement, or unrealistic expectations of your child.

Now you must work on your own assets and liabilities; if you are to help your child change his behavior, it is important for you to examine what you may have done to help create it.

OPTIONS   Suggest some options to your Baby Bully, if he cannot think of any, for earning back your goodwill. These can include a host of household chores, which he must complete on a schedule of joint choosing. He can also get a job. Moreover, he must not miss school, and one option is for your child to speak to each teacher to discuss his efforts to reform in class. Another is for him to get involved in some after-school activities, such as sports, the school newspaper, and community service.

BRAIN-   Give your child a chance to add some suggestions of his
STORMING   own.

AGENDA   As he begins to improve his behavior, you can begin returning to him certain privileges: the use of the car once a week, or the opportunity to go on vacation with you, or the resumption of use of the telephone on a limited basis. Don't give him all these privileges at once—restore them one at a time as he changes his attitude. Tell him about this plan.

The point is to encourage his positive steps toward curbing his liabilities. Say to him, "We cannot control what you do
TRADE-OFF   outside the house. That is your decision. But at home we expect you to be a cooperative participant in the family." By being given ways to control himself, he will in time begin to internalize that control and make it his own—but not unless you make it very difficult for him when he does not.

All this sounds like Toughlove, and in a way it is: he

doesn't know about limits. Accountability is the key issue with a Baby Bully. If he has not been held accountable in the past, he knows that he must be now if he is to have your trust, emotional support, and financial generosity.

Part of wanting to be accountable is knowing that it is a choice. If your Baby Bully knows that the decision to shape up is his, and that the ways he can do so are also his, he will not feel such a desperate need to defy you.

With a Baby Bully, you must be consistent and firm. At first, it may take all your resolve to monitor his behavior and to remain cool, having set your limits and stated your bottom line. It will help you adhere to your strategy if you think of his future, something he has trouble doing: if you do not intervene now, he may have trouble in adulthood holding a job, forming loving attachments, and being a contributing member of society.

If your Baby Bully sees changes in you, he will begin to run out of reasons not to change himself. As he begins to feel good about himself—and the heart of his troubles has been that he does not, in part because you may not have helped him to do so—he will become a collaborator within the family, and not its archenemy.

As we have said, Baby Bullies need to be drawn into joint decision making so that they do not need to find inappropriate ways to feel a sense of control. One example of decision making that alarms many parents is outrageous appearance: punk haircuts and clothing and theatrical makeup, which appeal to the Baby Bully's dramatic personality, may grate against your conservative, buttoned-down style.

But it is wise if you do not make an issue of your Baby Bully's motorcycle-gang appearance. It is superficial and experimental, rather than a metaphor for his morality; and it is an acceptable choice, rather than a dangerous one.

We know a 16-year-old girl whose hair is a crew cut on one side of her head, long on the other; who wears five earrings in one ear; who wears only black. But she has her liabilities under control: she ranks high on the honor roll at **TRADE-OFF** school, she is responsible and courteous. We consider her appearance to be her rebellion, one that does not frighten her parents, because the trade-off for it is her collaborative nature at home.

Another Baby Bully we know wears his hair to his shoulders, about which his parents do not chide him. But they are adamant in their refusal to let him pierce his ear and to wear an earring. Since they have been understanding about his hair length, he has not defied their wishes regarding ear piercing.

Kid Tyrants feel most alive in a debate, and by the time they're teenagers, will have honed their considerable dialectical skills, as well as their uncanny ability to spot parental weakness; your possible indecision is what fuels them, and being right is the target they seek.

Says one 17-year-old Kid Tyrant we talked to:

Sometimes I wish I could shut up. I'll nag my parents about something I want, even though I know I'm not going to get it, and I just keep nagging, nagging, nagging. All of a sudden, BOOM! I can't use the car for two weeks. I'm sunk. Me and my big mouth.

By the time your Kid Tyrant is a teenager, he may well have corralled the resources and wit to outargue you. He props up his arguments by citing his outstanding scholastic record, his student government activities, and his hefty bank account, for which he's earned every penny.

Why, he argues, should you be upset because he wants to get tickets to a rock concert, which will mean standing in line all night in a seamy part of town, because the tickets will be gone by morning if he doesn't? Don't you trust him?

This is exactly what Penny, a 15-year-old Kid Tyrant, said to her parents, who still refused to let her go. Here, according to Penny, is what happened next:

I told my Mom I was sleeping at a girlfriend's the night the tickets went on sale, and three of us went into the city, and slept on line. I had the greatest time of my life—we met some really weird people; it was scary, but it was fun.

But we got caught. My parents found out that I wasn't at my friend's house, and my dad drove into the city, looking for me. He found us, and I was grounded for two months, which was really unfair—the other girls

weren't grounded, and they even got to go to the concert. Plus, the punishment included my birthday—I had
to stay home that night.

Here's what Penny's mother says about her caper:

> That concert was the turning point in our relationship
> with Penny. She'd always been defiant; she's like an
> exposed wire, always needing to have excitement. When
> she wants something, she's relentless—she'll just wear
> you down. What I say doesn't really matter. Last year
> she teamed up with some real difficult kids who had
> serious problems at home, and they were looking to get
> into trouble. These kids were just wild, running around,
> looking like a mess, lying to their parents, not being
> where they said they'd be.

BOTTOM LINE

> I've always given in to Penny in the past, but this
> time she pushed too far. The concert thing was the only
> time I really took a stand; she knew I meant business.
> And her father, who's usually a softie with her, blew his
> stack and terrified her with his screaming.

> Grounding her was hard for her because these kids
> were her only friends, and they left her out of things
> after that. They made fun of her, and that really tortured
> her.

> But after that incident, Penny began to change. Re-
> cently she came to me and said, "You know, about that
> concert—I guess I never realized how much you would
> worry about my safety. That's why I'd never do it
> again."

FISHING

Penny's parents followed up her grounding with a
huddle, and said to her, "We can't tell you who to be
friends with, but we think you can do better. Is this what
you really want?"

Penny says:

TAKING STOCK

> I guess I just wanted to be different. My brother was
> a jock, my sister was part of the "in" crowd, and I didn't
> want to be like them. But then I realized that just being
> different by hanging out with that crowd, and not really
> having fun, wasn't proving anything. When I decided

not to hang out with the bad kids anymore, I didn't have anyone. It was really a lonely time for me. But this year I got my act together. I made a new circle of friends, and a new me.

Penny was able to transform herself because her parents followed up in another important way. In the course of their huddles with her, they discovered that she was extremely insecure about her appearance; she was 20 pounds overweight, had bad skin, and hated her hair.

ZEROING IN

BACKUP

Their daughter made clear to them the anguish her appearance gave her, and they realized that a desire to look attractive and healthy was a positive step. So they took her to a dermatologist for skin treatments, allowed her to join a gym to work out, and, for a delayed birthday present—once her grounding had ended—treated her to a "day of beauty" at the beauty salon of a department store.

SHIFTING GEARS

Penny's parents negotiated her defiance very well, and in the process were themselves jolted into seeing how they had contributed to her problems. Her father has since begun trying to curb his rare, but frightening, explosions of temper; her mother has learned to pay attention to her instincts. Says she:

ERROR ANALYSIS

I knew when she was little that she was too immature to begin school. I should have held her back a year. By not doing that, she always felt inferior, and needed to prove herself in immature ways. And, because she's the baby in the family, we didn't realize she was growing up—we kept babying her.

The result of their family collaboration is that Penny finally understands, probably for the first time, the consequences of her rebellious behavior, and the reasons for her choice of friends. Her parents' apparent lack of authority—in the form of giving in to her demanding nature—served simply to erode whatever shaky self-confidence she had. By reaching their bottom line, they were able to behave in a way that left no doubt about where they stood, or what they would do if she stepped over their boundaries.

Because her parents helped her to examine the disadvantages of her friends and their lack of positive values, ultimately Penny realized she was far luckier than they. And because her parents addressed Penny's feelings, she was able to pay attention to her assets and to diminish her liabilities.

Not all defiance by Kid Tyrants is so alarming. But other ways of rebelling are no less irksome. We know a 14-year-old girl who makes a habit of correcting her mother's grammar, cooking, attire, and grasp of facts, even in front of company. "Sally's accurate to a fault," sighs her mother. "Righteousness is hard to live with."

This is the negotiation we suggested to this woman:

1. It is a strategic mistake to tell a Kid Tyrant, "You're right." Once you've said that, they tune out and lose interest in whatever else you have to say. Instead, say, "You may have a point."

2. Put a time limit on debate with a Kid Tyrant. If the issue is tangible—such as using the car, or borrowing a sweater, you can say, "We will discuss this topic for ten minutes. At the end of that time, this talk is over." Your Kid Tyrant is capable of devoting an hour to the correct way to butter a muffin. A time limit will help her define what's important to her. She'll learn to use the abbreviated time to set priorities and will have very little left over to try to wear you down.

ZEROING IN

3. The logical consequence for public embarrassment is private repentance. We advised Sally's parents to tell her that she could not join them when company comes because she doesn't know how to be polite to them. They said to her, "You can sit with us if you do not correct us—not even once." After they set that limit, she respected it.

ERROR ANALYSIS

4. Sally's parents need to examine why she feels she must be so accurate, in fact, so perfect. It is quite possible that she is unable to tell them about her fears of failure; this is quite common among today's teenagers, especially Kid Tyrants, who are perfectionists. Many parents only want to hear the good news of scholastic and sports accomplishments, and are too busy to hear the darker side of being a teenager—the doubts that good grades cannot always cure, the loneliness of being the "perfect" leader but nobody's

friend, the tempting and potentially risky business of sexual longing.

Several teenagers we talked to told us that their parents do not take their problems seriously. One Kid Tyrant said, "If I told my mom that I'm depressed, she'd laugh in my face."

Problems are never frivolous to a child, and, given the teenager's secretive and changeable nature, he needs only one dismissal to be discouraged from ever bringing up the subject of his unhappiness again. The Kid Tyrant especially needs to know that feelings are not a scorecard—rather, they are a matter of soul-searching and of finding answers that may be neither right nor wrong, but which are appropriate for them.

Defiance from *Loners* turns on their ability to create havoc in the family by silence and insensitivity. The Loner's most exasperating quality is his ability to tolerate other people's anger at him, and to deflect it by not allowing it to penetrate. But he also creates havoc within himself, because it is so difficult for him to get in touch with his needs and feelings. So when your monosyllabic Loner begins to rebel, it's hard to know where to begin to renegotiate your relationship with him.

One unusually perceptive couple we interviewed was able to contain their 13-year-old Loner's rebelliousness. Says her mother:

> In the eighth grade, Judy began to be surly and to speak to us rudely. It was a real departure for her— she'd always been fairly predictable, and we'd had an unusually good relationship; she'd listen to us.
>
> Now she wouldn't talk at all, and when she did, it was with a "you owe me" attitude. My husband and I let it go for a couple of weeks, because we wanted to get a handle on exactly what had changed in her, to find the one thing that was most troubling to us; it wasn't just leaving dirty dishes around, or not setting the table, or picking on her little brother, and it didn't make sense to punish her for every little thing.

TAKING A BEAT

ZEROING
IN

Finally we figured out that what we didn't like was that she wasn't being generous anymore. Judy had always been privileged—private school, camp, a computer, a ten-speed bike, those kinds of things. We wanted her to behave toward us with the same generosity with which she had always been treated, not just in things, but in our being considerate to her.

ZEROING
IN

SHIFTING
GEARS

BOTTOM
LINE

My husband knew that you can't talk a subject at length with Judy, because she tunes out, so he condensed our thoughts into one brief speech. He said, "You have been given so much, and you take it for granted. Your friends have to work after school for spending money, and even cook dinners for their parents who work. You have none of these responsibilities. But we don't owe you what you do have, and what we give, we can take away. We want you to treat us as generously as we have treated you—we want you to be giving at home. If your behavior doesn't change, we will withdraw, one by one, all the things you have been given, starting with the computer."

FINDING
COMMON-
ALITIES

Judy said, "Would you really take it away?" We assured her that we would. We told her that we understood how it feels to be a teenager, and that we knew her priorities were changing, but they did not have to be expressed in a negative way. Her selfishness was completely unacceptable. She got it. Within one week, there was a substantial change in her behavior.

Loners have a powerful mechanism, peculiar to their style, for acting out in their teens: They'll listen to what you have to say, then turn around and walk away. At this point most parents will become furious and stand there, sputtering.

You have a powerful response to this behavior: You *follow* your Loner and, within a set time limit—brevity is the key for negotiating with Loners—insist on his coming to terms.

The best place to negotiate with a Loner is in a car. He can't walk away from you when you're driving 50 miles an hour. Your strategy is to get him to divulge why he's chilling you

BRAIN-
STORMING

FISHING

and everyone else in the family. So say to him, "This silence is not healthy for any of us. How can we live together differently?" The main negotiating skill you will need with your Loner is fishing.

The temptation with Loners is to be as taciturn as they are: do not take on their liabilities—instead, persist and keep fishing, so you can help them draw on their assets.

The *Saint* will defy you in so many ways, most of them small, that you scarcely know where to begin: She *has* to borrow your belt, that's why she took it without permission; he *has* to do a project in school, that's why he took your car, even though you needed it to go to work; she *has* to help a friend who's just been dumped by her boyfriend, that's why she didn't call to say she'd be late.

Saints live on the edge, procrastinating about responsibilities, and, more than other styles, putting their own pleasures first. This skewed sense of priorities occasionally causes them to lie.

One Saint we interviewed, Marietta, a high school junior, was forbidden by her parents from getting into a car driven by any other teenager. (Note: Saints will be forced to lie if your limits are unreasonable.) One day a friend of hers wanted to go to the beach, and, without telling her parents, Marietta accompanied her. She says, "I came home and told my mom that my friend's mom drove, because I didn't want to get into trouble. But my mother ran into her mother, and found out."

At the same time, Saints tend to be a social worker to their friends, taking them in when they run away from home, advising them about sex, trying to help them get off drugs. You may worry because your Saint is attracted to the troubled kids at school, thinking that he may become more like them. And so you may discourage him from spending time with them.

Your Saint's defiance will generally come in the form of feeling indispensable to those friends, who "need" him, and so he will refuse to stop seeing them.

TAKING
STOCK

In determining how to negotiate with your Saint about what appears to be defiance, spend some time evaluating his history. Has he ever gotten into real trouble at school or with the police? Has he neglected his health or seriously violated your values? Chances are that the answers to these questions will be no.

The key to your negotiation is to realize that your Saint, while appearing at times to be scatterbrained or irresponsible, is a real survivor. He may appear to go along with his friends' values, but he knows how to get himself out of, or to avoid, terrible trouble. Remember, Saints are controllers, not followers.

Since there are always so many minor issues clouding the air with your Saint, it's easy to discount his problems, or to overreact to his frenetic and sometimes hysterical approach to life. The primary vehicle of the Saint's defiance—the way he blows off steam at home—is being fresh. Because of his empathy, he knows how to wound, and how to ignite your temper.

Here's how to negotiate your Saint's verbal abusiveness:

FISHING

TAKING STOCK

1. Begin by fishing. What is important to him? How can you help him determine what his priorities are—is the issue of what to wear really as critical as the issue of studying for a test? Help him weigh the difference.

BOTTOM LINE

OPTION

2. Tell your child that he will accomplish nothing by being insulting, or by swearing at you. Alert him that the minute he begins to do so, your conversation is at an end. He may rant and wail, "You're such a hypocrite! You say you want to communicate with me, and the minute I try, you give up!" Do not relent. Just say, "We'll talk again after dinner, if you're ready not to be abusive," and walk away.

ERROR ANALYSIS

3. Help your child become less overwrought about the pressures on him that he allows to accumulate. His abusiveness is a symptom of his stress. If you habitually bail him out of dilemmas, you're likely to feel growing annoyance at him, though you may not express it. Then you may overreact to his next urgent plea for help because of the anger that has built up within you.

BRAIN- STORMING

OPTIONS

Ask him to list the four things that are most important to him at the moment. It will be difficult for him to narrow them down, but the exercise will help him sort out what must be done now, what can wait, what can be delegated, and what he can do without. Your Saint is weak on critical skills—this exercise will help him become more discriminating and will aid him in setting priorities.

ERROR ANALYSIS

4. Employ mutual error analysis by saying to him (if this is the case) that, by being overprotective, you have not helped him become more responsible in the past. His emotionalism is often a controlling mechanism, and you may have perceived it as hysteria. Tell him that you are not responsible for his obligations—he is. And if he fails to meet them, you will not take them on.

Underdogs will seldom defy you openly; instead, they'll bury their anger, or rebellion, behind a smokescreen of lethargy, or tears, or illness, or television, or sleep, or drugs. These are all defensive gestures, but they are insidiously self-destructive ones.

Teenage Underdogs are not only carrying the weight of their own adolescence, they're also carrying it for their friends. Says one 17-year-old we interviewed:

> Sometimes I wish I had no friends. I feel like when a friend is upset, and I have my own problems, but I care about her, I can't talk to her because I have a lot on my mind, but she needs me, so I feel bad. That's pressure.

FISHING

You need to help your Underdog avoid being swamped to the point of depression by his indiscriminate empathy; you must monitor—while respecting his privacy—both his difficulty with asking for help and his tendency to shoulder his friends' problems. You also have to make sure he isn't trying to shoulder your problems—if you are troubled, try to talk to a friend, rather than your Underdog.

TAKING STOCK

The defiance of an Underdog takes the form of passive aggression: He rebels through apathy, or dependency, rather than being outrageous. He promises to do something and then forgets, and gives endless excuses for his undependability; you find yourself reminding, prodding, and becoming frustrated.

GOAL SETTING

Your strategy is twofold: first, to rob him of excuses; second, to get to the heart of his paralyzing inertia.

One way to accomplish your first goal is to give him time limits. If, for instance, he promises to get the car washed in exchange for using the car, and fails to do so within an afternoon because he had five favors to do for Baby Bully and Kid Tyrant friends, you can provide the logical consequence of his not using the car; one broken promise sometimes deserves another.

BOTTOM LINE

ZEROING IN

But let us say that none of your negotiating skills and strategies works with him—brainstorming, bottom lines, the lot. Now you have to go to your second goal: What's keeping him trapped in his inertia?

Here's the strategy for unclogging your Underdog:

TAKING STOCK

1. Ask him to list five things he wants to accomplish—they may include being popular, getting good grades, getting a job. It's possible that you are inadvertently applying too much pressure on him in these and other areas, and so he rebels by doing nothing.

OPTIONS

2. You want his self-esteem to grow as a result of being responsible. Give him a list of things you want him to do routinely as a participant in the family: cooking a meal, running certain errands, and tutoring a younger sibling in math are examples. Ask him which three things he is willing to do, and on which dates or days of the week; make

AGENDA

sure he understands that this is an informal contract to which he has jointly agreed, and that you expect him to carry out his promises. And be prepared to follow through with logical consequences if he does not. But build into your agenda time for his friends.

ERROR ANALYSIS

3. As your Underdog becomes more confident, ask him to assess his friendships and how they may hurt or help him. This style needs to learn how to be able to say no without feeling that he'll be abandoned (about which we'll elaborate in Chapter 16) and to voice his concerns openly.

Appropriate rebellion is stating what one does and does not like about life, attachments, responsibilities, parental expectations. Have frequent huddles with your Underdog so that he has a climate in which to ventilate and to be comfortable with discussing his feelings, rather than lurking behind and

**FINDING
COMMON-
ALITIES** ____ feeling overwhelmed by them. Tell him you understand how difficult it is to learn to stand up for oneself, and add an anecdote from your own teenage years—how hard it was to talk to your own parents, perhaps—that would illustrate your understanding.

**TAKING
A BEAT** ____   You want him to learn constructive defiance. So if he says something that wounds you, try not to react negatively—at first, you need to listen patiently while he tries on this new way of interacting with you.

The Underdog is the style most likely to join a cult if his withdrawn behavior continues without your intervention; since Underdogs don't believe in themselves, they tend to put their faith in other people. It is the "good kid" who worries you most—you long to have him become defiant, just to make sure he's okay.

Be aware that the important negotiating skills to use with this style are fishing, finding commonalities, and finding options. You want to help your Underdog define himself, rather than being defined by others, and thereby becoming their victim.

CHAPTER 15

GRADES (GEARING UP FOR COLLEGE OR FULL-TIME WORK)

According to a 1986 national survey conducted for an ABC Television program entitled "ABC Notebook: The Great American Teenager," the most important problem teenagers face is getting good grades in school—indeed, 84 percent of the high schoolers polled said it is "very important."

As we discovered in our own survey, it is even more important to students than many parents realize. Much has been written about the stress experienced by high school students who are anxious about being accepted by a good college, or *any* college, because of the competition in the job market.

And for students who are not ready for college yet, or who plan to go instead into a trade, the assumption that they *ought* to be planning for college can make them—and you—feel like failures or disappointments if they do not have such plans. Forcing kids whose interests are nonacademic onto a college-bound track rather than training for a trade or other work also causes stress.

But pressure for success in high school also includes involvement in sports as a credential for college entrance or to obtain an athletic scholarship, or as an end in itself. Some parents—to whom achievement at football or basketball or track is of great importance—become enraged if their teenager doesn't make the team, or is cut from it.

Said a 15-year-old Underdog boy:

My father always puts pressure on me about football. He thinks I am the next Lawrence Taylor [New York Giants]. He pushes me really hard, and demands that I put in extra practice time so I can make the team. I'm big, but I'm no jock, and I can't possibly live up to his expectations. My athletic ability has never been good enough for him, so what's the point of trying any sport, even just for fun?

Teenage stress is often exacerbated by parents who worry about their teenagers' futures, a concern that hangs in the air in many families and is impossible for kids to ignore. Many of the students we interviewed said that grades, even more than sports, are the single greatest source of arguments with their parents; indeed, parental pressure to get top marks often goes to extremes, and can backfire.

An 18-year-old Saint described her parents' pressure about grades this way:

Even when I was little, they pressured me; in the fourth grade I'd actually study for hours at night—I was afraid they'd yell at me if I didn't.

Now, I'll be watching a television program, or having a snack, and my mom will say, "Don't you have some work to do?" I'm on the high honor roll, and I've been accepted by an Ivy League school, but she still finds ways to pressure me, like saying, "I hope you'll keep your grades up when you get to college."

The parental rationale for applying pressure about grades, according to the mother of a 15-year-old Loner, is this:

She's always been a good student—not a very top student, but basically an A student. But last quarter her grades fell. She went from an A minus to a B plus in science, and from a B plus to a B in math. So I was really angry. I said, "This is completely unacceptable. A girl who has done so well should not be so distracted that her grades fall that much." She ended up crying. I grounded her, and I was angry for quite a long time about it.

This is one issue that could easily be dropped entirely from the list of things you argue about with your teenager, for this reason: your child's school work is his "job," not yours, and his decision to work or not to work is his alone. You are not doing him any favors by putting the screws on regarding homework, or report cards, because he's already putting a tremendous amount of pressure on himself.

This does not mean that you do not take an interest in his academic progress, or that you do not have certain standards about it. Certainly, you do not want your child to flunk out of school, nor do you wish to condone any irresponsibility—say, his daily habit of watching television for hours rather than studying—by witnessing it without comment. You need to strike a happy medium: you monitor his progress, but you don't nag; you fish, but you don't interrogate. You have the right to see your teenager's report cards, but you don't yell at him if he gets a B instead of an A.

Parental pressure for high marks comes in all forms: raising an eyebrow when a child gets a C on a test, insisting on typing and editing his papers, paying him for A's, expecting more from him than he is able to deliver, terrifying him with tales of professional failure or with titanic rages upon receipt of a report card. We spoke to several parents who even wrote their teenagers' college application essays for them, doing considerable research in the process.

Do not imagine that your child is indifferent to his school progress. Indeed, kids compare grades the way adults compare incomes, and it is nearly impossible to overstate their importance to teenagers.

Your child is acutely aware of his class rank. He's discussed it with his teacher, his guidance counselor, his coach, his friends, his friends' parents. *He knows*, and your lecturing, or arguing, or punishing will not help him take on the responsibility for studying if he is not prepared to do so.

Pressure to achieve may produce good grades—and trophies—but it can also produce a crisis elsewhere. If, for example, your honor roll, varsity-soccer-playing Saint breaks up with her boyfriend, the event will have much greater impact than it would if you have not applied pressure. She's already trying not to fail with you; if she fails in a relationship, her self-esteem may be shattered, rather than merely badly bruised.

The best negotiating agenda you can formulate regarding your teenager's school work is this:

- Helping him see what his priorities are
- Helping him deal with the school's and the culture's pressure for success
- Helping him to narrow his choices
- Helping him set goals

At this point in his life, that goal probably centers around going to college, or he may want to train instead to develop a skill so that he can go to work upon graduation. How well he fares in high school will depend in part on how well he gets along with his teachers. It is in these years that a clash of styles between teacher and student may produce a range of difficulties for your child, from inability to learn to eruptions in class.

Just as your child is becoming an adult "person," he needs to learn that his teachers are human beings, with the same pressures, biases, and ambivalences as the rest of us. Your child will need to learn how to work within the system—in this case, high school.

This does not mean that, occasionally, you do not intervene at school. If, for instance, your female teenager is harassed sexually by a teacher, either through flirtation, or, as in one case we know of, by being pulled onto her teacher's lap, or outright seduction, it is imperative that your child tell you so that you can take immediate steps by reporting such behavior to the school administration and, possibly, to the police. The same applies to teachers or coaches who are abusive to your child, male or female, in any way.

Your teenager may be a mini-adult, but there are some situations in which he cannot, and should not, be expected to negotiate for himself. Be alert that your passive teenager may not tell you immediately of such problems: here is one area where you need to be acutely aware of changes in his moods or behavior, and of his style. He may be in trouble and not know how to tell you.

You can help your child retain his individuality through negotiation with adults—in this case, his teachers. You may need to brainstorm options, rehearse strategies, role-play conversations or negotiations with him, and have him write down his plan of action.

Here's how to help your child succeed in the classroom, and to get along with the "boss"—which will be of incalculable help in reducing pressure he feels to succeed in school—by style:

> *Baby Bullies* want to achieve in school because they're born competitors, but their grades may slip as a result of taking on too many challenges, such as sports and making money after school. You need to help them narrow their choices of areas in which they compete.
>
> One woman handles her Baby Bully's grades this way:

ZEROING
IN
   We discuss his report cards. When a teacher says, "Is capable of doing better work," I remind him that working harder is not for me; I don't have to go to school any more. It's for him. I never punish him for poor grades. I just try to steer him toward being more responsible in those subjects where he has a natural gift.

Many Baby Bullies create problems for themselves in school because they antagonize their teachers. The biggest complaint teachers make about them usually has to do with their attitude: He's cocky, he's a showoff in class, he's arrogant, so he's constantly in trouble.

Your Baby Bully may have provoked his teacher once too often, and the teacher may then pick on him or be withholding of praise or help because your teenager is so abrasive. Remember: Baby Bullies tend to blame everyone else for their troubles, instead of taking responsibility for them.

Baby Bullies fly off the handle and make snap judgments; they need to learn how to see gradations and subtleties, not only in their studies, but in their teachers. If your Baby Bully becomes crazed over a grade on a test and wants to

ZEROING
IN
assault his teacher, remind him of his tendency to affix blame, and help him negotiate with the teacher to improve their relationship.

Here's how your Baby Bully can establish a better working relationship with his teacher:

He can have an after-school huddle with his teacher and say, "I'm really not getting this subject. Will you give me some help before or after school to find out where my

TRADE-OFF
weaknesses are and what I should be concentrating more on? I'll stop acting up in class, and start taking my work more seriously."

Baby Bullies can be so charming that most teachers will respond well to this approach of candor and willingness to try. They will also respond when they see an underachieving Baby Bully shift his attitude by curbing his tendency to be a big mouth.

BACKUP   Your Baby Bully may be unwilling to attempt this kind of reform in school. Indeed, he may have a history of getting kicked out of class, or off the team, or even of being suspended. It may be that he needs another kind of school—say, one that has a looser and more creative structure, or a **OPTION**   trade school—rather than the highly structured atmosphere of many competitive high schools geared to college preparation.

If these options do not appeal to him, or if it is not possible for you to offer them, you need to help your teenager see what opportunities are available to him in the event that he does not want to play by the rules of his current high school.

BACKUP   Give him a list of jobs that do not require a college degree, such as working in a gas station or doing construction work. Then say to him, "These are your choices. Perhaps you should try one of them over the summer, or for a year after you graduate, to see whether you prefer them to college. You can always get a degree later on. But whatever **BOTTOM** you decide, you cannot do nothing. You can either get a job **LINE**   or change your attitude about high school. There are no other options."

You have to have the courage to follow through on these options. You may imagine the risks of doing so—that he'll run away, for instance, or that you will be embarrassed if he is not college bound. But by the time he is a senior in high school, his future is his responsibility. You must help him chart a course for himself and see the consequences of his decisions, rather than reward him—and penalize yourself—by avoiding the issue altogether.

Kid Tyrants often have personality clashes with their teachers, mostly because they want to demonstrate that they know more than the teacher does. When they are disgusted with a teacher, they may decide to clam up in class as punishment.

Teachers should be given medals for their accommodation of outspoken Kid Tyrants. Says one high school senior we interviewed:

I'm politically conservative, much more so than my parents. I have opinions on just about anything, and I'm not afraid to share them.

I've never had a teacher who agrees with me politically, so I'm always going against them in class. We disagree on just about everything—abortion, affirmative action, Star Wars, women's rights. But I do it in a friendly way. I make friends with most of my teachers.

And, in all likelihood, those teachers kick the dog when they get home at night.

ZEROING IN

Your Kid Tyrant may go too far in throwing his weight around in class. Point out to him that teachers have emotions, and that styles differ, and he needs to learn to get along with a variety of people as he gets older. If the teacher is a sensitive or passive sort—which Kid Tyrants despise—it doesn't mean that he or she doesn't have a great deal to impart in class. In any case, the teacher is the "boss."

TAKING STOCK

FINDING COMMON-ALITIES

And so the negotiation with your Kid Tyrant could be this: Appeal to his need for control and to his agenda for his future by saying, "You will need your teacher's help in getting into college [or getting a job]. If you antagonize him, you are cutting down your options for teacher recommendations. You are also making it harder for yourself to listen and to learn. Perhaps you should speak to him and try to sort out your differences. You may discover that you have a lot in common with him."

The issue here probably isn't grades—Kid Tyrants usually do well in school. The issue is team playing, which is difficult for this style, because he wants to be captain of the team.

By encouraging your child to settle his problems with his teacher, you are helping him learn how to get along with authority figures, who will have a great deal to say about his future career path, as well as with peers, whom he will want to motivate and lead. You can't motivate through coercion; you can motivate through persuasion. Kid Tyrants potentially are gifted in swaying opinion, but need to work on their tendency to try to railroad people.

Loners may be having trouble in school because they have a keen ability to honestly assess their work, and their assessment may differ from their teachers'. This is not altogether bad. One artistic Loner we interviewed said this:

My art teacher praises all my work, but I can cite some pieces I consider magnificent, and he'll just say, 'Oh, they're all right.' That's because the struggle to do them isn't so obvious, as obvious, for instance, as the work I did that won prizes. But I know how much effort the others took.

At the same time, your Loner may create problems for himself because he likes to do things his own way, and may fail to see that a wider context—the school—has its own, perhaps differing, way.

For example, a Loner may get so involved with a science project that he'll spend weeks exploring one aspect of it, and become something of an authority. That tenacity is a fine thing, but the deadline for the project may have come and gone, and his other school (and family) obligations may get sidetracked.

Many teachers will applaud this kind of intellectual curiosity and ambition; some, who are more by-the-book, may not, wishing their students to adhere to their instructions and schedules, and will balk. So might your Loner. Says one 16-year-old Loner:

If I find I've got a teacher who will not accept any opinions that are not her own, I just won't work as hard. If it's a difficult teacher, I simply won't put forth the effort. But if the teacher is reasonably good to straight-out excellent, I'll put out every effort.

Your Loner will need to learn to accommodate his teacher's style—but he can still negotiate according to his own, **TRADE-OFF** say, by requesting to do a project for extra credit, and at the same time learn how to bring his assignments in on time.

How this negotiation will turn out depends in large measure on the Loner's ability to communicate his needs—his difficulty in doing so, of course, is his biggest liability. If your Loner is to achieve his goals outside the family, he needs to explain to those people who are important to that achievement exactly what his goals, as well as his feelings and thought processes, are.

Loners expect you to read their minds, and they can be punished, in the form of poor grades or poor sportsmanship or misconstrued attitudes, for their inability or refusal to communicate. Help your Loner to be open with his teachers about his enthusiasms and interests.

Help him do the same kind of communicating with you. If our theoretical Loner with the science project closets himself, refusing to show up for meals or to do his chores, he may need to negotiate with you, or his siblings, to set up some trade-offs while he is working on the project.

TRADE-OFF You might, for instance, agree to let him off the hook for one week regarding taking out the garbage, if at the end of that time he will help you clean out the garage or attic. Says one studious Loner we talked to:

> My parents have been really nice about my spending a lot of time doing homework. I just lock myself in my room after dinner and work until midnight. They kept reminding me of the things that hadn't gotten done, but they gave me the time to do them later.

Do monitor your Loner during his obsessive periods. We interviewed one 17-year-old Loner whose happiest hours are spent running:

> I enjoy training hard. I know my limitations, and if I'm not working to the top of my capacity, I feel somehow that I'm being lax. I'm pretty stubborn, and I keep going. It's a challenge. But sometimes I work too hard and put in too many hours at the track. This year I shot my health to hell because of that.
>
> I had a small breakdown this year because I was working too hard—I cried hysterically for three days. It terrified my parents. They badgered me because I had chosen to try for a marathon. I thought I could handle it, and I was wrong, but they shouldn't have given me a

TAKING STOCK

guilt trip. I might have stayed on a more even keel and would have managed my time better if I hadn't had to devote so much time to cooling down after our fights about my running.

This Loner has a better awareness than her parents of logical consequences, although their concern over their daughter's health is understandable. Allowing your child to make her own decisions regarding her sports—or studies—can make even harsh consequences easier to bear and reduce your Loner's stress. In this case, stress led to physical illness and an anxiety attack, some of it of the child's own making, some of it caused by a lack of support for her decisions.

Saints, by the time they reach high school, will be paying heavily for their attention to everyone else's agenda but their own. Now they are up against a daunting list of demands that are anything but social: preparing for the PSATs and SATs, visiting colleges and filling out applications, trying to get their grade point average up and to choreograph the "right" sports and activities for those applications.

Some Saints try to address all of these pressures at once, and manage to do it all: honor roll, star of the school play, captain of the soccer team, summer internship on a newspaper. But their difficulty in setting priorities can land them in the hospital.

This is what happened to one Saint we interviewed who is trying desperately to please her parents, who are extremely demanding and who apply enormous pressure for her to get into an Ivy League college. Because she is active in a variety of after-school activities, and is on high honor roll, she often studies until 2 A.M. At one point she was taken to the hospital for extensive tests because she exhibited symptoms of mononucleosis. She says:

It was overwork. I hate my school—the competition is ruthless; kids with a ninety-three average will cheat on tests to get a ninety-four, while I just study really hard.

I really got fed up with my mother, because she

makes matters worse by imposing such high standards for me. She'll say, "You should be working harder, your room's a mess, your bathroom's a pigsty." So I finally yelled at her and said, "Mom, we're two different people. Please just leave me alone."

The thing is, I'm driven. But what I hate is that she pushes me to do well in school and part of me says, "I don't want to do it because you want me to," and part of me says, "But I'm only hurting myself." And then when I start studying, I feel like I'm giving in to her. I'd like to do something that makes *me* happy. My parents don't agree with that.

ZEROING IN

SHIFTING GEARS

Your Saint needs an emotional payoff for exerting effort, and so your task may be to help her set goals for herself, rather than to please you, and to budget her time so that she doesn't become sick or overly anxious. If college is her goal (and it may not be—be prepared to help your Saint evaluate the option of taking a year off to allow for more decision-making time on this subject), then she needs to rearrange her priorities and learn how to budget her time.

Your Saint may not be able to set scholastic priorities because other things are crowding her emotional agenda, such as lack of self-esteem. Getting poor or average marks is especially troubling for your Saint if she is in an extremely competitive school, and if she is very insecure. We interviewed one Saint whose senior class of 129 students had 7 valedictorians—they all had straight A's. She said:

I'm so lazy. Both my sisters get better grades than me. My boyfriend goes to an Ivy League school. I feel like a loser because I don't get good grades.

My Mom said, "You have other qualities, too." I said, "Name them."

"Well," she said, "first of all you care about people, and all your boyfriend cares about is cars."

Something in me doesn't care about being the best, only being happy. But I don't know how I'm going to be able to earn a living because I'm no good at anything practical.

While concerns about the future are epidemic among today's high school students, they are staggering for some Saints, whose nurturing style is often alien to the aggressive, fast-track campus and marketplace.

BRAIN-STORMING

You need to help your Saint, who is so good at manipulating and persuading people, to learn to apply that same intuition to herself. Ask her: "What do you want? What are you interested in? What are you good at? What do you like to do that makes time fly?" These are the same kinds of questions that career counselors ask adults, and they are invaluable for narrowing choices and finding options.

If your Saint can begin to answer these questions, have her write her replies down on paper and put them away. The ages of 14 through 18 are not necessarily when your child will have answers—indeed, many adults in their thirties do not have them. But if your Saint keeps this list and pulls it out every few months to reevaluate and edit it, as she nears her senior year, when college and career decisions are made, she will begin to have an idea.

OPTIONS

But even if she doesn't, a liberal arts education provides four more years of narrowing options. Taking a break from school and getting a job also provides more time for this task. Most colleges and universities have special programs for people beyond traditional college age who are seeking degrees, often at the same time that they are working part- or full-time.

Do not force your Saint—or, for that matter, any style—to commit if she is not ready. Your job is to show her that she *always* has options, and one of them is to wait until she is ready to make a commitment about college or a career.

Underdogs may fall into many of the same traps as Saints, but the difference is that Saints have stronger egos and better survival instincts. As we have said, Underdogs are the most vulnerable of styles, and most in need of your support.

It is this style that tends to be shy and unable to confront, or even talk to, teachers. Underdogs may experience enormous academic problems in a highly competitive high school, because they tend to feel overwhelmed by pressure, and the idea of jockeying for scholastic position may unglue them.

Their hardest job is trying to survive a teacher who is exacting, demanding, and merciless with those people who seem to be giving less than their best. Some people thrive with such teachers and rise to the challenge of pleasing, or proving wrong, an unpleasable person; the Underdog is not one of them.

Underdogs like their teachers to be mentors. They look to them for guidance, as well as for understanding—even friendship. Their neediness can lead to crushing disappointment and self-destructive behavior.

Here's how one 18-year-old Underdog described his relationship with his favorite teacher in his junior year:

> The only course I failed was English. I had a big personality conflict with my teacher. In the beginning of the year, we were great buddies. I write very well, and he had told me that I was very talented. I had a whole drawerful of things I'd written at home, and I took some of them in to show him. He started asking me a lot of personal questions about my family and making me nervous.
>
> My mom helped me write him a letter to say that I used to be able to count on him for someone to talk to about my writing, or to just shoot the breeze, but that now it really hurt me when he embarrassed me by putting me on the spot about my family. Even after he got the letter, he kept doing it.
>
> So I copped an attitude of, "I don't care about your stupid class." And I deliberately flunked.

Your Underdog may be indiscriminate about befriending authority figures—as this young man was—and will be devastated if his hero worship goes awry, or if the teacher cannot give him the attention he craves. It may be that his lack of discrimination stems from a paucity of attention at home, and you will have to consider whether or not he is being given enough. Or he may never have been encouraged to make decisions or shown how to solve his own problems,

**ERROR
ANALYSIS**

because you have been *too* sympathetic about his victim personality.

Underdogs need help understanding that teachers, like bosses, are not teenagers' friends or parental substitutes, although some of them may be friendly and even sympathetic. But one kind word does not mean that the teacher is his patron saint. Underdogs' instincts about such things are shrouded by their insecurities.

Before your Underdog has such a long history of rejections that he gives up making any effort in school, you must give him opportunities to achieve, such options as volunteer work, or music, or writing. This may include hiring a sensitive tutor for those areas in school in which your Underdog is having trouble—one who is strong enough not to be caught in your child's web of sadness and who can keep a friendly distance.

**GOAL
SETTING**

Underdogs tend to be emotionally and socially delayed—many of them don't, in the teen years, date or go to parties. Often they just aren't ready for it. So you need to help them reach some attainable goals in those areas in which they *are* ready.

Once your child begins to have solid successes, even minor ones, to point to, he will be much less inclined to allow a teacher, or boss, or friend, or lover, to break his heart, or to construe criticism as rejection.

Rather than pressure him for good grades, you persuade him to find something that interests him, and give him every opportunity to do well at it. Success breeds success, and you want your Underdog not to be overwhelmed in school—you want him to discover that he can set a course and accomplish a goal, one piece at a time, under his own steam.

If you can afford to send your Underdog to a low-key private school with small classes and understanding teachers, he will have a tremendous advantage. But if that is not financially possible, you will have to help your Underdog negotiate for himself.

Let's say he has a history exam coming up, but he's terrified of his teacher, and he's afraid he'll flunk. What he may not understand is that his terror is getting in the way of his ability to learn—if you can cure the terror, you can help prevent a failing grade.

ZEROING IN

Have your Underdog list the things he doesn't like about his teacher, and also the things he understands and doesn't understand, say, in his history class. If the teacher is abrupt, or seems not to take time to answer your child's questions, role-play with the child so that he can talk about it with his teacher in a private meeting after school.

> *You:* "What do you want to have happen with your teacher?"
> *Underdog:* "I want him to get off my back."
> *You:* "What would you like to say to the teacher?"
> *Underdog:* "Drop dead."
> *You:* "If you do, he'll get angry. What about saying, 'It's difficult for me to do my work because I'm frightened of you'?"
> *Underdog:* "I'd rather die than say that."
> *You:* "What would you be willing to say?"
> *Underdog:* "You scare me."
> *You:* "Terrific."

Your child has to use his own words when talking to his teacher. If you get him to rehearse those words, he won't forget what to say.

However, your Underdog may balk at the idea of confronting his teacher in this way. You can suggest these options:

OPTIONS

1. He can write the teacher a note saying approximately the same thing; if your child asks, you can help him write the letter.

2. He can arrange to have a meeting with the teacher with you present. Although we don't recommend this alternative for most teenagers, your Underdog is, in many ways, still very like a sixth-grader in his people skills. Tell him you'll attend, but you'd like him to try to do most of the talking. In the meeting, you can tell the teacher you are there at your child's request to lend moral support, not to be a watchdog.

3. You can ask the guidance counselor to arrange a

conference with you, him, the teacher, or even with all his teachers. Most schools will accommodate you in this request. We know of several such conferences in which the faculty had not known of a student's emotional problems or difficulties at home and, once informed, willingly altered their treatment of the student. If a teacher lacks information, he cannot know what he is doing wrong, or change it; most teachers will shift gears if they have information.

4. If your Underdog wants someone to change, he has to do the work; if he's stronger and more decisive, people will respond to the changes in him. Tell him that the next time you want him to negotiate for himself, having intervened on his behalf this time. If he approaches his teachers honestly and directly, they will usually respond in kind.

BOTTOM LINE

It is extremely important for Underdogs to learn how to negotiate now, because soon they will be on their own, and you won't be able to intervene for them. You don't want to set up your Underdog for failure by not attending to this important skill—negotiation—now.

CHAPTER 16

PEER PRESSURE (DRUGS, ALCOHOL, SEX)

This is the area that gives parents of teenagers the greatest anguish. Most parents are acutely aware of the proliferation of drugs and alcohol, and of the sexual activity of youngsters. The increase in teenage drug overdoses, deaths at the hands of drunk drivers, teen pregnancies, herpes and AIDS, is hardly news.

Parents fear the worst in the abstract, but they often deny their own children's involvement in these areas: our survey indicated that teenagers are more involved than their parents imagine.

Nevertheless, virtually all the teenagers we interviewed said that if they did not want to experiment in these areas, no one pressured them into it. As a high school junior put it:

> There's no peer pressure in my high school. But you can put peer pressure on yourself, by thinking, "I want these people to think I'm cool." No one would ever say, "If you don't do this, we won't hang out with you." You give in to pressure only if you're insecure.

There is no question that alcohol, drugs, and sex are more available to teenagers—in cities, suburbs, and communities across the country— than they were to their parents' generation. With over half of all mothers in the work force, teenagers have more opportunities to become involved in unsupervised activities than ever before.

But availability does not equate with use. The difference is in the teenager's ability to make decisions. If he has been prepared for decision making, from the position of a strong sense of self and of individuality, he is far less likely to make the wrong choice.

For example, if a teenager is at a party where cocaine and vodka are served, and the teenager says firmly, "No, thanks," the matter is usually dropped and, according to some adolescents we talked to, the abstainer is even admired, by users and nonusers alike. The pressure is rarely as great as you think.

If that is true, why are so many teenagers involved in these things? According to most child psychologists and researchers on this subject, the reason is this: adolescents who do not feel as though they are indispensable partners within the family—whose parents do not spend enough time with them or set loving limits and provide logical consequences—may choose the quick fix of peer approval.

Children who give in to peer pressure generally have parents who fall into one of three categories:

- Parents who are unable to be consistent—who threaten but do not follow through—and who feel powerless
- Parents who are overprotective, and do not allow their children to learn from minor mistakes so that when the big decisions come along, they will not make big mistakes
- Parents who are overcontrolling, and who have unrealistic expectations of their children, rather than accepting their styles and helping them find options

In all three categories, the teenager may feel out of sync with his or her family. Such children look to their peers for the acceptance they are not getting at home.

According to researchers who have studied teenage suicide, 90 percent of suicidal children turn to friends, rather than to parents or counselors, for help. And those teenagers who are of the more passive (unable to solve problems) or competitive (impulsive) styles—Baby Bullies, Saints, and Underdogs—are most vulnerable to peer pressure and self-destructive behavior.

As psychologist Dr. David Elkind observed in *All Grown Up and No Place to Go: Teenagers in Crisis*, "People who have a strong sense of self do not lose it even under the most trying circumstances."

It is in this troubling and potentially life-threatening area that it is imperative for parents to know their child thoroughly, even if they have, for whatever reason, failed to do so before.

As one 17-year-old girl we interviewed put it:

It's never too late to start paying attention. If your mother or father suddenly became loving and caring, even if you were in your forties, wouldn't you respond?

The big problem is that parents don't spend enough time with their kids to just talk to them. Kids need to know that you've been there, that you've had the same kinds of experiences and problems, to hear your stories about those problems when you were growing up.

A kid won't open up to someone who hasn't opened up to him. So they turn to their friends, who understand, because their friends are going through it, and will talk about it. If you open up to your kid, you can help him through the bad times, because you've been through it and you understand. And the kid will become more aware of what your needs and feelings are.

As we have said, if you are not schooled in your child's style, his assets and liabilities, his interests and his behavioral patterns, you will not notice changes in him that are clues to experimentation with drugs, alcohol, and sex. The problem is not solely those temptations: the problem stems from your teenager's style and his feelings about himself, which are either a barrier to, or an invitation for, pressures to become involved with them. If you find that your child is veering increasingly toward the liabilities of his style, and if his assets seem to be receding, you have a clear signal that he is in trouble emotionally, possibly with self-destructive activities.

But it may be that his dramatic behavioral changes *are* signs of drug abuse. Most parents want to see such changes as rebellion and deal with it as an interpersonal problem, when in fact what's wrong with their teenager may be that he is drug dependent, and nothing you do, including negotiation, will work.

You cannot deal with your child's liabilities if they are caused by drugs; you have to deal with the substance abuse itself and get medical and psychological help immediately.

And so, destructive behavior may be a matter of peer pressure and rebellion, or it may be a product of and motivation for drug usage. By knowing your child thoroughly, and by paying close attention to his style and the changes in him that may or may not be appropriate to that style, you will be able to tell the difference.

There isn't a great deal that you can do about your teenager's decisions outside the house, but there's quite a lot you can do in it.

If, for instance, your child wants to have a party, you can call a huddle and say this: "These are the ground rules: No booze, no drugs, and no going up to a bedroom and closing the door. If any of these ground rules is violated, the party is over."

This negotiation doesn't always work; in many communities, kids may arrive empty-handed, but they have stashed bottles of booze in the woods, or in their cars, and, even in a blinding blizzard, will slip out from time to time to get a drink. Many parents do not want to have to stomp through the snow, keeping an eye on their teenager's guests, and so they forbid parties altogether.

But parents may encourage their children's illegal use of alcohol in other ways. In those same communities, some parents will allow parties on their lawns—in the vague belief that if the kids are not actually *inside* their houses, the parents are not culpable. Other parents, with a misguided sense of supervision, will serve and drink booze with their teenagers and their friends.

Your adolescent cannot begin to set limits for himself if you have not been abundantly clear about your thoughts and values. If your child has a party, *be there*, and be prepared to enforce your rules. He and/or his friends may find ways to break them—but, as one father put it, "I don't have to help them by being indefinite on the subject."

Many parents are reticent about stating their values because they do not wish to appear to be uncool or antediluvian to their hip teenagers. Once you have taken that position, you have jettisoned any possibility of negotiation and collaboration; you have capitulated.

So if your values include an uneasiness about your teenager having sex with his or her love interest in the house—even though you know full well that they can find other places, and other hours, to couple up—you have the right to say, "It makes me uncomfortable, and this issue is not negotiable. If your friend spends the night, he [or she] can sleep in the guest room, or on the couch in the den."

It's your house, and you are under no obligation to defend your values. You do have an obligation to state them, so that there is no possibility for confusion on your child's part or doubt as to what you expect of him under your roof.

Here's how teenagers respond to peer pressure, by style, and how you can help your child navigate through it:

> *Baby Bullies* are impulsive, and seldom think before
> they act. Because they want to be on the cutting edge of

things, they are likely to accept dares. Given the availability
of drugs, it is not surprising that they do more than their
share of experimentation. They are often the first one to
say, "You haven't tried it [booze, drugs, sex] yet?" as
though it were a contest they must win. They are not afraid
to get and use fake IDs or to be big shots by buying pot
from their local dealer.

Baby Bullies need to prove themselves as risk takers.
They're prone to becoming involved in risky business because of the intensity of their style: they are least able, of all
the styles, to postpone gratification, and to see cause and
effect.

But if you don't say no to your Baby Bully, and point out
the consequences of his behavior, he won't be able to say
no to himself. And he will be disinclined to take no for an
answer from someone else.

It is the male Baby Bully, for instance, who will try to
coerce a girl into having sex with him. But he is usually
more interested in the chase, and the conquest, than in a real
relationship. If the girl says, "I'm not ready," or "I don't
want to," he'll use every persuasive trick in the book: a
classic is, "Don't you like me?"

You can go to your bottom line regarding your values in
a series of huddles with the Baby Bully.

**BOTTOM
LINE**   If you think he's sexually active, say to him, "Sex is
adult behavior—it is not kid stuff—and if you are sexually
involved, you have to know what you are getting into.

**ZEROING
IN**   "It is your responsibility to respect whomever you want
to have sex with—if a girl says no, you have no right to
persist. And if she says yes, it is your responsibility to be
protected with birth control, or to make sure that she is.

"If she becomes pregnant, you are responsible for talking with her to her parents. If that happens, and you do not
tell her parents you are involved, I will tell them."

AGENDA   Nothing could be clearer: you have firmly stated your values, and you have given him a nonnegotiable agenda for
what will happen if he fails to take responsibility for his
sexual activity.

The same applies to alcohol. You can set an example by
not drinking with him and by not drinking to excess in front

of him, and by seeing that there is always a designated nondrinking driver when you go out with friends.

OPTIONS   Moreover, you can sign a contract with your child that if he is ever drunk somewhere else, he can call you for a ride home with no questions asked, and that if you are drunk, you can call him as well. Such contracts are available through your local Safe Rides chapter, and are an example of healthy collaboration with your teenager.

In addition, you can make sure your teenager always has money in case he needs to take a taxi home, rather than get into a drunk driver's car. Or he can spend the night at a friend's house if he is unable to drive. Or you can teach him, through role playing, to ask to be let out of a car in which he feels unsafe.

Make sure he understands that there are numerous options if he finds himself in a jam regarding excessive drinking and/or being with friends who are drunk. The most important thing is that you want to save his life.

On the morning after, you can follow up by having a huddle about drinking in general, without discussing the previous night's revels, to find out why it is important to him to drink so much, and to help him learn other, healthier ways to compete.

BOTTOM LINE   The bottom line with your Baby Bully—as with any style—regarding drinking is that if you discover he has had a single drink on a night when he has been given the car to use, or if he gets into a car whose driver is inebriated, then he loses driving privileges for one month. The same applies if you discover he has purchased any alcoholic beverage. The logical consequence for breaking the law is the loss of certain adult privileges, and the car is one of them.

If your Baby Bully becomes involved with drugs, you may have to do what this courageous family did. A 16-year-old Baby Bully had marijuana in his book bag, which his father discovered accidentally one evening when it spilled onto the floor in the hall, where the boy had left it. The father made his son tell him the names of the boys from whom he had purchased the drug and called the school to inform the principal.

The school had its own machinery—a hearing with the superintendent of schools, the high school principal, and the boys and their parents, and levels of punishment, including suspension of varying lengths—to deal with the problem. The Baby Bully was suspended for 1 week; the dealers were suspended for 6 months. All the teenagers were required to go into therapy to avoid expulsion.

BOTTOM LINE Then the father told his son that if he did not call the police himself to inform them of his drug purchase, the father would. The boy turned himself in but, since the amount was so small, and since he was a minor, there were no legal repercussions.

The consequences of the Baby Bully's behavior were these: the boys he "finked" on threatened to beat him up; the other boys' parents were furious with his father, who was unmoved by their refusal to face the fact that their sons were in terrible trouble. And the Baby Bully himself was flabbergasted that his parents would, as he put it, turn him in.

And yet turning him in was exactly the appropriate thing to do. As it turned out, his marijuana caper did not go on his permanent school record. But for the other boys, it did. That's a consequence for selling drugs, and the boys, and their parents, were forced to face it.

Interestingly, once this episode became common knowledge within the community, several parents called the Baby Bully's parents and thanked them for taking a stand, one that they could hold up to their teenagers.

Now the Baby Bully does not dare hang out with unsavory kids or to dabble in pot or booze because, as he told us, "I'll get killed—I'll have to do community service for the rest of my life."

Kid Tyrants do not want to lose control, but they do want to be included in peer activities, and so if they drink, or use drugs, or engage in sex, it is usually in moderation. Some Kid Tyrants will take a stand by refusing to become involved with drugs and booze—if not in sex—and will take a leadership position to persuade other kids to follow their lead.

It is often the Kid Tyrant who starts a chapter of Students Against Drunk Driving (SADD) in his school, or who spearheads and runs a Safe Rides program in his community, or who seeks and negotiates for a leading authority to come to the school to talk to parents and kids about the dangers of drug and alcohol abuse. Indeed, if you find that your Kid Tyrant is tempted to become involved in drinking or drugs, possibly as the supplier rather than user of either, you can guide him into this leadership position—it appeals directly to his style.

Loners, if they drink or use drugs, will do so in private, and not as a social activity. Such usage is totally alien to their style and is, in their case, symptomatic of real depression or crisis, and requires immediate intervention.

The Loner is the least likely style to experiment with illegal substances. According to the study about adolescent drug use mentioned in Chapter 13, the teenagers most immune to this kind of peer pressure have these characteristics: conventionality (i.e., not rebellious), achievement motivation, control of emotions, and social isolation. All four are vintage Loner qualities.

Some parents can unwittingly contribute to the erosion of those qualities. We have in mind one Loner whose parents were concerned about her lack of friends and a social life. Says the 17-year-old:

My Mom definitely wished me to be more social. She encouraged me as much as she could to get together with friends on weekends. She was absolutely thrilled when in tenth grade I actually started going to parties and hanging out with boys.

I'm willing to drink occasionally, and my parents are absolutely delighted. But I don't really like to drink. Yet they've been encouraging it, while I've been saying, "No, no, I really don't want a drink, thank you anyway."

If your Loner doesn't want to go to parties, or to drink, do not push him. It would be far better to respect your child's style and to take advantage of his built-in cautiousness than to undo the very qualities that protect him in the teenage years.

As for sex, when Loners do form attachments, they are few and deep. If your Loner has a boyfriend or girlfriend, he or she will take the relationship seriously. At times, these romantic attachments can become obsessive, as anyone who has read Scott Spencer's *Endless Love* knows.

TRADE-OFF

One Loner we know of broke into his girlfriend's house after she terminated the relationship. His parents were shocked at his behavior, because he'd always been so muted in his demeanor, and they simply didn't understand his style. The girl's parents did not press charges, in exchange for the boy's parents insisting he go into psychological treatment, which he agreed to do.

ERROR ANALYSIS

The Loner needs to deal with his feelings, which are often unexamined, in order to prevent his veering sharply toward his liabilities, including obsessiveness. You can help by asking this question: "What can we do to encourage you to tell us how you feel, and how have we made it hard for you to open up to us?" If you did not negotiate with your Loner when he was younger, you can assume that he has trouble being open with you now. This kind of question will make it easier for him to learn how.

Saints, like Baby Bullies, are impulsive and want to be in the center of things; unlike Baby Bullies, they are impulsive to please, rather than to show off.

A girl Saint, for example, may be reluctant to be open about her activities, her temptations, and her experimenting, because she doesn't want to worry you and because she'd rather advise you than have you advise her.

OPTIONS

If you think she's sexually active, do not ask her whether or not she is, because she'll say, "Would *I* do such a thing?" Instead, give her the phone number of Planned Parenthood, or arrange with your gynecologist to give her birth control upon request. You will not be able to prevent her from becoming sexually involved—of all styles, she is most likely to believe in romance.

TAKING STOCK   But romantic love is not always what it's cracked up to be. You can have huddles with your Saint—whether male or female—about "love" and about having respect for one's body, as well as helping him or her get in touch with his or her instincts and real needs, as opposed to peer identification and social wants.

Most teenagers who are sexually active have, as their hidden agendas, the need for intimacy, gentleness, warmth, and caring. For them, sex is frequently a way to get close, as opposed to a need merely to "get laid."

Your Saint may need help in learning how to say no. You can suggest these lines:

OPTIONS   "No, that's not what I want."

"No—I'm scared, and I'd like our relationship to go a little slower."

"No. I'd rather be your friend."

"No. If you insist, I may not be the person for you."

You can encourage your Saint to role-play and to rehearse these lines; chances are he will feel uncomfortable doing so with you. But you have given him some negotiating options to draw upon, and he may rehearse them with friends.

ZEROING IN   The Saint is a flirt and, often, a tease; help him understand that either is encouragement to think he means bed, when he may simply be trying to attract interest.

As for booze, your Saint may learn the hard way the consequences of excessive drinking—in the form of a hangover or social embarrassment—since excess is a prime ingredient in his style. Since he wants to be part of the social whirl, in addition to teaching him to say no to sex, you may have to teach him to "fake" drink; ginger ale looks like scotch or beer. He can also take a drink, dump most of it, and fill up his glass with water.

But follow up with a huddle to examine with him why he thinks that he is socially acceptable only if he has a drink in his hand.

In the long run, however, it is the Saint's need to be needed and his controlling nature that will probably save him from severe consequences of his behavior. He'd rather hold a friend's head than be the one whose head is held; he'd rather advise kids not to take drugs than to be stoned out of his mind; he'd rather have a friend who is his slave than to be mistreated by one.

TAKING STOCK

However, because he tends to be spontaneous and initially indiscriminate about friendships, you will need to teach him how to spot a phony, or a bully, or a liar. If he can identify these types up front, he will spare himself terrible hurts and potential physical harm.

TAKING A BEAT

The issue for you, and for your Saint, is trust: he needs to gain your trust by being open and honest with you. And if your Saint decides to be candid, and to discuss his or her drinking or sexual activity, do not overreact; instead, help the teenager see the consequences of his or her behavior, and point out that there are other options for becoming popular.

OPTIONS

These include getting good grades, being active in sports and student government, getting an after-school job. If your Saint is involved with these kinds of activities, he simply won't have time for unattractive or unsavory peers. And if your Saint's self-esteem is boosted in a healthy way, he won't need to choose unhealthy means to bolster it.

The *Underdog* is the style you have to be most concerned about, because it is the one most likely to give in to peer pressure regarding sex, alcohol, and drugs. Says the mother of a 16-year-old Underdog:

> I'm more concerned about Carl than my other two kids because he's the most insecure. I know he wants to be popular, and I worry that he wants it so much that he'll do things that he shouldn't do. He shows none of the outward signs of drinking or drugs, but you still wonder: when he goes to weekend parties, what are they doing? Especially when he sleeps at someone else's house. When he sleeps at home, at least I'm there to smell him when he comes in!
>
> I found a marijuana wrapper in his room one day

when I was cleaning it. My husband said to ignore it. I said, "You're out of your mind. I'm going to confront him with it. I have to know."

When Carl came home from school, I called him into his room and said, "I want you to know I was not in your room snooping, I was vacuuming; and I found this." He said the wrapper belonged to a friend who came over recently.

I believed Carl about 85 percent. You want to believe your children. But still I worry.

To cite again the above-mentioned study regarding drug usage among adolescents, the kind of teenager who is at greatest risk has these Underdog personality traits: depressiveness, anxiety, difficulty in maintaining good relationships, and lack of achievement motivation.

Without a stable family environment with solid values, consistent parental behavior, attention to the child's feelings, and ability to involve the child in problem solving—all of which create self-esteem—the Underdog is highly likely to abuse himself through destructive peer attachments and activities.

BOTTOM LINE

While it is crucial with other styles to learn to collaborate with them in their confidence building, with the Underdog it may be a matter of life and death. This is an alarming and frightening thought; but if you have not intervened before, now is the time you must begin.

Underdogs are often defined by their attachments to people, and have enormous difficulty making decisions about whom to befriend; anyone who pays attention to them is a "friend."

ZEROING IN

You need to help your Underdog become a problem solver by first helping him define problems. Encourage him to discuss his friends, and to tell you what he likes and dislikes about each one. He may be reluctant to take a stand regarding his dislikes, because he's not sure he's entitled to be critical; indeed, he feels that he will be abandoned if he is, that somehow negative thoughts will come back to hurt him. The Underdog is the style most prone to this kind of anguished magical thinking.

The female Underdog has terrible troubles being discriminating in romantic attachments, and is vulnerable to coercion by partners. For her own protection, you need to help her to become more critical, and more discriminating.

If she has a boyfriend, ask her questions that require more than a yes or no response:

"How do you like to be treated by him?"

"How does he show you that he cares about you?"

"How is he like a best friend—can you talk easily to him?"

"What happens if you tell him you don't want to drink, use drugs, or have sex with him?"

"What decisions do you make about what you do and where you go?"

Rephrase these questions, and perhaps add to them, about your Underdog's friends.

ZEROING IN

If the answers to these questions are negative—and be prepared to dig for the answers—you will need to point out to your Underdog that she is not capable of making a commitment to anyone until she puts a higher value on herself. Indeed, her willingness to blend into someone else and to become invisible makes her not much of a partner to begin with, because she's feeling so insecure.

FINDING COMMONALITIES

With the Underdog, you begin your negotiation by an expression of your fears and possible culpability in her insecurity. If she sees that you can be candid, and critical of yourself, it will be infinitely easier for her to feel that her negative thoughts about herself are permissible, and even useful, because they are the first step to salvaging her self-esteem.

BOTTOM LINE

With an Underdog, the issue is never sex, or drugs, or alcohol: the issue is her lack of self-esteem. If your Underdog is seriously involved in any of these areas, full-scale intervention is urgent because she is most at risk for harm, emotional and/or physical.

Once your Underdog is able to expose her demons, she can learn that they do not have the capacity to terrify and paralyze her without her help. It is the awful imaginings that create such panic; and it is the sympathetic examining of them that renders them harmless.

BACKUP____   Tell your Underdog also that the flip side of her fears is her enormous gift of creativity; most people who are phobic, for instance, are creative—it is their vibrant imaginations that create the panic they feel. You might want to encourage her to begin keeping a journal, or to enroll in a writing course. Many of today's finest novelists were once Underdogs.

We are acutely aware of the terrifying and daunting difficulties of raising an adolescent today, and know how easy it is to have a gnawing sense of powerlessness with teenagers.

At the same time, we believe fervently that you are not without influence with your child. Even the most outrageous teenage behavior can be dealt with, if you negotiate. It is never too late.

Remember: Your teenager needs love and limits. He does not want to be the authority figure in his family; he wants you to be.

Your denial of his difficulties will only increase his efforts to test your authority. He may do so just to make sure it exists. But he does not want to take it on, because instinctively he knows that he is not yet an adult. He still needs you—in some ways, more than ever.

At the same time, you need to know that he is beginning to become an adult, and is entitled to assume certain responsibilities, tasks, and decisions. You must respect his growing autonomy. All the values you have taught him, skills in which you have trained him, problems you have helped him solve, have been internalized in the teenage years and are solidly intrenched.

And even if you are new at negotiating, it is possible, even probable, that in time your teenager will learn to value himself, and to value you as well.

PART VI

EXPERIMENTAL
THEATER:
SPECIAL
NEGOTIATING
SITUATIONS

CHAPTER 17

DIVORCE

Shirley Adams, 37, is the mother of two children—Lauren, 17, and Seth, 7. Divorced for six years, she works as a secretary in a personnel agency. Her income barely covers the expense of raising two kids—she gets minimal, and sporadic, child support. After six years, one would think she'd have gotten used to the stress of being a single parent and the lack of routine in her children's lives.

She hasn't. Says Shirley:

A couple of Saturday nights ago Seth and I finished eating dinner around ten-thirty—Lauren was out—and it was a beautiful night; the moon was almost as bright as the sun. I said to Seth, "Do you want to take a walk?" We strolled all over town, went down to the town ball field and ran around. It's my outlet, a respite from worrying. I worry about five million things, and money, all the time. So when we walk, we talk—he talks best on our nighttime walks, because he doesn't get distracted.

But Lauren gets the short end of the stick, because Seth's so young and needs me more, and she's so independent. Sometimes I think I'd love to go into Lauren's room, after Seth gets settled in bed, and just sit there and talk to her. But there are always so many other things I have to do—go to the laundromat, buy groceries, get the car fixed. The next day I say to myself, "Tonight I'm going to set aside some time for Lauren." But then I'm so beat at the end of the day, and I just want to read for half an hour in bed. And Lauren will come bebopping into my room and I want to say "Leave me alone, I'm so tired, I just need some time to myself." But I can't do that. Not with a good conscience.

Of all the problems faced by single parents, none causes them as much anxiety as the paucity of relaxed time with their children. It is this anxiety that wipes clean your negotiating slate: where once family routines followed a certain predictable pattern, now uncertainty about the future and trying to be two parents at once cloud your agenda. Negotiating with your child seems like an intellectual luxury, pushed by concerns about mere survival to the bottom of your list of priorities.

These are the things you worry about now:

- Money—if you are the female custodial parent, there's as much as three quarters less of it
- Responsibilities—the kids have to pitch in, not as a character-building exercise, but because if they don't, the household chores (cooking, cleaning, errands) just won't get done
- Your child's fears—if Daddy's gone, will Mommy leave too? Is it okay to love them both?
- Curiosity of and abandonment by friends—yours and your child's
- School—your child may act out there because he's afraid to at home
- Dating—parenting and finding a partner seem mutually exclusive
- Setbacks—your child may have reverted to bedwetting, and his grades and appetite may take a nose dive; you may take up smoking again
- Your ex-spouse—how to get him or her to cooperate with you regarding the children
- Guilt—am I entitled to a new life, and are my kids going to be scarred forever? How do I meet my needs and theirs, too?

From this partial list, it is clear that, in addition to all the other developmental issues your children face, and all your good intentions to design strategies to keep them on an even keel, there is this new, agonizing monkey wrench: this is a time when kids need parents most, and parents have the least to give. Children are sent reeling by the blow of divorce to the family, and may veer sharply toward the liabilities of their styles, while you are just trying to keep body and soul together.

Set against the context of loneliness, financial insecurity, and a gnawing sense of panic, a phone call, for example, from your child's teacher regarding his sudden misbehavior is the last thing you want to hear or feel able to deal with through negotiation.

The majority of divorcing parents are hurt in tandem with their kids, and may revert to adolescence, ignoring or denying their children's pain.

Styles of parents and of children suddenly shift as though slammed by a bulldozer.

You may feel like a teenage version of your adult style. Recalls one woman:

> Recently my teenage son told me that during the divorce, when he was eight, I scared him to death. I had a bad temper—I'd get upset and yell.
>
> One time during the summer we were having lunch, and I was looking at a bunch of photographs spread out on the kitchen table. He spilled a glass of milk on the pictures, and I went bananas. I grabbed him by the shirt so hard I ripped it; I yelled at him to get out, to go to the public pool, and he had to ride his bike with one flat tire. I didn't even let him put on his shoes.
>
> Afterwards I felt so bad, I didn't know what to do. I cried all afternoon, but I didn't know how to apologize.

Or your style may soften. If, for instance, you were a Dictator in your former life, now you may become a Big Daddy/Big Mamma because you don't want your children to hate you, or you don't want to be the "heavy." Where once you set limits, now, in an effort to lessen their pain, you may overlook their tantrums, or their bossiness, or their bedtimes.

Your child, on the other hand, may seem to undergo a complete personality change. That's what happened to Tony, whose parents divorced when he was 10. Now 14, here's how he describes the change in his style:

> I was raised mostly by my father—my mom didn't have that much influence over me—who is really macho, a blue-collar type of guy, into outdoors stuff, football, poker every Wednesday. We were inseparable. I was always dirty; I was like a tough little guy.
>
> Then when my folks split up, I hardly saw my dad at all. So I radically changed everything about me. I became passive and extremely nonviolent. I haven't hit anyone in the past four years. I didn't want to be anything like my father.

Even if your child seems to be relatively the same at home, he may be having trouble in school, his behavior mirroring his liabilities. For example, Baby Bullies may get into fist fights; Kid Tyrants may jettison their typical logic to become verbally abusive; Saints may lose some of their sweetness and boss their friends around; Loners may become sarcastic and acerbic to teachers and buddies; Underdogs may make daily visits to the nurse's office, pleading illness.

The primary reason your child may act out in these ways is that he wants you and your ex-spouse to get back together again (unless, of course, the child was battered by one of you, and sometimes even then) and because his emotional foundation is crumbling. Says one woman we interviewed:

> I've noticed that when my ex-husband brings the kids home on Sunday nights, they won't leave us alone for a minute. They don't want us to talk without their being there. A friend of mine who's divorced says the same thing happens with her kids. I think it's because they're hoping we'll patch things up.

And so your child will put you through the wringer, and manipulate you, either to bring about a reconciliation or to find out where he stands in the modified family constellation.

Here's how each style may try to "play" you during and after the divorce:

Baby Bullies will give you the guilts, demanding new toys, saying that the absent parent spends more money on them than you do, pitting mother and father against each other.

Kid Tyrants will try to assume a leadership position, and behave like *your* parent. They'll interrogate you about every aspect of your life: "Who'd you go out with?" "Are you sure you should spend money on that?" and "Why were you late getting home from work?" are typical Kid Tyrant questions designed either to put you on the defensive or to dominate you.

Loners, sinking deeper into their remoteness, will use silence to express their anger, as though to say, "If you feel free to ruin my life, why should I tell you anything?"

Saints will rise to the occasion with liabilities blazing: in the name of concern, they'll want to hear all your problems, advise you on your love life, tell you what's good for you. They may also "tattle" on your ex-spouse by saying such things as "Gee, Dad's new girlfriend isn't as pretty as you are," and reverse the compliment to the absent parent, in an effort to control you both.

Underdogs will become needier than ever, not daring to complain and exhibiting physical symptoms—such as headaches, belly aches, and/or insomnia—of their stress, as well as depression. They are so afraid of being abandoned by either of you that they'll do anything to please you both.

And so your child's and your own styles will, during this trauma to the family, undergo changes and alterations.

Since the family and its parts have been reshaped, so, too, are your negotiations. You now have three new agendas:

- Renegotiating your relationship with your child
- Teaching your child to negotiate with the absent parent
- Trying to collaborate with your ex-spouse regarding your child

Because the vast majority of mothers retain custody of their children following divorce, we will discuss these issues from the woman's point of view and, in a later section, address the special problems of being a single, noncustodial father. Having said that, many of the following issues apply to both parents.

RENEGOTIATING THE RELATIONSHIP WITH YOUR CHILD

TELLING YOUR CHILD ABOUT THE DIVORCE. Imagine that when you go to work on Friday, in your paycheck is a pink slip announcing that you have been let go, with no advance warning. You are filled with shock, rage, desire for revenge, panic, a sense that this is all a bad dream and soon you will awaken from it.

Now imagine how your child feels when he or she discovers that daddy left in the dead of night with a suitcase, never to return. Or, as very often happens, your child returns from summer camp to suddenly find that Daddy no longer lives at home.

If it is possible for you to do so, do not spring such news on your child without warning. But before you inform him, do your homework: you have to be able to answer his questions and to formulate strategies for his adjustment to his new life, and so you need to gather information about what changes in your life and his will be wrought by your divorce.

Here's how one woman prepared for her divorce:

First, I sought out a therapist for emotional support. Then I read every book on divorce, and its effects on kids, that I could find. Then I consulted a matrimonial attorney to find out what my rights and legal options were. Forget about telling the kids—I did all this a year before I told my husband that I wanted a divorce. *Then* I told the kids.

After gathering information, you and your spouse should call a huddle and tell your children, together, about your plans to divorce. Be specific about what will happen: where Daddy will be living—the address and telephone number; where you will be living—preferably in the same house or apartment, or the same community; where you will be working (if you have not worked before) or that you will be looking for work; how you plan to arrange visitation; that the children can call Daddy anytime; that there is *nothing they can do to prevent the divorce, and that it is not their fault.*

Your children will respond to this news in a variety of ways:

- The Baby Bully may scream, rage, and blame you both
- The Kid Tyrant may ask why he was not consulted
- The Loner may go to his room and stay there all day
- The Saint may try to get you together again
- The Underdog may beg you to change your mind

The ages of your children will also contribute to their reactions to the news. Children in elementary school will imagine immediate horrors of abandonment; high schoolers will imagine future deprivations, such as loss of college tuition or trade school fees, or your or your spouse's remarriage.

Be prepared for a period of rocky transition, and do not formulate long-term strategies or make large decisions, such as moving away, during it. This is the time to take a long beat—perhaps for six months.

Allow your children to be angry and to grieve in their own ways; until the mourning period is permitted to run its course, their recovery and regrouping—and yours—will be stalled. If you know their styles, you will be aware of the ways that they will express sorrow and anger, and be able to anticipate and to respect them. Their behavior will be variations on a stylistic theme, with liabilities expressed in new ways or with new volume; still, they will be within the child's style.

If your ex-spouse will not join you in this information-giving huddle, or if you feel his attendance would be unwise because he tends to be violent, to lie, to blame, or to lose his temper, you will have to handle this meeting alone.

Be prepared to answer any and all of your children's questions. As to "Why?" which is usually the first query, be as honest as possible without demeaning your spouse or unduly frightening your children. One way to put it is this: "I'm a good person, and your Dad's a good person; we just aren't good together, just as you and [name a friend of your child's] were friends last year, but aren't friends any longer. We fight all the time, and we tried very hard to be friends, but it didn't work. So we've decided that the best thing for us is to live apart. That's what has changed. What hasn't changed is how we each feel about you. And you will still be taken care of."

Sometimes your ex-spouse can't be painted in such rosy hues—if that is the case, selective candor is in order. Just as you do not bad-mouth an ex-boss to a prospective employer, you don't have to go into detail to your child about your or your spouse's extramarital affairs or the times he beat you up. The information will serve no purpose, and may come back to haunt you, particularly if your child repeats it to the absent parent.

But you can state the broad outlines for your unhappiness—Daddy's seldom home, we don't like each other, he's too rough (if you are a battered spouse, it is no secret to your kids). You can add that by living apart, you will in time become happier and have more to give to your children—to be a better parent with the source of friction removed.

Says a divorcée who could no longer bear her husband's remote and judgmental nature:

> The day I told the kids their dad and I were separating, I decided to be truthful. I told them how I felt. They saw my deep emotional turmoil; I was not in total control, and it was better that way.
>
> If you feel sorrow, you should share it with your kids. I think mine were grateful because I told the truth all the way down the line. They trust me because of that—they never have to be anxious about not knowing.

Make sure that your children understand that there will be a lot of changes in the household, but that one thing that won't change is that you love them and will be there for them, and that you'll never leave them.

But just as you have been honest with them, allow them to be honest with you; painful as this procedure is, it is far preferable to having their angriest and most terrifying thoughts and feelings lay beneath the surface, like a bomb waiting to be detonated. Their honesty will help you determine how and when to negotiate with them.

Many divorced parents err in making "pals" of their kids during this trying time. Some discuss their love lives, or their financial troubles, or their fights with their ex-spouse, or their insecurities, as though to an adult friend. If you make your child your peer, he or she will be thrust into the position of premature adulthood.

Says Freddie, a 12-year-old boy we interviewed:

> My mom drank a lot toward the end of the marriage, and a lot after the divorce, and she'd complain all the time about my dad. When she drank, she had a really bad temper. One time when I was little I remember my dad leaning on the kitchen door frame, laughing, while she was screaming and throwing dishes at him. I heard all the dishes breaking and she was screaming and I thought she had cut herself. After a few months, she quit drinking.
>
> Now she can make a six-pack of beer stretch out over a week. But I watch it. If she starts drinking too fast, I say, "Mom, you bought the six-pack yesterday, and you have only two left."
>
> I'm like a peer to my mom. She doesn't have to be a mom, because I'm pretty independent. For instance, she doesn't ask me to turn down my stereo. Instead, I have to say, "Mom, I'm trying to study, can you turn *your* stereo down?" It's neat. But it's odd.

Children do not want, nor are they prepared for, this role; moreover, to whom will they turn for support if they are busy propping you up? You lose authority with your child when you make him your peer; you cannot negotiate with him if, at the same time, you are seeking his permission to behave like a child yourself. As Freddie's mother told us, "I lost control over my son, because I was so busy trying to get on with my life that I lost track of his."

Tell your child as much as he needs to know, but not so much that he feels *responsible* for your problems and the solutions to them.

PARENTING ALONE. The good and bad news of being a single parent is that you don't have to check routine decisions with your spouse—at the same time, you do not have a spouse to help enforce rules, or take the kids while you rest or do chores, or simply to back you up in your decisions.

And, of course, there is the lack of time to thoroughly monitor your kids' behavior, to evaluate the changes in them, or even, perhaps, to see much of them. You may have a sense of not really knowing what is happening to them, either at school or emotionally.

In order to negotiate with your children, you need one skill more than any other: fishing.

Sometimes this requires heroic measures. Said one woman of her 7-year-old Loner:

> After my divorce, my daughter stopped talking about school. She'd say, "Oh, it's fine." I knew it couldn't be "fine." So I took her shopping, and when we got home, I said, "You are not getting out of this car until you tell me everything that's going on in school—your teachers, your friends, everything." It took a lot of digging, but she finally talked.

Your kids may think that you don't want to know what's going on—they see your anguish and don't want to contribute to it. Even small children—4, 5, and 6 years old—know intuitively not to bring you bad news. Be aware of the double messages you are giving.

As one woman put it, "My lips said, 'Come to me, darling, with your troubles,' but I really didn't want to know, and my daughter knew it." Remember, your children are still subconsciously afraid that you'll get so fed up with them that you'll divorce them as well. This fear cannot be overstated.

And so your negotiating skills at this point involve not only talking in a certain way, but also *listening;* you need to assess just how much information your children are taking in and the ways in which they may be tuning out. You have to know what your children are capable of hearing, so that you can tailor your negotiations accordingly. Kids have only one agenda item—how will the divorce affect my life, and how many more losses are in store for me?

And so, even as you listen, think of those friends to whom you can ventilate, or dump, and do it with those people, rather than with your children. By clearing your emotional head, you can better concentrate on your children's needs, to hear them, and to summon your negotiating skills.

When you are fishing with your children, do so in the spirit of interest and concern and affection, rather than in an effort to pick them clean, depriving them of the privacy they need to deal with change. Respect their styles at the same time that you are trying to help them.

In addition to fishing, you will also, more than ever, need to set limits. Your child may push you to the wall, trying to find out where he stands in the scheme of things, testing your capacity to parent alone. He cannot be allowed, however, to abuse you, or to flagrantly violate your rules. He needs as much consistency and routine as possible.

In this area, it is vital that you engage outside help. Inform the school immediately of your change in marital status and, if you have moved, of your new address. Give your child's teachers and guidance counselor as much detail as possible about his behavior and fears to help them help your child adjust to his new life.

Here's what one particularly imaginative teacher did in response to a divorcing mother's candor about her 6-year-old daughter's fears and regression. The teacher knew the child was creative, and so she designed a special, extra-credit project for her: to write a book of short stories. Once a week for 6 weeks, the teacher stayed after school for an hour to discuss the project with the child; it emerged as a fully illustrated, 20-page booklet that the teacher had bound and put on permanent display under "fiction" in the school library.

Anyone reading the book today and knowing its author can read between the lines of the fantasies and fables about animals, the dangers they faced, and how they survived them. The book was the child's way of working through, in a creative, school context, her problems at home.

Incidentally, when the girl was 10, the school began an after-school rap group for children of divorce, and she was asked to be an advisor to other children in the discussions. It was a role she willingly assumed, and she was able to act as a mentor to her troubled friends, showing them not only that they were not alone, but also that, in some ways, life after divorce becomes better. This responsibility had an enormous impact on the girl's self-esteem.

It is also important for you to get help, in the form of therapy, for yourself so that you can take your terror out of the family milieu and constructively examine and ventilate it. Many communities have clinics where psychiatric social workers are available for family and individual therapy on a sliding scale of fees. For children, fees in some clinics are as low as $5 per session.

HELPING YOUR CHILD HANDLE QUESTIONS ABOUT THE DIVORCE.   Your child will become a curiosity to his friends and, perhaps, to yours: well-meaning people will want to advise him; not-so-well-meaning people will want to pump him for information—including some of his teachers.

We are reminded of one fourth-grader whose teacher, in front of the entire class, said to him, "Oh, I'm so sorry to hear that your Mom and

Dad are getting a divorce. What happened?'' Her insensitivity immeasurably contributed to his stress.

At the same time, your child's friends may become curious because they are afraid that *their* parents will break up; often, upon hearing that a classmate's parents have split up, many children go home to take the pulse of their parents' marriage, just to make sure it's okay.

Having said that, your divorce is no one's business, unless you choose to make it so. You can help your child field questions from the interested, the concerned, and the merely voyeuristic.

Here's how one woman helped her 7-year-old daughter, Christie, to do so:

> A classmate of my daughter's started asking all kinds of questions and offering unsolicited advice to Christie. She told me she didn't know how to stop it—she was very shy—so I said I'd help her rehearse what to say, and she wrote it down and practiced with me.
>
> The next day the friend again questioned her, and Christie said, "I don't like being asked about that. It makes me uncomfortable." The friend stopped probing.
>
> Christie's teachers tell me that since then she's become more assertive and outgoing, able to say what she needs, and to stand up for herself.

RENEGOTIATING FAMILY FINANCES. According to sociologist Leonore J. Weitzman, in a 1981 article for the *UCLA Law Review* entitled "The Economics of Divorce: Social and Economic Consequences of Property, Alimony and Child Support Awards," a year after divorce the standard of living for women drops as much as 73 percent, while that of husbands increases up to 42 percent. While these statistics may not apply to everyone, for the majority of single mothers one of the first issues they must deal with is that of money—that is, the lack of it.

Renegotiating finances after a divorce is best accomplished by making your children partners in decisions regarding how much money they need, how much they want, where it will come from, and how it will be spent.

Here's how one mother negotiated her children's financial wants, having established that their needs were her responsibility:

> At first, I felt so much guilt about the divorce that I was handing out money to them right and left. But I couldn't continue to do that, because there was a limit to what I had.

So I sat down with my two kids to discuss our finances, and I asked them what the one thing was that they wanted most. Nancy, my 17-year-old, wanted to go on a three-week teen tour of Europe for the summer, a fifteen-hundred-dollar trip; Andy, my 12-year-old, wanted a computer.

I told Nancy I would help put out the word that she wanted to babysit at night. And I took her for an interview for a waitressing job five blocks from our house, and told her she could walk to work and I would pick her up when she got off. I agreed to lend her half the money for the trip—I borrowed it from my parents—but she had to pay me back from her jobs when she got back from Europe. She took the agreement very seriously, and I was reimbursed within six months of her return.

Andy agreed to forego his allowance—two dollars a week—as well as Christmas and birthday presents for six months, in exchange for a lump sum, and I helped him negotiate with his grandparents to give him checks instead of gifts. He also got a paper route.

We went comparison shopping at discount stores, and did research together in the library. When he had accumulated five hundred dollars, which the computer he picked out cost, he bought it. These "deals" had a fascinating effect on them. Before my divorce, they took money, and their possessions, entirely for granted, assuming that there was more to come. Now they respect it more, and take better care of their things.

Another woman, realizing she had to earn more money, explored the possibility of starting a mail order business in her home to augment her income as a teacher. She says:

I talked with my kids and gave them this choice: "If I am going to increase my income, I will have less time with you; if I spend more time with you, we'll have to learn how to tighten our belts."

The kids came up with this solution: to help me run my mail order business. My teenage son, who has a driver's license, said, "I'll make deliveries." My daughter, who attends a local community college, said "I'll be the bookkeeper." My other daughter, who is 11, said, "I'll take phone messages and wrap packages."

It was a joint family effort as our family went through a struggle together; and it made us closer than we've ever been.

Negotiating your finances after a divorce requires a realignment of priorities. If, for instance, you want to remain in your community to allow your children to continue in their schools and to have the continuity of their friendships, but you cannot afford your current residence, the trade-off may be a move into smaller—and more affordable—housing.

If your children know what's at stake—the possibility of moving away—they will be more willing to collaborate with you regarding budgets and cutting back in order to stay where they are. This does not have to be a somber or dispiriting business.

You can engage your children in ways to have fun on less, as well as ways for them to make money. Many imaginative children make their own Christmas presents, for example, or plan camping trips for vacations; one enterprising seventh-grader told us he plants a garden in the summer to grow vegetables for his mother and himself and to sell the rest, a project that gives him a great deal of pride.

NEGOTIATING TIME FOR YOURSELF. According to many single mothers we interviewed, one of their primary adjustments was putting themselves first. As one of them told us, "It was always the kids, my husband, and me, last. Now I've moved up the ladder one rung."

At first, this rearrangement of rank can be heady, and many parents go overboard socially for a time following their divorce, neglecting their children because of an urgent need to discover whether or not they are still "marketable" in the dating scene.

While we don't recommend a nonstop social calendar, we do believe that it is extremely important for you to have some time to yourself in order to refuel—to take a beat, if you will—for the daunting demands of being a single parent.

Here's how one woman we know negotiated a limited social life—one evening out per week—with her 8-year-old daughter.

Patty went to three birthday parties in as many Saturdays. On the fourth Saturday, I hired a baby-sitter and prepared to go out for the evening. Patty sat on the stairs and wailed, "Mommy, don't go out," something she hadn't done for years. I went, but I didn't have much fun—I called home twice, and came home early. I felt guilty. But I also felt angry.

The next day she had another birthday party to go to. When her ride came to pick her up, *I* sat down on the stairs and whined, "Patty, don't go out, I want you to stay home with me."

She was shocked. Then I said, "I'm just kidding. I know you want to see your friends, and I know how important it is to go to their birthday parties. It doesn't mean you don't love me. I like to see my friends, too. Of course you can go today, but let's talk more about this when you get home. Have a good time.''

By finding this important commonality, this woman and her daughter were able to sort out their social needs, and to come to a new understanding of one another.

If you fish and are aware of your child's liabilities, or insecurities, you'll know the difference between manipulation and the real need to have time with you. If your child is experiencing emotional setbacks, you can negotiate by taking the child with you on certain outings, or by trading off, say, a trip to the circus with his grandparents for an evening you wish to go out.

And if your child is in middle school or older, you can negotiate time for yourself in other ways. Here's how one woman was able to carve out recreational time:

> I go bowling every Tuesday night, and my 13-year-old son, Ben, baby-sits for his 2-year-old sister. I tell him on that night he can eat anything he wants—Doritos, sodas, pizza—because he's in charge of the house and can make the decisions. And I made him a special mug with his name on it, which he calls his Big Shot Tuesday mug. He only drinks out of it on Tuesdays.

You may find that your child's neediness keeps you close to home for a time; if you are engaging him or her in problem solving and joint decision making in appropriate areas, as well as having frequent huddles, this period will be temporary.

Studies show that the child of the single parent who sets strong guidelines and establishes consistent, albeit new, family patterns and traditions, is the child who fares best.

For this reason, you do not have lovers spend the night, and you do not involve your children with romantic partners unless it becomes very clear that yours is to be a permanent relationship.

Small children, particularly Saints and Underdogs, may find themselves becoming attached to or dependent upon the man in your life (or the woman in your ex-husband's), and if your relationship ends, they will be devastated by yet another loss.

As for teenagers, they can make dating difficult or uncomfortable for you, because they do not want to be confronted by your sex life during those years when they are trying to come to terms with their own. Boys, especially Baby Bullies and Kid Tyrants, may become irritable, or sarcastic, or protective, or insulting to your romantic partners. One woman told us, "Every time my kids take a message from a man, they say, 'This nerdy guy called you.' "

Girls may even be jealous. As one 17-year-old told us, "Mom and I talk about our boyfriends—the fact that she has one, and I don't."

Most children will be threatened by the thought of your "replacing" Daddy.

It is wise to keep your social life private; meet your date anywhere but in your home. The revolving door of attachments only serves to compound whatever confusion your children already feel, and to erode whatever authority you have established.

This does not mean you do not have a sex or social life; it means that you conduct it apart from your children.

RESENTMENT TOWARD YOUR CHILDREN.   Your negotiations with your children can be sullied by a buildup of your unexpressed anger. It is inevitable that the pressures of your children's adjustment, and your lack of privacy and freedom, will produce occasional feelings of resentment toward them. Every decision is now yours, since you are the day-to-day parent, and many women try to do too much in an effort to protect their children from the realities of family changes after divorce.

To reduce your resentment, you need to engage your children in sharing the family responsibilities. Here's how one woman handled her stress overload:

> I was doing it all alone: shopping, car pooling, basketball games, school conferences, all the things in the orbit of my children's lives. My biggest problem was time, especially with three children all having their own schedules. We had a family meeting and I told them I was going to delegate some of these responsibilities. I told my 12-year-old that she had to take care of her own car pools, and arrange for her own rides to her activities; I said, "You know you have to go someplace on Sunday. Arrange for your ride today."
>
> My 17-year-old now shops for her own clothing. I wrote a letter to department stores where I have charge accounts giving her permission to use my card.
>
> When my 18-year-old wants to use my car, the trade-off is that she has to take her younger sister for her haircuts or to certain appointments.

The result of my delegating these kinds of chores is that we have more time together at the end of the day when I get home from work. I am more relaxed ever since I made them my allies and partners.

But what about the resentment you feel about the child who *reminds you of your ex-spouse*? What if all you can see in him are his liabilities— the irritating characteristics that so annoyed you in your husband? Since temperament is relatively equal parts of nurture and nature, any similarities are not surprising.

Surprising, no; painful, yes. Says the mother of two children, a 12-year-old Kid Tyrant girl and a 10-year-old Saint boy:

> I have to face the fact that my daughter is a clone of her father, a man for whom I have absolutely no respect. Before she opens her mouth, I have a negative mind-set toward her, and I struggle with it every day. When she makes me angry, fifteen years of fury toward her father flash before my eyes. She brings out the beast in me.
>
> For example, she was sick today. If it had been my son, I would have been chatty and loving. She does not elicit in me the warmth I am capable of. I know that at some level she feels my hostility. It makes me feel horribly guilty.

This woman's postdivorce hostility and guilt were getting in the way of her seeing her daughter's style clearly, and negotiating accordingly. Just because a mis-fit in marriage can lead to divorce, it does not follow that a mis-fit with your child is insoluble. The issue is not so much that her daughter reminds her of her ex-husband, it is that the child's liabilities—like the father's (he is a Dictator)—are qualities that are annoying in anyone.

Guilt skews your negotiations when you are a single parent. So does unresolved rage toward your ex-spouse, something you may not have worked through yet, and which will muddy your relationship to the child who resembles him.

Older children pick up on your ambivalence in this regard. Said a 16-year-old:

> I think my mom sees me as like Dad; when I yell at my brother, Mom feels I am attacking him the way Dad does. So when she's defending my brother against me, even for little things, she is also defending herself against Dad.

If you can concentrate on your child's style, and his assets, rather than on his similarity to your ex-spouse, you can collaborate with him, using your skills of limit setting and joint problem solving, as well as attention to his feelings.

If you've had therapy, for instance, you probably know the ways in which you resemble a parent you may despise, as well as the ways that you are your own lovable, intelligent, creative, capable person. Try to see your child the same way: where there are similarities to your ex-spouse, there are also differences. When you can concentrate on the positives of your child's style, the negatives can be contained.

Part of the problem here is making the divorce final in your head: if your ex-spouse can still push your buttons, even circuitously through your child's similarity to him, you are still married, at least emotionally.

TEACHING YOUR CHILD TO NEGOTIATE WITH THE ABSENT PARENT

For those custodial parents whose ex-spouse is cold, or demanding, or stubborn, or insensitive, this is the most painful aspect of divorce. When your separation agreement requires you to allow the absent parent time with your child—especially if your child doesn't have a very good time with that parent—you feel miserable, because you can't do anything about it.

We are reminded of a woman who watched her crying child go each week to the father's house. It wasn't that he was a cruel man, it was that he was a Silhouette who didn't talk and had no patience with the Saint child's insecurities. He would park the child in front of the television set while he read or did chores in his apartment. Had he been physically abusive, the mother could have taken him to court to prevent visitation. As it was, mother and child were in miserable limbo on weekends.

This child was 5 at the time of the divorce, and too young to be able to summon the toughness that is required to address a Silhouette's blindness to other people's feelings.

But when the child is older, you can help him sort out differences with the ex-spouse—whatever the father's style—through negotiation. You want to make visitation as pleasant as possible for your child, since you cannot control what goes on during it, and because you want to try to keep the damage of divorce to a minimum.

Incidentally, many parents will pump their children about the absent parent, asking questions about new boyfriends or girlfriends, the ways in which they spend money, and the like; these questions serve no purpose for the child except to make him feel used, as well as to be guarded about anything he might wish to convey spontaneously. If you find yourself doing so, make every effort not to—such curiosity will hinder the negotiating process with your child.

You and your spouse may no longer get along, but he may be loving, attentive, and responsible as a parent. If that is the case, you are fortunate indeed, because he can collaborate with you regarding your child, even in absentia.

But if he is an amalgam of his style's liabilities, you will have to help your child learn to deal with those liabilities. Until your child is a teenager, when few courts would force him to visit the noncustodial parent, and assuming that the absent parent is not abusive, you will have to teach your child to negotiate with him in order to improve their relationship.

The baseline of your child's negotiation with the absent parent is this: the child cannot change the other person—he can only change how he responds to that other person, by stating his feelings and needs and setting boundaries to how much he can be manipulated.

Let us say, for example, that the absent parent makes a habit of bad-mouthing you to your child, attempting to use the child as a weapon against you. You can role-play with your child to make sure that manipulation stops.

Here's how one mother accomplished that goal:

My son, Billy, who is 14, wanted to take a skiing trip with his school ski club, and his father had said he would help pay for it, but only if I kicked in some money too. He told my son that I am too protective, and my son felt torn apart. So we talked about what he could say to his father. I asked Billy what he wanted to say. He said, "I hate it when he puts you down. You're my mother, and it hurts me. I don't like it when he says you won't let me do this or that, even though sometimes I agree with him. I just don't want to hear it from him."

So I said, "That's exactly what you should tell him. You can also say that you want me out of the middle, that anything you want from me, you and I will work out; and anything you want from him, you and he will work out."

That's what Billy did. His father stopped talking about me in front of him. And I started to let go a bit and be less anxious about my son.

Some differences between your child and ex-spouse are not so easily surmounted. We interviewed a father who was able to negotiate very well with Jeffrey, his 7-year-old son, with whom he was a "fit," but less well with Amy, his 14-year-old daughter, with whom he was not.

Jeffrey used to call him from time to time to complain that Amy was "not being nice to me." The father would reply, "You have to work it out. I'm not there, and I don't want to take sides if I'm not there."

With Amy, however, there was on the father's part an inability to respect her style. Says the father:

> When a certain amount of time goes by and I don't hear from her, I feel abandoned. I'm an emotional person, but she is very possessive about her feelings. If I delve too far, she'll push me away by debating me.
>
> Recently I sat her down to talk about it. I said, "I don't feel loved by you." She said, "What do you mean?" I said, "I need you to tell me, to hold me, to give me kisses."

The fact is that his daughter does express her feelings for her father, but she does so in a way that mirrors her Loner style: she writes notes, or sends cards.

You can help your child understand his own style, and to state to the absent parent what he is able to do, and what he is unable to do, in expressing it. As for the above example, the teenager can say this to her father: "It makes me feel uncomfortable to love you in only one way, the way you want me to. I show how I feel in other ways that are more comfortable for me. Please don't push me to be something I'm not."

Her father told us, "My kids are going to get me the way I am." If he can respect his own style in this way, perhaps he can learn to respect his daughter's style as well.

You can help your child negotiate with the absent parent by fishing to find out what troubles him in the relationship, and then by role-playing to find the words with which he would feel most comfortable in expressing his concerns. The following samples of negotiating language are given as suggestions only—which you can help your child rephrase into his own words—and are geared to your ex-spouse's style:

Jungle Fighter: If your ex-spouse makes a habit of criticizing you to your child, the child can say, "I don't like it when you put me in the middle. I want to have a good time when I'm with you, and I can't if you're always angry at what Mom did."

Dictator: If your ex-spouse constantly pumps your child for information about you, the child can say, "I'm willing to answer all your questions about school, or my friends, or sports. I'm not willing to answer your questions about Mom."

Silhouette: If your ex-spouse is uncommunicative with your child, the child can say, "I have a hard time being with you because you don't talk to me; it makes me feel as though you don't like me."

Big Daddy/Big Mamma: If your ex-spouse is overly protective of your child, the child can say, "You make me feel like I'm 2 years old and that you don't think I can take care of myself. What have I done that makes you feel that way?"

Soother: If your spouse makes promises to your child that he does not keep, your child can say, "It's hard for me to trust that you will keep your word. I'd rather be sure of what you are willing to do than wonder about what you aren't."

It may be a tall order for your child to confront the absent parent in this way. But if you can help your child address his feelings regarding a mis-fit, even if, out of guilt or fear, he is unable to express those feelings, at least he will be secure in the knowledge that his feelings are sacrosanct.

This awareness may not improve the relationship with the absent parent, although it will help in your child's other relationships, and it may be necessary for you to intervene in your child's behalf with your ex-spouse.

NEGOTIATING WITH YOUR EX-SPOUSE

It's vital that you make every effort to negotiate with your ex-spouse, because he or she may be in your life forever, since you have children together. The child's stability will be greatly enhanced if you can establish at least a civil relationship with your ex-spouse and learn to collaborate with him or her to insure a degree of continuity in your child's daily life regardless of whose house he is in at the moment.

This is an important goal; it is not an easy one to reach. In all likelihood, an inability to connect with your spouse led to your divorce in the first place; having to maintain contact, even for the sake of your child, can be unnerving.

Some parents are able to accomplish it. We spoke to one man who regularly talks to his ex-wife to find out what their child's bedtime and meal routines are, whether or not he has homework to do, and what punishments (say, no TV for a week) should be enforced when the child is with him, so that they do not inadvertently sabotage each other's parenting efforts.

Others are less able to negotiate together. Says one woman, "My children would like it if I were better able to confront their father, to stick up for them. I have a tremendous amount of trouble dealing with it, because I hate confrontations, and with him, everything is a confrontation. I just fall apart."

Even at its best, you'll find that, at first, your negotiations will be strained because you both are still emotionally wounded. But if, in time, you can concentrate on the task—collaboration—rather than the feelings—retribution—you will see the negotiating issues more clearly. You already have the most profound commonality: your child's well-being and his regard for you both. It's a good beginning for your negotiations.

When you begin your negotiation with your ex-spouse, these are some of the items that may define your strategy for collaborating with him:

1. Keep your eye on the goal, which is to create as much consistency for your child as possible. Every time an issue comes up between you and your former partner, filter it through this question: what is best for our child?

2. Be aware of the ways in which you may be sabotaging each other's parenting efforts. It is useful to take your pulse immediately following a divorce, and to examine patterns in your behavior regarding your ex-spouse. Do you, or your ex-spouse, do any of the following?

- Make comments to your child regarding late child support payments?
- Arrive late when bringing the child home?
- Permit your child to do that which is against the other's wishes or values?
- Talk critically of your ex-spouse to a friend, either on the phone or in person, within hearing distance of your child?

If you can spot these patterns in yourself, and stop to consider the logical consequences of these tendencies, which is to create confusion and insecurity in your child, you will be able to terminate them. Sabotage does nothing to move forward a negotiation.

You can address the issue of sabotage by asking your spouse to have a meeting with you, in a neutral place—a coffee shop, for example—and saying to him, "I realize that I tend to be late getting Johnny ready when you come to pick him up [or some other undermining mechanism], which must infuriate you. But there are things you do that create the same anger in me. I'll try to always have Johnny ready on time. Can you . . . ?"

Your spouse may deny negative behavior, perhaps in heated terms. One man we interviewed said he attempted, without success, to negotiate with his ex-wife:

> She has tried to freeze me out of any kind of decision making or closeness with my daughter, so there are decisions, such as where she will go to camp, that she makes without consulting me. She's tried to withhold her from me on weekends. Our separation agreement is a worthless piece of paper, except when she cites part of it to our child and says I haven't done what I was supposed to do, which is a lie.
>
> I realized we were getting nowhere, so recently I said to her, "Maybe we should try to talk about things for Michelle's benefit more openly, and try to help each other." She looked at me and said, "I think you're the scum of the earth, and I don't want to talk to you ever again about anything." Our only negotiations are through our lawyers.

When this imbalance occurs, the only thing you can do is to keep trying. But there needs to be a time limit to your entreaties, because of the toll they will take on you.

Once you've reached your bottom line, *cut your losses* by being certain not to dwell on your ex-spouse's liabilities. Instead, concentrate on the main event, which is your relationship to the child. Even if your ex-spouse continues to sabotage you, your child isn't stupid: he will know who cares about him, and who cares about using him to hurt you.

Says a young woman about her parents' divorce when she was 7:

> Every Saturday when I went to visit my father, my mother would say, "Tell your father he's behind on child support payments." When I was with my father, he'd say, "Your mother doesn't spend the money on you—she spends it on herself."

The upshot is that today I have no relationship with either of them, because they were more interested in hurting each other than in loving me.

3. Most negotiations are not so hopeless. If you know your ex-spouse's style, you can still negotiate with him, in private, apart from your child. These negotiations apply, whether you are the custodial or noncustodial parent:

Jungle Fighters are great party parents, lavishing expensive gifts, vacations, and dinners on your child; but they will, if they are the noncustodial parent, often ignore your child's schedule, and pick him up or bring him back late. If they have custody, they may not be home when the noncustodial parent delivers the child. Go to your bottom line and say, "The next time you do that, I will hire a baby sitter and send you the bill," or "If it happens again, I will take the child back home and you will have to come get him." If the pattern persists, keep a record of each time your ex-spouse is late and have your lawyer send him or her a letter about it.

Dictators are the style most likely to interrogate your child about your life. Do not take a moral position regarding these intrusions or be intimidated—rather, stick to the facts by saying, "Your grilling our child is not helping him in school, because he is under stress, or in his desire to talk to you, because you overwhelm him. How are you willing to change?"

Silhouettes will give you little or no information about your child that would help you in your parenting, so don't expect much. If you do communicate to your ex-spouse, put it in writing, and be specific, with requests such as "Please send me Jimmy's report card," or "Please tell me what his adjustment problems are." Silhouettes care about their children, even if they won't talk, so they may write back.

Big Daddies/Big Mammas will try to keep your child dependent by saying, "Call me when you get to Dad's," or "I'll be thinking of you every minute until I see you again." They also try to get the child to choose sides. Say to this style, "I've noticed that Sharon feels guilty when she's with me, and worries about you. What can we do to make her feel better about being with either of us?"

Soothers will promise your child the sky, but will fail to deliver—they are glad-handers and can be unreliable, for example, about visitation, and not show up when they said they would. Say to this style, "Perhaps we should renegotiate the visitation schedule so that it will be more convenient for you."

If you have made every good-faith effort to negotiate with your ex-spouse and have gotten nowhere, you will have to learn to focus instead solely on your relationship with your child, and try to get rid of your anger through therapy or some other means. The important thing is not to deny your child your love and emotional support, whatever the outcome of your negotiations.

In extreme cases, however, you may reach your bottom line in the form of suing for custody with no visitation, if you feel that your child's life or mental health are endangered. *Do not fail to do so if that is the case*. If you cannot afford a lawyer, you can get a court-appointed one; moreover, your underage child, in many states, is entitled to his own legal representation and his lawyer, also court appointed, can sue on his behalf, even if you have a separation agreement.

But if there is no clear and present danger, don't use your lawyer or the courts as a vehicle to harass or punish your ex-spouse; doing so means that you are still married in some way, and that you need to exact retribution. Such needs will be barriers to your own growth and the rebuilding of your life, and will destroy any negotiations you have with your child.

WHEN YOUR CHILD WANTS TO LIVE WITH DADDY. The ultimate threat is when your child says, "I hate you and I want to go live with my father!" It is the Baby Bully and the Saint who are most likely to play on your worst fears in this way. You may even be tempted to take advantage of this opportunity, because you are financially and emotionally overwhelmed, or because you honestly believe the child would be better off.

Or you may simply be fed up with this constant threat from your child. One woman we interviewed said of her 16-year-old Baby Bully:

> For three months, whenever we had a fight he would tell me he couldn't stand me and he wanted to live with his dad. He refused to abide by my rules or to respect my wishes. He'd leave the house at night and not tell me when he was coming back—sometimes, he wouldn't come back at all. Finally one day I reached my limit. After he went to school, I called his father to tell him that his son was moving in with him, to which he agreed.
>
> When my son got home, I met him at the door. There were three shopping bags on the floor that I had filled with his clothes. I said, "Here are your things. Your dad is on his way over to pick you up. This

is what you wanted, and you've said it so often that I finally believe it.''
And off they went.

But in three weeks, he was back.

In another case, a daughter moved in with her father, and discovered
to her dismay that he really didn't want her there; he had his own life, a
girlfriend, a demanding job; she had no friends, and she spent much of
her time alone. Says her mother:

> When she left, I was on the floor—I was devastated. I felt as though
> someone had stabbed me through the heart, and that I had lost her
> forever.
>
> But guess what? In about a month, I started to enjoy it—no hassles,
> no clutter, no waiting up nights when she didn't come home, no sarcas-
> tic comments about my friends. So when she called, after four months,
> and asked to come back, I said, ''I'll be honest with you; I'll have to
> think about it.'' She was stunned.
>
> I wasn't playing games; I was assessing whether or not we could
> have a life together; whether or not she would end up ruining my life. I
> had discovered that I wouldn't die without her; so if she was going to
> come back, it had to be on my terms.

This woman laid down certain ground rules for the child, which were
the conditions for her being allowed to return home:

1. She could put neither parent through this manipulation again.

2. She had to let her mother know where she would be if she was
out, to phone if she was detained, and abide by a midnight weekend
curfew for 6 months; after that it would be removed, providing she did
not once break it.

3. She had to pitch in each week with chores that they would jointly
agree upon.

4. She had to begin talking civilly to her mother about her feelings,
rather than through insults.

This negotiation worked, and the child is still at home and thriving.
By being pushed to her limits, the mother began to establish logical
consequences for the first time; having been burned once, she was not
about to allow that to happen again.

Note: If you, your ex-spouse, and your child agree to a change in
living quarters, get in writing that this is a *trial period*, rather than a
relinquishing of permanent custody. You can negotiate the terms, perhaps put a time limit on it—but you do not want your ex-spouse, if he is

a vindictive sort, to use it as a means to punish you through the court system, or to provide legal grounds to sue you for violating the separation agreement.

FOR FATHERS ONLY: WHEN YOU ARE THE NONCUSTODIAL PARENT

The saddest part of being the noncustodial parent is that you simply are not around your children enough to see the subtle changes in them that are indications of their maturity, growth, happiness or unhappiness, triumphs or defeats. So much is lost to you in the time between your visits together, and it is the losses that are so painful.

And so you will have to maintain your relationship in other ways, through phone calls, or letters, or visits. One father told us:

> I made an arrangement with my kids to have daily contact, even though we don't live together. Wherever I am, there isn't a day I don't speak with them on the phone, if not see them. Even so, I don't always pick up on all the changes in them. But I try.

If you have negotiated with your ex-spouse and have a polite relationship with her, the chances of playing a greater role than a separation agreement outlines—say, taking the child on a business trip if it doesn't interfere with school, or extending the vacation time with you—are greatly enhanced. This is the biggest motivation for continuing to negotiate after a divorce.

Moreover, in most states, you have a legal right to have copies of your child's report cards and other school materials sent to your home. Contact your child's school to determine what other rights you have in terms of keeping track of how your child is faring.

There may come a time in your child's life when he wants to live with you. It is important for you to fish with the child, and to have huddles with your ex-spouse, to determine whether this is mere manipulation of both parents, or a genuine, or even urgent, need for him to move in with you.

The teen years are when many such changes of venue take place, sometimes with the mother's permission, even enthusiasm, as we discussed above, sometimes against her wishes, sometimes because the teenager is under the assumption that life will be idyllic with you and he will leave all his troubles behind.

You will need to have a series of huddles with your child to examine his motives and needs. Ask him to list the ten things he hates about living with his mother, the ten things he likes, and the ten things he thinks will be different with you.

For your part, you can list the ten things that you expect of your child if he comes to live with you: they may include the rules you will enforce, the limits you will set, the freedoms he will have (and lose if he doesn't abide by your rules).

This is an extremely serious negotiation, one for which your child needs to take his share of responsibility. Such decisions require a measure of maturity, which the teenager has, at least chronologically. It may turn out that change is not what he needs, and that private school, or your encouragement of his mother to learn how to set limits and to negotiate, is what is really in order.

But it may also turn out that the best thing for him is to live with you. Establishing the ground rules for this change—and letting him know that you will respect his wishes if he changes his mind—will make the transition easier for both of you.

There should be this bottom line: your child cannot treat you (or your ex-spouse) like a puppet, moving in for six months, moving out for two, moving back in for three months, and so on. He needs to address his problems and not try to run away from them.

IT'S NOT ALL BAD NEWS: HOW CHILDREN FLOURISH AFTER DIVORCE

If you've ever been fired or laid off from a job, you are familiar with the sequence of emotions: grief, mourning, anger, acceptance. We add this emotion: hope. Unexpected changes have this payoff—you are forced to examine and explore options in a way that your set patterns precluded. Change can be a series of opportunities.

So it can be with children of divorce, particularly if they are jolted into a new awareness of themselves, or their parents, and of the possibilities, rather than the losses.

One woman told us about the positive changes in her two daughters and in herself following her divorce:

> The biggest change is that my kids' mother has come home. I'm no longer running out of the house—to meetings, to work late, to visit friends—to escape from my husband. I love to be home now. I'm with my kids more than I ever was, now that I'm divorced, and we're closer than we've ever been. And the kids? They're flourishing, flying! My 15-year-old, who used to be so lethargic, and who let everything slide, has changed to a take-charge person. She suddenly matured. My 10-year-old, who used to play it safe by being so sweet to everyone, has learned to express her anger. She is able not to be so goody-goody. The other day she said to me, "Mom, stop calling me twice a day from work. I can handle myself."
>
> After a year of sadness and grief over the loss of my marriage, they have adapted to the change in our lives. They had their pain, and they overcame it. They've each told me that they have come out of it stronger.

A father told us:

> Until my divorce, I left all the parenting to my wife—I didn't really know my kids at all. Now that I get to see them regularly, alone, we have a relationship for the first time.

Research shows that five years after a divorce many children are fully recovered and are getting on with their lives. There are variations within that recovery period. The children who fare best are those whose parents have negotiated and collaborated with them in the ways we have discussed.

If you can remember that it is their styles, more than any other quality, that determines their recovery and their ways of demonstrating their happiness and unhappiness, negotiation will be the most viable parenting tool that you can employ during and after a divorce.

When you collaborate, guilt and rage can become optimism, and your relationship with your children—having survived the worst—can be better than ever.

CHAPTER 18

STEPPARENTING

A young man stands at the microphone on a platform, reading his valedictory speech to his fellow graduating high school seniors and their families. Crowded into the first row of seats before him are his beaming family: his mother, stepfather, and their children from this and their previous marriages; his father, stepmother, and *their* kids and stepchildren; and four sets of grandparents. In all, the teenager can count 15 close relatives in his entourage of celebrants.

This is the modern extended family. Thanks to the divorce and remarriage rates, it is estimated that a third of today's children will sometime in their lives be stepchildren; by the last decade of this century, according to another estimate, stepfamilies will outnumber traditional ones.

On the face of it, where there are children involved, remarriage would seem to redress some of the losses of divorce, providing stability, a larger family context, an extra pair of parenting hands, and a fresh perspective.

Indeed, sometimes stepparenting does have this positive effect. Says the stepfather of an 8-year-old girl:

> I deal with her as though she were my own daughter. When I think she's right, and her mother's wrong, I say so. I help her with her homework, alert her that bedtime is coming up, tuck her in. She's happier here than she is with her father, because she doesn't like him or her stepmother.

But even at its best, stepparenting is an uneasy peace, with the threat of "You can't tell me what to do—you're not my *real* mother [father]!" hanging in the air.

And so, says this same stepfather:

I'll be honest with you. I look forward to the weekends, when she goes to her father. As much as I love her, it's nice to get a break. As a stepparent, I get all the responsibility, but few of the rewards, of being her mother's husband. There's no way my love for my stepdaughter is going to be returned.

For most stepparents, their experiences more closely resemble the following two examples:

Glenda Ferris's husband, Arthur, has a 10-year-old daughter, Maggie, by a previous marriage. Maggie's weekend visits have put a strain on the marriage. Says Glenda:

> Maggie is absolutely the center of Arthur's life. His attitude toward her is, "Do anything you want, and I'll automatically love you." When she comes to visit us, we will have made all these elaborate plans, and she'll say, "I don't want to do that." She's the ultimate manipulator. Constantly adjusting myself to her moods drives me crazy.

When Dudley Cramer married a woman who had two children from her previous marriage, he became an instant parent. He says:

> I've had to learn how to be a parent from my wife. I remember the first school day after we got married; I had to get up at six to get them to the school bus at seven. They were jumping around—they knew what they had to do to get ready. But I didn't. I'd never gotten kids off to school before. I remember thinking, "I'm paying the rent here, and I can't even get into my own bathroom."

As confusing as it is to be a stepparent, it is no less bewildering to be a stepchild. When parents remarry, authority lines are rerouted, children don't know where they stand, and they are expected to like, or at least be polite to, someone they may hardly know.

If the new spouse fits the description of a "wicked stepparent," the child's identity is further shaken. A weeping 13-year-old girl put it this way:

> I see my dad on weekends, but I don't like it much, because he always sides with my stepmother. When we're together, he gets mad a lot, but it's really my stepmother who gets mad; she puts him up to it. She once said to me, "You're not the little girl I used to know," just

because the birthday card I sent to her arrived a day late, and then he got angry about it, too.

I've tried to tell him I'd like it if we could spend more time alone together, but she's always there. My dad and I aren't that close at all, and I think we should be. I mean, he's my father.

Often, however, the "wicked stepparent" moniker is undeserved. Says a stepfather about his stepson:

When my wife and I were first married, Ricky was 6, and he hit me a lot. I didn't do anything about it—I knew why he was hitting me. *He* didn't know why he was hitting me. He wanted his parents to get back together, and he just wasn't going to get that.

But two years later, Ricky and I still clash. For example, my wife and I may punish him for something, and even if it's a joint decision, he focuses his anger on me, not her. No matter what goes wrong with him, he always blames me. My active participation is perceived by him as interference, because he doesn't believe I have any authority.

At its best, moving into an already established family is rough; you, and not your stepchildren, are the new kid on the block. The children have a history of family traditions with their parent that predates you. They also have a history of interactions: depending on their styles, your spouse and his or her kids have developed patterns of trust and affection and, possibly, hostility, and are used to them.

Now you come along and upset those patterns, like a drop of food coloring falling into a glass of water. The water remains essentially the same—but its tone changes. Until the blending is complete, the new element is a visible intrusion, even though it shares the same space.

It is your nebulous parental identity, and how you can negotiate your place within the stepfamily, that we will address in this chapter.

As a stepparent, you have three agendas:

- First, you need to negotiate your new marriage, which includes more than just your spouse. As you adjust to your spouse's style, you have to adjust also to his or her commitment to the children from the previous marriage.
- Second, you need to invent your role with your stepchildren. You are being sniffed and tested and observed by them, and your acceptability is on trial. By definition, you do not have a fit with

any of them, because, in all likelihood, it was not their idea that you be part of their family.
* Third, if both you and your spouse have children from previous marriages, you need to help them develop positive relationships with one another. Theoretically, stepsiblings are more than friends and less than kin—when, in fact, they are practically strangers.

These three items call for sensitive and skillful negotiations.

NEGOTIATING WITH YOUR SPOUSE

While you may not be a full-blooded parent, you are certainly one of the adult authorities within your blended family. You are being asked a great deal: to help parent someone else's kids. It is a tall order and, at times, a no-win one—you deserve a lot of credit and empathy and support for undertaking it.

It also requires a lot of planning.

In the current climate of marital skittishness, the vogue of prenuptial agreements—whereby you negotiate what happens to property in the event of a divorce *before* you marry—is an understandable, if unromantic, hedge against financial mayhem.

Similarly, when embarking on the business of becoming a step-parent, it's a good idea to negotiate, though not necessarily on paper, your emotional stakes and those of your stepchildren-to-be before you make it legal. Here are some useful questions to discuss with your future spouse: What is expected of me? Am I to be a parent, or a friend, or a roommate? How do I define my role? How do the children define their relationship to me? What are our goals, and how will we achieve them?

These are the kinds of questions Rachel and Stan Lewis discussed before they got married. Rachel had a son, Marty, by her previous marriage; this was Stan's first marriage. Their strategy was to make the transition from divorce to new family as painless as possible for all of them, and to design negotiations as a kind of preventive medicine for future family troubles. Says Stan:

> The first thing we agreed on was that we would not impinge on each other's authority with Marty, and that we would give each other the room to work out our separate relationships with him—we wouldn't interfere with the other's decisions.

The second thing we agreed on was that if she and I did have a disagreement about him, we would settle it outside of Marty's hearing. Once we decided on a course of action, we'd stand united—we'd back each other up.

Third, we determined that when she and I had kids, there would be one class of children, not two—"real" and "step-". Marty, and our future children, would be "our kids."

Finally, we made an agreement with Marty's father. He is always welcome in our home, and I never impinge on his authority or put him down in front of his son. He agreed that when Marty goes to his house, he would enforce punishments begun at our house, such as no TV, and that he would not bad-mouth us.

Such all-encompassing prenuptial harmony is rare. And even where it exists, no matter how ironclad and heartfelt these agreements may seem, they are always subject to revisions. In the journey between good intentions and the reality of living with stepchildren, you travel over unfamiliar terrain, and often reach impasses.

Your spouse's parenting style will not change when you marry, and so it would be useful for you to review Chapter 5, "Your Parenting Style." When you understand how your partner negotiates within the family, you have a starting point for your negotiations with him or her.

The most important negotiating skill when marrying into an established family is shifting gears. Your marriage has built-in stresses that do not exist when two people marry for the first time. These stresses, which are listed below, are the agenda items you and your spouse need to discuss and negotiate.

There will be times when you'll want to have huddles, or brainstorm, or employ error analysis with your spouse in order to sort out these stresses. But you must do *something:* try a variety of negotiating skills, depending on your and your spouse's styles. If you ignore these stresses, you're setting yourself up for negotiating failure.

GREAT EXPECTATIONS. Your style determines your expectations and fantasies of what the stepfamily will be. It is these expectations that skew your negotiations before you even move in.

Sam Graham, a Big Daddy, knew when he married Ruth and became a stepfather to Michael, her 7-year-old Loner son, that this was, as Sam puts it, a "package deal." What he didn't anticipate was the constant feeling, even after 10 years of living with his wife and stepson, of being an outsider. Sam says:

When we got married, I wanted nothing more than to be a father to Michael. But Ruth and Michael have a very close relationship, and I always feel left out. I've supported him for years, and what I get back is a degree of respect, but no sense of his thinking of me as a father. Because of this feeling of deprivation, I tend to come down hard on him for things like not turning off lights, or leaving dishes in his room. If I didn't feel deprived, I'd probably like everything about him—I'd certainly be more forgiving, the way natural parents are.

Eleanor Raymond, a Dictator, sailed blissfully into marriage thinking she had enough goodwill, commitment, and intelligence to make her relationship with her stepdaughter work. She says:

I expected to be able to handle everything, and I did. My husband was the kind of man who was happy to have me take over. So I did it all—disciplining, going to teacher's conferences, listening to her problems, telling her how to talk to her father, taking her shopping—without his help—until finally, I burned out. I said to my husband, "I've had it. It's your turn."

He wasn't prepared for getting back into the fatherhood role. My mistake was expecting too much of myself, and not including him in the parenting process. It's one of the reasons our marriage ultimately failed.

You can spare yourself a great deal of grief and disappointment if you are aware of the way your stylistic liabilities dictate your stepparenting expectations. And you can make your role easier if you can concentrate instead on your assets, which offer a great deal to the blended family. Here are summaries of stepparenting behavior, by style:

Jungle Fighter. This style sweeps into the family like a tidal wave, with little or no regard for its former incarnation and patterns. Jungle Fighters expect everyone to adjust to them, rather than the other way around. They'll bark orders and, in a flash of charm, break their own rules to demonstrate their spectacular generosity.

But Jungle Fighters also have a genius for imparting a sense of adventure and fun, and for getting the family out of the doldrums.

Dictator. This style stalks into the new family full of rules and ideas for reform. He is going to shape up this family, no matter what, confident in the belief that his is the best way—surely better than the absent natural parent's.

But Dictators have this valuable asset: they will provide for the family stability that it probably lacked when it was in marital disarray.

Silhouette. The only thing this style expects is respect for his privacy; any infringement on it is regarded as a lack of regard or outright malice. Because they are sometimes perceived as uncaring, this expectation can become reinforced by the stepchildren's compensating cautiousness or neediness.

At the same time, Silhouettes provide a sense of continuity in their loyalty and commitment to the new family; almost nothing the stepchildren could do will cause them to retreat.

Big Daddy/Big Mamma. This style will buy, do for, and give to the stepchildren—until they cross him, and then he withdraws all the goodies. His expectation is that the kids will find irresistible his titanic heart; he will recoil, as though struck, if they do not, and exact a heavy punishment in the form of guilt.

But the Big Daddy/Big Mamma also gives the family a burst of warmth and, being an extremely social sort, the excitement of a new set of adoring friends.

Soother. This style will do almost anything to avoid the anger and resentment of the stepchildren. Eager to keep the peace rather than to set limits, Soothers will quickly be exploited by the children, who will send them on errands or demand favors, to which they are loathe to say no.

But Soothers will also be worthy mediators for disputes, and will listen to both sides in the interests of justice and compromise.

DIFFERENT PARENTING STYLES. The complexity of the stepparent/stepchild relationship is compounded by your different styles. If your stepchildren are used to one way of parenting—say, the slack of a Big Daddy/Big Mamma, Silhouette, or Soother—and you are more assertive—a Jungle Fighter or Dictator—you and your stepchildren will be a mis-fit. They expect you to be indulgent and/or casual, and will not easily adjust to your more direct or pragmatic approach.

Let's say the kids bring friends over to spend the night without consulting you. You say, "You should have told me; it's inconsiderate not to ask my permission." They reply, "What's the big deal? Mom [or Dad] doesn't care about that stuff."

STARTING IN THE MIDDLE. "Do not ever give me the rowboat scenario," the mother of a 6-year-old said to her bridegroom. "You know, 'Who would you save if the boat overturned? Me or your kid?' Believe it: I'd save my daughter.'' The daughter is now 14 and in a state of high adolescent dudgeon—she's often obnoxious—so the woman would at least pause if asked that question today.

Nevertheless, stepparents do marry a "package deal," a gnawing fact of remarried life, because you *know* who comes first, and it probably isn't you, especially if your stepchildren are very young. As a result, many stepparents often feel disenfranchised. Without a "vote," they do not want to feel even more isolated than they already do. And so they put the natural parent in the middle, while they stand on the perimeter, artfully dodging the flak that stepchildren send up, letting the natural parent take the shots.

Says the stepfather of Lauren, a 10-year-old girl:

> For the first couple of years of our marriage, whenever I had a complaint about Lauren, I'd go to her mother and tell her to do something about it. She'd say, "Why don't you tell her yourself?" My perfectly reasonable excuse always was, "My relationship with her is already tenuous. I get home so late, do you want me to spend the little time we do have together screaming at her?"
>
> For a long time, she bought it, and fought my battles with Lauren for me, which I loved, because it made me the good guy. But it made my wife a wreck. Finally one night she burst into tears and said, "Do you realize that every night when you come home, all you do is complain about Lauren? You've got to stop making me the referee." I realized that I was jeopardizing my marriage by not getting my hands dirty and risking Lauren's anger.

For their parts, many natural parents *allow* themselves to be in the middle because, apprehensive about the possibility of putting themselves and their kids through another divorce, they try too hard to keep peace within the new family. Here's how one woman describes that indelicate balance:

> I can recall vividly the day, about six months after we got married, standing in the kitchen. My husband was on one side of the house, calling for me. On the other side of the house, my daughter was calling for me to come into her room. I stood there, feeling torn in half, not knowing who to go to first: my new husband, jealous of my relationship with my daughter, whom I was trying to make feel important? My daughter, jealous because she now had to share me, who was the innocent casualty of a divorce?

It took me a long time to realize that I didn't have to choose between them.

The natural parent's guilt and/or inability to share authority can keep him or her in the middle. Says a stepfather:

My wife is the third party in my relationship with my stepson. She never gives us a chance to develop our own relationship. If I ask him to do something, she'll say, "He doesn't have to do it now," and I'll say, "See? You're doing it again. You're stepping in. This is between him and me." But she's so protective, afraid I'll do something wrong, that she never leaves us alone.

When remarried couples begin their lives together in this artificial way, with little or no direct communication between stepparent and stepchild, anxiety and anger accumulate on both sides and undermine any hope of negotiation, let alone friendship.

UNDEFINED ROLES. Diane Fields was, in her childhood, a stepdaughter, and so thought she'd have an advantage when she married Andy, the father of two children. She was wrong. Says Diane:

I had a preconception of what it would be like to be a stepmother. But I'd been through it as a kid—I didn't have any idea what it was like from the stepparent's point of view. You don't know where you fit in. These kids already have a mother. So I feel I need their father's permission to do any disciplining at all. He's got a real fear that if he disciplines them, they will hate him and not come back to see him. So he tends not to set any limits.

It's very difficult to sit back and watch that. I save it up and then explode at him. It is the one bad area of our relationship, his being afraid to confront his kids.

A stepfather puts it this way:

Being a stepfather means wanting my stepdaughter to understand that I'm a parent, but not her real father. It's a strange line. It's a problem that never gets resolved in some ways, because if you take on the role of her father, she will resent you forever. How can you love her as a parent and not be her father?

On the other hand, if you become uninvolved, you lose all credibility when it's time to get involved—say, in a crisis.

There are no rules for this kind of relationship. It's very hard to structure it so she comes out whole and you do, too. So the only thing to do is the best you can, and hope it works out.

LOGISTICS. The venues of visitation, either to your place on weekends, if your spouse is the noncustodial parent, or to the ex-spouse's place if they live with you, can be dizzying. Rules, discipline, and routines are disrupted every week as your stepchildren shuttle from one house to another. The kids go through mood changes—like the transition from deep water to the surface for skin divers—as they adjust from one parent's style and routines to yours, and you are as upset by these disruptions as they are.

If your spouse does not have custody, when your stepchildren come to visit you may feel less than even a stepparent and more like a servant; you often get all the scut work and little or no appreciation.

Says a stepmother:

> Instead of being a family, we have houseguests—my husband's kids—on weekends. We don't deal with them in the real world. We feed them and make nice on them and try not to make waves, and then we take them home, and they just take it for granted.
>
> I haven't gotten much out of my relationship with them. It makes me wonder what is wrong with me: I feel as though I'm not worthy of attention.

If your spouse has custody of his or her children, you are intimately involved in their day-to-day activities and problems, but still are made to feel like an interloper. Says a stepfather:

> Sunday nights when the kids return from their father's are the worst for me. The kids walk into the house and look at me as though I had just stabbed them. I am public enemy number one, because I happen not to be their father.

DEALING WITH THE ABSENT PARENT. Your spouse's ex-husband or ex-wife, although out of the domestic picture, is not out of your life. By comparing yourself to him or her, and by wishing away the ills, or benefits, of the children's relationship to that parent, you make yourself unnecessarily unhappy.

It's important to begin your strategies regarding the absent parent with this reality: he or she is the children's natural parent, and there's nothing you can do to change that fact. You can, however, change how you feel about it.

For example, one of the issues that causes enormous anxiety and rage within the blended family is that of child support. It is a matter of statistical record that the majority of noncustodial American fathers do not support their children, or are late with support payments, particularly when those fathers remarry and begin new families.

If this is the case in your family, you have two options: the first is to accept it, unless you and your spouse wish to incur the extraordinary legal tariff of going to court. We interviewed a stepfather who put it this way:

> I decided, when I married my wife, that I would be fully responsible for the kids' financial needs. Whatever their father contributed, I would consider as gravy. So I never get upset when he refuses to pay for such things as orthodontia—which he has—or other items that are not spelled out in the separation agreement.

The other option is that you negotiate with the ex-spouse directly. He or she very likely does not have excess emotional baggage regarding you, and the chances of reaching compromises in the children's best interests are greater with you than with your partner.

This can be accomplished in a neutral place, such as a restaurant, and by being direct, as well as understanding. One man we know asked his wife's ex-husband, who refused to pay for his children's summer camp, to have lunch with him, and said the following:

> We all want what's best for the kids. I realize you have financial obligations, other than the children. And there's a limit to what I can afford. Is there a way we can both cut back somewhere in order to split the costs of camp?

Where the direct approach is not even remotely possible, it's important for you to be aware of the ways in which the ex-spouse will try to sabotage your parenting efforts and the new family, so that you can defuse those efforts. These are the styles of ex-spousal sabotage:

Jungle Fighter. This style often uses money as a weapon—by withholding or delaying child support and by buying lavish gifts for the children instead. Jungle Fighters also may make little or no effort to help in the continuity of your rules and punishments when the kids are with them.

Dictator. This style may criticize you to the child by saying such things as, "Your stepfather doesn't know what he's talking about. I know what's best for you." Dictators believe they are always right—which makes you always wrong.

Silhouette. This style usually adheres to the letter, rather than to the spirit, of the separation agreement. Since the Silhouette's credo is, "A deal is a deal," do not expect one cent more. One well-to-do Silhouette father we know of, who in 10 years was never late in sending support checks, refused to pay for psychiatric help for his suicidal son. Only after painstaking negotiation on the part of the stepfather did he agree to pay half. Silhouettes will not give more than they have contracted for—but at least you don't have to worry about getting less.

Big Daddy/Big Mamma. This style wants to out-love and out-parent you because he or she wants the adoration of the children. In the guise of concern, the Big Daddy/Big Mamma will say to the children, "Oh, your stepfather and mom didn't take you with them on their vacation?"

Soother. These apparently well-meaning and loving parents will promise, for example, to pick up the children on Friday at 6:00, and at 8:30 will call to say they were detained—or not call at all. Soothers will make elaborate plans, but will then forget them. To live with this undependability, you need always to have backups—as, say, hiring a baby-sitter in case you have to go out and the ex-spouse does not show up.

Since you know how each style is likely to behave, you base your expectations accordingly and reduce the possibility of cumulative rage or anxiety. You also clear the way for an honest and loving connection with your stepchildren apart from their relationship with the absent parent.

If, for instance, your stepchildren want to complain about the abuses or neglect of that parent, you can say, "I know how that must hurt you. But we are not like that. Try to concentrate on what you do have—the good things—and not let the bad stuff take over."

If, on the other hand, your stepchildren compare you unfavorably to the absent spouse, you can say, "It's wonderful that your dad [mom] can do so much for you. Enjoy it. But we don't operate that way—we do other things that are special, too."

Either way, you have stated your position—that you and the stepchildren have a separate relationship, and that the absent spouse has nothing to do with that, nor can he or she damage how you feel about them.

There's very little you can do one way or the other to change how the children feel about the absent parent; as they mature, they will see for themselves whether or not the parent loves and cares about them—and they will make up their own minds about you as well. In any case, it's not a contest.

When you consider all the pitfalls that come with the territory of stepparenting, it's not surprising that 60 percent of remarriages end in divorce.

These problems make negotiation with your spouse not simply useful, but imperative. None of your strategies with your stepchildren will work, nor will your marriage, if you have not worked them through.

Once you have anticipated and resolved how to deal with the potential negotiating hurdles within your marriage, you can address your relationship with your stepchildren.

NEGOTIATING WITH STEPCHILDREN

You need to define your role with your stepchildren so that the structure of your new family, and your place in it, is secure. But it will not happen overnight—the transition period of your acceptability to your stepchildren, and theirs to you, is a long one. If you can keep that in mind, your expectations for the long and short terms will be realistic, and so will your negotiations.

For the long haul, you want the children to have a degree of stability and a sense that you are a significant source of guidance, encouragement, and affection—not as a parent, but as a concerned and caring friend.

Do not expect to be thanked for that friendship. It may not occur to the children, until they are grown, how significant your presence is; but most stepchildren whose stepparents refuse to give up on them in time come to treasure the relationship.

With that in mind, your long-term goals can inform your short-term negotiations. No, you are not a natural parent; yes, you do have a right to be treated with respect and courtesy in your own home.

It helps if you know that your stepchildren's hidden agenda is to bring about a reconciliation between Mom and Dad, or at least to have the natural parent all to themselves. The reasons for this hidden agenda cannot be overstated: they are afraid of another divorce and *another loss;* and they are afraid that they will be replaced by you in their parent's affections.

And so, your stepchildren may try to derail or manipulate you in the following ways:

Baby Bullies are the most likely style to say "You can't tell me what to do!" They will, for example, deliberately exhibit disgusting table manners, or barrel into your room without knocking, or not let you know where they are.

Here's how Fran Douglas describes her relationship to Jason, her husband's 9-year-old Baby Bully son:

> For the first year, Jason barely acknowledged that I was alive. He'd act like a barbarian, and his father wouldn't do anything about it. And I was not the nicest person to Jason, because he would bring out all my latent Germanic instincts. I used to joke, "You can call me 'Mommy Dearest.' "
>
> It was the strangest thing; the firmer and tougher I got, the more Jason seemed to like me. As it turned out, he and I were more alike temperamentally than he and his father, who is a softie.

It takes time to tame a Baby Bully, and you will need two negotiating skills above all others: taking your pulse, so that your anger doesn't reach out-of-control proportions—which would delight the Baby Bully—and the bottom line of insisting on adherence to ground rules.

Fran Douglas instinctively knew that the way to deal with Jason was to let him know that she wasn't going anywhere, and that he was dealing with someone who was as intransigent as he was. She and Jason are a fit; because of that, she has been able to create changes in his behavior by appealing to his assets.

She has also encouraged her husband to become more assertive, rather than Jason's doormat, so that the relationship between him and his son has improved. Jason's style and behavior cried out for loving limits; Fran, who understands him, provided them.

Kid Tyrants will react to your joining the family as though they are being busted to buck private. Until you came along, they were probably the dominant person in your spouse's home life, particularly with the custodial parent, who may unconsciously have encouraged their decisiveness by giving them a great deal of responsibility.

With you, they stand to lose their stripes. Consequently, they will—in your presence—talk about you as though you weren't there. Or they will ignore or debate your decisions. And so you need to have frequent huddles with Kid Tyrants, to assure them that their valuable leadership abilities can still be exercised, but in different ways.

We interviewed Pamela, the uncommonly perceptive stepmother of Rachel, a 12-year-old Kid Tyrant. Says Pamela:

> I took Rachel to lunch one day and put it to her: "What bothers you most about my having married your father?" She said, "I used to get my way all the time. Now I can't do anything, because Dad always discusses everything with you first, instead of me."
>
> I asked her, "What do you want more than anything?"
>
> "To make my own decisions!" she said.
>
> "Okay," I said, "you got it. Here's where you can do that: your homework, your bedtime, your friends, your clothes—all those things are your department. Here's what's your father's and my department: everything else. But we won't make any final decisions without consulting you first. Deal?"
>
> "Deal."

Loners will give you the feeling that if you were found dead on the driveway, they would barely break stride as they entered the house and headed for their room. They give the impression of supreme indifference to your presence—or absence.

If you dig deep enough, and have the patience to have huddles, to brainstorm, and to fish with your unresponsive Loner, you will find that the impression is entirely superficial.

Brenda Hewitt broke through her Loner stepson's facade this way:

> I wrote him a letter, which said, "My mother remarried when I was seven, and I resented it a lot. It took a long, long time for me to understand my stepfather and to find out it was okay for me to like him, that it didn't mean I was being disloyal to my father. I know exactly how you feel about me, that you may even hate me, because I felt the same way, at first, about my stepfather.
>
> But now I have a problem, and only you can help. I've never been a stepmother before. I need you to let me know what I'm doing wrong so I

can change it. Please write back to me and tell me how we can work together to make it better for all of us.''

Brenda tailored the extremely effective skill of finding commonalities to her stepson's style by communicating on paper, rather than in person. Loners who have been through a divorce may have sunk deep into their naturally withdrawn natures; confrontations will only drive them deeper. But writing and receiving notes will make it easier for them to emerge, because it allows them to express themselves in a way that is nonthreatening.

Saints will welcome you as though you were a long lost comrade, because they want to diffuse any possibility of your rejection. And so they may seem to become your best friend and biggest booster.

At the same time, they will be devious in their efforts to undermine your marriage. "Gee, Dad, we went to Bloomingdale's and spent a fortune! Mom never does that!" is typical Saint behavior, designed to bury, rather than to praise you.

Be aware of the Saint's manipulation; in the guise of flattery he will try to put you in a disadvantageous light with his parent. Saints like to divide and conquer.

One way to deflect the Saint's true intent is to say, in answer to a request (other than for you to pass the salt), "Have you checked this out with your father [mother]?'' Another is to tell the child you'll do so yourself.

Underdogs will meld into you as though you are the ideal parent for which they have always longed. One Soother woman we interviewed recalled her desperate need, when she was a child, to be immediately engulfed by her Silhouette stepfather. She recalls:

> I voluntarily changed my last name to his. I got up in the morning to make his breakfast because my mother always slept late. I introduced him to everyone as my father, rather than stepfather.
>
> It all made him very uncomfortable because he wasn't demonstrative; he was embarrassed. But his remoteness only made me try harder. I allowed myself to be swallowed up by my fantasy of the kind of father I wanted him to be—which made little difference to him, but cost me, as I look back, a great deal.

You may be in a better position even than your spouse—the child's natural parent—to help the Underdog find his identity and to nurture his assets, because the emotional investment in you is less than in his parents, and so he has less to lose by being open with you. Gentle fishing and lovingly finding commonalities can help bring this child out from behind the barricades of his neediness.

You can begin this way: "I think we are a lot alike. I feel out of place, because I'm not your real parent, but I'm not exactly just a friend either. You may feel out of place too, and not just with me. What do you think? Where else do you feel you don't fit in?"

Your Underdog stepchild may welcome this sympathetic line of questioning. At the same time, you can zero in in a way that his family may not have by retaining a certain optimism about him. He is so used to being a victim, and having that role reinforced by the excuses and low expectations of his family, that your belief that he is capable of more may come as a pleasant, although initially unsettling, surprise.

You can make gentle demands of the Underdog by setting time limits on his procrastination; by asking him to do one thing, rather than three; by not bailing him out of his chronic undependability. With you, he has no track record of such behavior, and you can help keep him from slipping farther into his negative view of himself.

In any negotiation with a stepchild, your goal is to help him get beyond the turbulence of his insecurities so that he can return to the agenda that is appropriate to him: his friends, his schoolwork, and his growth. These negotiations will help ease him away from worries about his future so that he can return to the present—his childhood.

INSTANT SIBLINGS

Your difficulties in dealing with stepchildren pale in comparison to those of your and your spouse's children in dealing with each other. As forced as being an instant parent feels, it is nothing in contrast to how children feel when they are compelled to live with kids they've never met before you came along.

If you and your spouse both have children from your former marriages, your collective heirs become "instant" siblings, and, in all probability, none of them will be crazy about this arrangement.

Adapting to the new marriage is made geometrically more difficult for the children because they are being dragooned into coexisting with peers they may not like, and certainly don't know very well. Where once they may have had a room all to themselves, now they may have to share it. And if you both have custody of your children, either your or your spouse's kids may have had to move and adjust to a new community and a new school system.

The *fait accompli* of your remarriage gives new meaning to the term *sibling rivalry*. It is one thing to become accustomed to a new stepparent, who may take special pains to endear him- or herself to the children. It is quite another to deal with new stepbrothers and sisters, who may have no such ambition.

You now have a negotiating situation that is as complex as any on the front page of your newspaper, because you start off with a bottom line that reflects your goals, not the children's: no matter how kindly you put it, your message is, "This is the way it is, kid—you better get used to it."

Your trade-offs are minimal: How do you sweeten the sibling deal, which, at best, they want no part of? What can you offer that will assuage the anger they will inevitably feel? The only thing that might appeal to them—and which is totally unacceptable to you—is divorce, so that they can go back to a simpler time when they had to deal only with their parents and their own brothers and sisters.

Negotiations begin before the wedding in private huddles among the children and their natural parent, during which the kids can state their fears and anxieties. Depending on your and your spouse's abilities to reassure, and your respective children's stylistic abilities to express their apprehensions, these meetings can start to address those apprehensions.

But they won't cure the problem. You and your spouse need to follow up with a *series* of huddles—as often as once a week—with all the children. These huddles are crucial because of the diversity of styles and of histories in the stepfamily.

In your first huddle you can address the children's feelings by saying, "This all probably seems weird to you. It's new for us too. But we are going to be a family now, even if it's different from what you're used to, and we all need each other to figure out the best way for us to be happy."

If you deal with the problem head-on, without lacing it with phoniness—as in saying, "Isn't it nice to have a new brother and sister to love?"—you acknowledge the chaotic emotions and impotence that the children feel not only about the new marriage, but about each other as well.

The agenda for your first huddle is to have each child write on a piece of paper what his fears and hopes are, in two separate columns.

The ground rule for this meeting is that each child can and must be honest—but not deliberately cruel or insulting. Fair game, for instance, is saying, "I wish none of this were happening," or "I wish you'd never met." If they don't list this fear, you can express it for them as a possibility, because they surely feel it.

Both parents can list and state their own applicable feelings, pro and con, in order to establish a commonality with the kids, who might recoil from being so candid: for example, you can say to a stepchild, "I'm concerned you won't take the time to get to know me, that you'll make a snap judgment and won't give me a chance."

The children may balk at this exercise because it feels as though they are being asked to help you engineer their own worst case scenario. But the purpose of these huddles is to open doors, not close them; you will have planted a collaborative seed, and they may come back to you later, privately, to open them further and to connect with you.

If the first huddle goes badly, don't give up: it's imperative that you follow through with your strategy. You can say, "Let's try again in a few days. Maybe you need some time to think about what you want to put on your lists. Here's something else you can add. One of the things we need to know is what you want, such as how you'd like to rearrange your rooms, for instance. At our next meeting, we'll see how we can each help you get it."

Negotiating stepsibling relationships involves bringing everyone into the decision-making process, with no exceptions. The Loner and the Underdog, because of their stylistic reticence, need especially to be encouraged to solve their problems, since they are the most likely to try to run away, emotionally, from the coercive nature of creating an instant family.

Style aside, it is this initial, and urgent, resistance—which all stepchildren share—that must be dealt with before any other negotiating item.

You can provide other ways to pave the way for collaboration. For example, you can put up a suggestion box into which the children can place their anonymous ideas, thoughts, recommendations, complaints, hurts. These pieces of paper are invaluable: they form your agendas for future huddles.

Without naming names (although you will probably recognize the child's handwriting), you can say at the next meeting, "It's come to our attention that some of you are taking other people's clothes out of the laundry. How can we solve this problem?" One solution is to have a laundry basket for each child, and nametags on everyone's clothes so that no violation of belongings occurs.

At a certain point, however, you have to allow stepsiblings to work out their own problems. If you allow their conflicts to undermine your marriage and sabotage the new family, the emotional consequences will be enormous. So you may have to give this bottom line: "You'll have to learn to live with each other and make it as easy on yourselves as possible."

You can, from time to time, provide tie breakers, as in saying, "You have one hour to solve this disagreement. You have lots of options—find one that you can both agree on. If you cannot, you will have to abide by our decision—one that neither of you may like."

One couple we talked to was able to diminish the stepchildren's chronic and debilitating conflicts by taking the entire family to neutral territory.

They carefully planned a camping trip and asked each child to name the one thing they wanted most to do: one wanted to go fishing, another wanted to go rock climbing, a third wanted to see some animals. The ground rule for this list of activities was that everyone had to participate in each item.

The kids planned the menus and the food, and each child was responsible for one meal, which the other children had to help prepare and serve. And each child was responsible for planning one night's entertainment—either storytelling or games that everyone would play. Finally, each child was given $20 to spend any way he or she liked—on souvenirs or junk food.

The beauty of the trip was that there were no television or telephones to distract the family from collaborating and coexisting. Where there were disagreements, they were settled in the evenings around a campfire. And disagreements there were.

But overriding and transcending those disputes were the momentum of the trip and the variety of things to see and do, which helped to give this new family a sense of collective purpose and pleasure that they could not have attained at home. They returned with a sense of camaraderie and team effort that had not existed before—and material for a scrapbook of photographs and memories that chronicled the trip and, in a sense, proved that they were, indeed, a family.

Making a remarriage work is, if anything, more challenging than succeeding at a first marriage because of the disparate parts of the whole. It is hard to imagine a configuration more complex and more in need of skillful negotiation.

But it is also hard to imagine a sense of achievement greater than meeting that challenge and making it work. If you pay attention to everyone's styles, feelings, assets and liabilities, and collaborative strengths, you can create from the blended family a bond that, because it has been put through so many tests and come through them stronger, has rewards that can last a lifetime.

EPILOGUE

Our culture does little to support and applaud your decision to have and raise children, or to give that choice the same prestige as, for example, being a highly paid professional.

And yet, no other choice is as important. When you negotiate for time with your family and set goals in your career that are compatible with family goals, you reestablish your parenting authority and worth.

But in a larger sense you also have an impact on the world: by helping your children to become adults who will think and feel and act on issues beyond themselves, you insure that they can make lasting contributions to humanity through their ability to bring out the best and noblest efforts of their families, friends, and colleagues. The future concerns of a community, or even a nation, are reduced, in however small and unheralded a way, when one parent takes the time and makes the commitment to love and collaborate with one child.

INDEX

Achievement, 242
Adolescence. *See* Teenagers
Affection, 54, 82
Age
  and negotiation, 18
  and style, 28
Alcohol, 41, 283–296
All Grown Up and No Place to Go, 284
Allowance (money), 228–232
Ames, Louise Bates, 28, 34
Anorexia nervosa, 12
Arguing, 256

Baby Bully, 50, 52, 53, 54, 56–58, 125–126, 133–136, 179–180, 185–187, 191–192, 194–195, 197, 202, 206–208, 214–217, 223, 227, 249–256, 270–272, 286–289, 340
Bandler, Richard, 206
Bedtime, 178–183
Body language, 53–54, 94
Brainstorming, 112–113, 187, 195–196, 210, 211, 219, 223

Chess, Stella, 25
Chores, 130
Cleanup, 194–196
Collaboration, 2, 11, 201–202
Communication, 42, 93
Community activities, 245
Control, 2, 12, 237–238

Conversation, 95–98
Cooperation, 202
Criticism, 102–103
Crying, 174–175
Curfews, 247–248

Defiance, 247–266
Denial, 154
Discipline, 17–18, 173
Distrust, 16–17
Divorce, 299–326
  children who flourish after, 325–326
  child's living arrangements, 322–324
  father as noncustodial parent, 324–325
  finances, 309–311
  handling questions about, 308–309
  negotiating with ex-spouse, 318–324
  parenting alone, 306–308
  renegotiating relationship, 303–315
  resentment toward children, 313–315
  teaching child to negotiate with absent parent, 315–318
  telling child about, 303–306
  time for oneself, 311–313
  See also Stepparenting
Dreikurs, Rudolf, 19, 123, 128
Drugs, 41, 283–296

Elementary school. *See* Grade
  schoolers
Elkind, David, 284
Emotions, 26–27, 173, 204–205
Encouragement, 128

Failure, 16
Family meetings, 129–131, 344–346
Family priorities, 159–161
Fatigue, 102
Feelings. *See* Emotions
Finances, 309–311
Food. *See* Meals and food
Fraiberg, Selma, 18, 174
Friends, 214–221
  See also Peer pressure

Ginott, Haim, 114
Grades, 267–282
Grade schoolers, 200–232
Grinder, John, 206
Guilt, 248–249

High school, 244–246
  See also Grades
Homework, 205–213
Honig, Bill, 160
Huddles. *See* Family meetings

Infancy, 174–176
Intervention, 15–19
  to implement family values, 17
  psychological, 15–16
Intuition, 113

Junior high school, 243

Kid tyrant, 50, 52, 53, 54, 58–59,
  126, 136–139, 180–181,
  187–189, 193–197, 202, 208,
  217, 224, 230–231, 256–260,
  272–273, 289–290, 340–341
Knowing your child, 32–54
  extent of knowledge, 36–43
  questionnaire, 36–50
  style of child, 43–54

Language, 52–54
  assessing, 104–105

body, 53–54, 94
conversation, 95–98
keeping negotiation going, 100–101
of negotiation, 89–105
opening negotiation, 99–100
phrases, 94–95
stopping negotiation, 102
talkers and nontalkers, 95–97
tone of voice, 93
Listening, 52–53, 103–104, 307
Logical consequences, 19, 123–125
Loner, 51, 52, 53, 54, 60–62, 126,
  138–141, 181–182, 189,
  194–198, 202, 209–212,
  219–220, 224–225, 231,
  260–262, 274–276, 290–291,
  341–342
Love, 17
Lying, 18

Magic Years, The, 18, 174
Manners, 190–194
Marks. *See* Grades
Meals and food, 183–189
Mental disturbance, 15–16
Messy room, 226–228
Money, 229–232

Name-calling, 101–102
Needs, emotional, 26–27
Negotiation, 1–19
  according to style, 3, 10, 12–15
  agenda, 108–110
  with Baby Bully, 57–58,
    125–126, 179–180, 185–187,
    194–195, 197, 206–208,
    214–217, 223, 227–228,
    230, 249–256, 270–272,
    287–289, 340
  backups, 116–117
  bottom line, 117
  brainstorming, 112–113
  with Kid Tyrant, 59, 126,
    180–181, 187–189, 193–197,
    208, 217, 224, 230–231,
    256–260, 272–273, 289–290,
    340–341
  of child with parent, 167–168

Negotiation (*continued*)
  definition, 11–13
  in divorce, 299–325
  error analysis, 117–118
  family huddles, 129–130
  finding commonalities, 112
  fishing for answers, 112
  goals, 11–13, 108
  with grade schoolers, 200–232
  intervention, 15–19
  issues, 111–112
  language of, 91–105
  with Loner, 61–62, 126, 181–182,
    189, 194–198, 209–212,
    219–220, 224–225, 231,
    260–262, 274–276, 290–291,
    341–342
  nonnegotiable issues, 17–18
  opening, 99–100
  options, 113–114
  with partner on child's behalf,
    161–164
  with preschoolers, 171–199
  priming of child, 110–111
  questionnaire, 42–43
  with Saint, 63, 126, 182, 189,
    193–197, 208–209, 217–218,
    227–228, 231, 262–264,
    276–278, 291–293, 342
  shifting gears, 110–111,
    240–241
  silence, 113
  skills of, 106–121
  and stepparenting, 327–347
  stopping, 101–102
  strategies, 122–132
  taking stock, 115–116
  with teenagers, 233–296
  tie breakers, 118
  trade-offs, 114–115
  with Underdog, 65–66, 126,
    182–183, 189, 193–198,
    212–213, 220–221, 228,
    231, 264–266, 278–282,
    293–296, 342–343
  as way to know your child,
    36
  with winner, 66

Outside help, 131–132, 203–204, 244
Overachievement, 15

Parenting style, 68–87
  child-parent fitness chart, 79
  dividing and conquering, 154–155
  denial, 154
  dependency needs, 156
  differing, 148–168
  and divorce, 299–325
  encouraging animosity between
    partner and children, 153–158
  expression of, 80–83
  and helping children, 83–84
  and hurting children, 84–85
  inappropriate family priorities,
    159–161
  mixtures within family, 77–80
  negotiation with partner, 161–167
  questionnaire, 71–77
  resolving differences, 157–158
  teaching child to negotiate with
    partner, 167–168
  types, 69–72
  women's/men's role, 154–156
  See also Divorce; Stepparenting
Peer pressure, 283–296
Personality, 29
Phrases, 94–95
Politeness. *See* Manners
Praise, 128
Preschoolers, 171–199
Priorities, 159–161
Privacy, 226
Punishment, 17–19, 123–124

Readiness, 127–128, 204
Rebellion. *See* Defiance
Reward, 17–19, 124
Risk taking, 16
Rituals, 172–173
Room, messy, 226–228

Saint, 51, 52, 53, 54, 62–63, 126,
    141–143, 182, 189, 193–197,
    202, 208–209, 217–218,
    227–228, 231, 262–264,
    276–278, 291–293, 342

Scapegoating, 154
Self-esteem, 12, 15
Sex, 41, 283–296
Sharing, 2, 12, 193
Siblings, 132, 222–226, 343–347
Silence, 113, 194
Single parent. *See* Divorce
Sloppiness. *See* Messy room
Speech patterns. *See* Language
Stepparenting, 327–347
    absent parent, 336–339
    expectations, 331–333
    logistics, 336
    negotiating with spouse, 330–339
    negotiating with stepchildren,
        339–343
    siblings, 343–347
    styles, 333
    undefined roles, 335–336
Strategy
    with Baby Bully, 133–136
    with Kid Tyrant, 136–139
    encouragement, 128
    family huddles, 129–131
    implementation with others' help,
        131–132
    with Loner, 139–141
    negotiation, 122–132
    readiness, 127–128
    with Saint, 141–143
    with style, 133–147
    time lines, 126–127
    timing, 125–126
    with Underdog, 143–146
    with Winner, 146–147
    See also Negotiation
Style, 3–4, 10, 12–15, 23–31
    and age, 28
    assets and liabilities of types of,
        50–52
    child's, 43–67
    components of, 24–31
    definition, 23
    and emotional needs, 26–27
    expression of, 29
    loving, 54, 82
    mixtures within family, 77–80

and parental influence, 27
of parenting, 68–87, 148–168
questionnaire, 43–50
of stepparenting, 333
and strategy, 133–147
and temperament, 24–26,
    28–29, 30
and values, 28–29
ways of revealing, 52–54

Teachers, 131
Teenagers, 233–296
    community activities, 245
    control, 237–238
    defiance, 247–266
    grades, 267–282
    high school, 244–246
    junior high school, 243
    peer pressure, 283–296
    renegotiating relationship,
        238–241
Temperament, 24–26, 28–29,
    30
Thomas, Alexander, 25
Time lines, 126–128
Timing, 125–126
Toddlers. *See* Preschoolers
Toilet training, 196–199
Tone of voice, 93

Underachievement, 15
Underdog, 51, 52, 53, 54, 64–66,
    126, 143–146, 182–183,
    189, 193–198, 202, 212–213,
    220–221, 225–226, 228,
    231, 264–266, 278–282,
    293–296, 342–343

Values, 17, 28–29, 248, 286
Verbal language. *See* Language
Voice tone, 93

Winner, 52, 53, 54, 66–67,
    146–147
Wietzman, Leonore J., 309
Workaholics, 157–160
Working parents, 159–161

For information about WINNING WITH KIDS
seminars (for parents and teachers)

contact
Dr. Tessa Albert Warschaw
15 W. 53rd Street
New York, New York 10019